John Steinbeck, the Good Companion

HIS FRIEND DOOK'S MEMOIR

John Steinbeck, the Good Companion

HIS FRIEND DOOK'S MEMOIR

Carlton A. Sheffield

Introduction by Richard H. A. Blum
Edited and notes by Terry White

CREATIVE ARTS BOOK COMPANY
Berkeley ~ California

Acknowledgment gratefully made to Michael C. Sutherland, Special Collections Librarian, and Jeane Paule, College Archivist, of Occidental College, Los Angeles. Thanks also to John Hooper of the Steinbeck Library, Salinas, California; Jill Wood of the Harry Ransom Humanities Research Center, Austin, Texas; and Rene Spicer of the Stanford Alumni Association.

For information contact:
Creative Arts Book Company
833 Bancroft Way
Berkeley, California 94710
1-800-848-7789

Library of Congress Cataloging-in-Publication Data

Sheffield, Carlton.
[Steinbeck, the good companion]
John Steinbeck, the good companion : his friend Dook's memoir / Carlton A. Sheffield ; introduction by Richard H.A. Blum ; edited and notes by Terry White.
p. cm.
Originally published: Steinbeck, the good companion. Portola Valley, Calif. : American Lives Endowment, c1983. With new introd.
Includes bibliographical references.
ISBN 0-88739-350-0 (pbk. : alk. paper)
1. Steinbeck, John, 1902-1968. 2. Steinbeck, John, 1902-1968--Friends and associates. 3. Novelists, American--20th century--Biography. I. White, Terry, 1950- . II. Title.
PS3537.T3234 Z8663 2001
813'. 52--dc21

2001042517

BOOK DESIGN BY STEVEN ZAHAVI SCHWARTZ
Printed in the United States of America

For Mark Dalrymple, 19, for fighting the good fight

and

For Dick Blum, friend and good companion, fighting it now with his usual grace, humor, and courage

Table of Contents

Introduction

by Richard H. A. Blum

The first introduction to the 1982 publication of Dook's memoir accompanied a limited distribution of *Steinbeck, the Good Companion.*[1] Sheff had given his memoir to me as Chair of the American Lives Endowment (ALE was then a fledgling, non-profit organization in the humanities). One of ALE's major goals is to encourage via publication and archival maintenance grass roots or otherwise unrealized life-writing—that is, biography, autobiography, family history and memoir. For instance, the memoir of Steinbeck written by my neighbor Sheff, and most fitting for ALE to sponsor.

We had hoped to provide the *Companion* with full-fledged publication, but the fates and the Reagan view of Government support for the humanities, were against us. However highly ALE was regarded for its splendid goals and the excellence of its Board, unhappily none of us knew how to raise money, an especially difficult task in the humanities (Today ALE manages to stagger along, philanthropically sponsored by Creative Arts Book Company).

When that anticipated grant from the American Endowment for the Humanities did not come through because President Reagan had cut its budget by half, our publication plans died. I submitted the ms. of *Companion* to major publishers. I later learned that Sheff himself had earlier gone the submission rounds with the best literate New York houses. One reason for rejection was that at the time of ALE's submission a major biography of Steinbeck was about to, then did, appear.[2] With an already narrow market interest in Steinbeck, a publisher would not push a then-minor, narrower work which could not compete with the major one. But, one must say it, Sheff was dull. Together those were hard odds to beat.

Things have changed now in the year 2000. There is no debate over Steinbeck's greatness. He is a prominent figure in American literature, his books are recognized as contributions to and portrayals of our America of that era—definitively so, for example, about the Great Depression or life near the canneries of Monterrey. His are novels sensitive and powerful; touching, painful and artistically realistic about lives in those harsh but not humorless days. Nowadays for academics Steinbeck is one of the great Americans to teach about, for readers simple or sophisticated. The Nobel was rightly awarded.

It is time then for an established press, one that still loves literature more than money, such as Don Ellis' Creative Arts, to make available for the now much larger audience readers, scholars, this important memoir. One grants that in later life theirs was a more ambivalent friendship, that is stated clearly enough in the Steinbeck biographies. Let that not affect our judgment of Dook's earlier importance. Steinbeck dedicated his Nobel address to Dook when sending him the ms. of his acceptance speech, telling him "all his books were dedicated to him." Dook was *the* major source of Steinbeck's earlier writing strength.

Two matters established then, and a third follows. One no longer argues the importance of Steinbeck to American letter; our history, national pride, or indeed, respecting the impoverished folk of the Great Depression, shame. Dook was for Steinbeck an immense resource as support, reader-critic, sporting-life companion and dearest friend in early manhood. The third fact, added by what we learn in this work, is the immense importance of Steinbeck himself to Dook, who in many ways defined his self-worth by virtue of that friendship, some contagious fame and identity in his having been an enhancing part of the writer's life. And Dook's life needed enhancing in middle and later years.

Let's consider that life. He hated work and could draw neither strength nor pride from any such achievements nor co-worker friendships. He did nothing well, nor did he seek to. He had given up women and wine; he was physically and civically inactive. He lived on the Andriano vineyard/orchard in semi-isolation but for the Andriano women and occasional visitors. Those lands then were just orchard country in back of Stanford University. Now upscale houses surround where he once lived. A freeway goes through his barn's living and my shanty's living rooms. He spent his time wood carving—terrible stuff—reading, welcoming with real warmth his few friends and visitors. He never complained. He was by now, by way of fame, Steinbeck's shadow. The Greek tragedians taught us that even the best of us succumb to envy. Sheff, bitter about himself, could be bitter toward others. I wonder if Steinbeck intuited a hint of envy.

One might argue Dook's salience to Steinbeck in the post-Nobel years; one can understand how it came to pass that Dook remains unknown until his own autobiography and memoir are presented in a much more readable form in this present work, albeit he is mentioned in every biography. The flat narrative is the style and the man. He suppressed excitement, chained whatever passions moved him and Steinbeck's as well. Empathy, if ever there were in Dook (and I do doubt that) is absent. Thus Dook-become-Sheff was ever so different from Steinbeck young and Steinbeck mature. The younger, wonderful friend to Steinbeck had become dull. Worlds apart. Steinbeck's visits to Sheff's barn became rare, harsh—even cruel—characterizations appeared. I know Dook disappointed himself; thus, I surmise he disappointed Steinbeck. How can a hard-working, compassionate, idealistic writer, a man of social import and personal conviction, an achiever and sometimes bon vivant—a man who could love life, women, ideals—how could Steinbeck not disapprove of his early friend become none of these? Sheff now a superficially contented almost-bore. Lazy. Living as fame's shadow, not much basking in that if the image is true. The foregoing is surmise on my part. I knew well the one, was next door when Steinbeck visited Dook but was not invited over. I know of his intimate Steinbeck only through our conversations, the *Companion* as memoir, and my own, perhaps over-psychologizing, inference. What the hell, I have been wrong before. But I did know Sheff well for over 30 years, and so do consider my views hypotheses for you to test from your knowledge of Steinbeck through his works and from the memoir itself here. Vico's rule: we know much about others because they are humans as are we.[3]

The foregoing challenge is one good reason to read this book. Consider the developments in these two lives in relationship to one another. There is a mystery there. Why that lazy withdrawal from work, liveliness, compassion, or any apparent effort to achieve competence doing anything? Each one of these traits so outstandingly contrasted in Steinbeck's life. This biography and memoir offer evidence for your consideration. If my poor inference is correct, no wonder there was separation! But if Steinbeck came to disdain, or at least be depressed by what his friend had become, why the hell couldn't—wouldn't—Steinbeck be the influence on Dook that Dook once was for Steinbeck, or indeed the two were for each other in their lively earlier interaction, adventure? Supportive. Energizing! Maybe you can solve the mystery. Even if you can't, read this book because for Steinbeck *aficionados* and scholars, Dook matters. This book is part of that Nobel.

There are also parallels in our own lives, our national evolution to what I have suggested about the later Steinbeck-Dook relationship. Somewhere along the 20th century way the simple, powerful, humane passions, tragic or joyful, those overall binding commitments to the good and compassionate, and that disciplined and masterful art which compels us to take note of the diverse depths of our being are being lost in our national spirit, and but for cinema, our art. If Dook had once such traits, Sheff in later life lost them but for his redeeming love of literature. Near my own mountain retreat lies Silicon Valley, the very wellspring and expression of man taken over by and absorbed in the machine. Recent studies suggest reduced social skills, human and creative artistic interests, increasing depression, are a corollary to the computer and television. (Ironic that some of the great Los Altos Hills houses of these masters of the chip, lords over ether—these antitheses of the interestingly human—were intrusively visible from Sheff's box house directly across the 8-lane, roaring freeway, the construction of which wiped out Sheff's barn, and my shanty. Sheff's colorless, plastic cottage was built by the state on remaining Andriano lands as a replacement for his barn. For Sheff and for much of our post-Steinbeck nation, we are losing as trait and experience that to which Steinbeck was most sensitive and communicated so powerfully. Consider most of our formulaic, market-oriented literature, the content of our television, the move toward violence and technological tricks. The human, the genuinely passionate beauty in joy and tragedy are gone. Steinbeck, viewing either our present times or Sheff's later life's lack of vitality and commitment would have been dismayed. Imagine how Steinbeck could have written about this shallower age. How can you write a book of passions, pain, or even pranks about folks who, buried in computers and their brokerage accounts, whose measure of leisure-time excellence is any television at all? Sheff by no means was that far gone, but in his later life blandness was prodromal.

The original foreword I wrote to the ALE 1983 edition is itself a pretty bad piece of work: saccharin, pretentiously folksy, phony as a $3 bill, uncritical, damn near hagiography, and gutless to boot. Dook and I *were* friends but much more ambivalently than that foreword would ever have allowed you to guess. I was a whippersnapper kid of a writer, Stanford lecturer, roustabout criminologist, half-assed politician, whatever. You will see as you read that I claimed to have responded to Sheff's sometimes bitterly sarcastic criticism of my stuff as though he were entirely right in his disdain. He well might have been. In any event utterly depressed by Sheff's criticisms of my drafts submitted to him, I threw away what Dook scorned. He scorned most of it. I stopped showing him my stuff and got it published instead. Not that I was ever a really successful writer, and God knows that, if Sheff had used Steinbeck as his gold standard, then I well should have, for the public good and the sake of letters or even entertainment, be forever denied possession of pen or typewriter/word processor. Even later, when a book or two came out which now and then a critic allowed as okay, Sheff was anything but interested or complimentary. Scorn, disdain—even though, as you will read, he had secretly kept a file of reviews, clippings, etc. featuring my work. There was a double side in him, a *Dopplegäng*ing so to speak, that held back pride and appreciation and replaced it with scathing criticism. At the very least Steinbeck had spoiled him for work such as mine.

It came to pass that, dutiful as I was in visiting him long after our shanty-next-to-barn days were over, I had become an academic, and all sorts of good stuff (as the Prince of This World might view achievement) were happening. He and I had ceased to be enthusiastic about each other. Might I have sabotaged convivial nights by my own need for praise from my older neighbor, drinking the Andriano Grignolino together—that is, until his ulcer dragged him onto the wagon, because of my own unmet need for praise from Sheff, a literary hero of sorts by virtue of his having been Steinbeck's first editor and goodfellow horseshitter? No damnit, I admit that the Andriano wine was not all that good, that we did joke, and talked many an evening away. Sheff was an uncomplaining, good companion. So there it is. I did like him and yet also, mostly later, simultaneously not.

You see it, don't you? The problem with biography, just as the journal *Biography*'s George Simson knows, writes, and teaches about, is that multiple appraising views of a person can be immensely varied or, in psychological terms, unreliably biased. Demographics, family, the luck of the draw predict most of what we believe and do anyway. And our times shape literature. The fact that I have a very different view now of Dook, or of his relationship to Steinbeck—may serve to tell you only that my memory is worse, my character as friend moreso, and that, flawed, I am a most uncertain mirror to other men. By 1985 when Dook was feeling both rich ($500K in the bank, he said) and chronically ill, things got worse. He was surely disappointed in me for not getting the *Companion* into public light. Can't blame him. Things had gotten so bad that I stopped visiting. And then a big fight by his proxy, or so I was told, toward the end. Someone promised him over the telephone that he could publish his memoir as a trade book, a big improvement over that small edition ALE had distributed at no cost to libraries, universities—and do it for $3K. That fellow necessarily wanted the ALE copyright transferred to him and even called me a bastard when I would not surrender it. (One cannot publish and market a trade book for $3K and, further negotiations were underway at last with a legitimate press.)

So much then for the reliability of biographies. Perhaps they are all inevitably revisionist. *Rashomon* being a fair model. Like Soviet history, Chinese capitalism, current politically correct thought, Catholic magazines' mascot painting of Jesus as black and a woman—Vico is right: the truth about a person is a shifting mental construct made of variegated stuff, Proteus before Plutarch. As for autobiography, I wrote one myself , taught life writing and psychology and foolishly claim to know something of those disciplines' literature, criticism. At the very least, Dook's own autobiography may be insufficient as full presentation of self (as Irving Goffman would have said). And the same for what went on with that dynamo Steinbeck. The events and portrait outlines are there, albeit disciplined, censored, suppressed, but as a "diary" quite likely reliable. Guts, color, the here-I-am-being-alive-of-it are missing.

So, speaking of intimate knowings and unknowings, I wonder about the contents of those undoubtedly fabulous letters Steinbeck and Sheff burned in that barn's back acre. Don't you see? One has to ask, Was it Sheff rather than Steinbeck who argued the match? That would have been typical of Dook-become-Sheff, and in relationship to Steinbeck I hold it possible as well. Burn the passions, deny the rich stuff, put a proper face on to fool the world. Nothing for a jury of your peers to hang you with. Now *there* is a mystery for you. I can't promise you the answer. I guarantee some clues from what you already know about human nature, fame, shame, lawsuits, marriages, self-disclosure. Could Steinbeck's good companion have been his moral censor?[4]

I write this near the place where Sheff and I lived, near the barn where the frontispiece photographs of Steinbeck and Dook were taken. As the Carmelites say, "Pray for me." And pray for all of us doing their best in life writing. Finally, thank you, spirit of Dook, for getting your friend John to keep writing.

Dick Blum
January 2000
Woodside, CA

Preface to the Reader

This is not a biography, nor is it a commentary or a critique. Those have been and will be provided by more competent and dedicated individuals who have analyzed and evaluated the life and works of John Steinbeck with scholarly thoroughness, sometimes with an assiduousness and penetration beyond my powers, although such studies might have puzzled him or driven him into roars of Homeric laughter.

Once, after the publication of his first book or two, he said, in essence, "I don't think it will ever be necessary, but if there ever has to be a biography of me, I want you to write it." At the time, in the flush of youthful enthusiasm about the potential of both of us, I agreed, but it was a promise I never fulfilled or really wanted to, particularly after I saw the erudition and explications that began to follow his rising star.

In 1938 I got a letter from Harry Thornton Moore, who said John had referred him to me because I knew more about John Steinbeck than he knew about himself. Flattered, I sent Moore two or three thousand words of jumbled fact, reminiscence, and comment, much of which was included in Moore's *The Novels of John Steinbeck*, the first book written about him.[1] It included an error or two that resulted from my inexplicitness and some that I couldn't be blamed for. I had no part in Moore's postulate that John had a breast fixation as demonstrated in the circular aspect of some of his titles and embodiments—*The Cup of Gold*, *The Corral de Tierra*, and other examples from his works. John was scornful of the idea.

As I mention below, I started saving John's letters because they were good letters, and I liked them—also, perhaps because I hate to throw things away, a quality on which he often remarked with some amusement. It is regrettable, both as a personal thing and as a documentary loss, that he later insisted I destroy the scores of letters he had sent me up to mid-1933, a period of his life least adequately covered in written records. They included one from Lake Tahoe about his disappointment in the unpublished *Cup of Gold*, and one to Ruth, my first wife, both in *Steinbeck: A Life in Letters*.[2] He was never secretive, but he refrained from gratuitous information about his plans and actions. And the explanations he did give often assumed a form that was more artistic or dramatic than the bare facts would warrant. In addition, he insisted that his memory was inaccurate and inadequate; that was sometimes proved when he disputed by version of something we had done together or that he had related to me.

During his life he occasionally referred other people to me as a repository of fact about him, and I have gladly given all the help I could to writers of books, articles, theses, and speeches, letting them examine and quote from letters, manuscripts, and other memorabilia I possessed. Frequent handling of such material, however, began to damage it, and I turned it over to the Stanford library, where it would have the best of care and attention as a collection available to students and scholars.

About 1950, with the growth of his reputation and following, I realized that our association over the years had been filled with many events that could be of interest and importance to developers of the Steinbeck saga, and with episodes that were of no importance at all except as humorous, even a bit reprehensible, sidelights upon a colorful career. And I was beginning to forget some of them.

As a result I started writing down without style or artifice a roughly chronological account of our association so that the facts as I remembered them might not be totally lost. Eventually I had piled up approximately 30,000 words of no literary merit, and not all the facts were unassailable. Then I put the whole thing away and almost forgot it.

During the last thirty or so years of Steinbeck's life, our communication was desultory. At times we corresponded frequently and at others, gaps of a year or two intervened. He was divorced by the wife I knew, acquired another whom I never met and who gave him two sons before a second divorce, and finally married Elaine Scott, whom I did meet four years before his death and continue to admire. With his winning the Nobel prize in 1962, critical interest in him and his work increased. In 1968 the Steinbeck Society was formed at Ball State University, Muncie, Indiana, by Tetsumaro Hayashi, Preston Beyer, and others. They began publishing the *Steinbeck Newsletter*, later to become the *Steinbeck Quarterly* with an ever-increasing list of subscribers. A number of new books about John were written, one of the first being Peter Lisca's *Wide World of John Steinbeck* in 1958, which was the product of much research and critical evaluation and served to stimulate further academic attention.[3] It had been preceded in 1957 by Tedlock and Wicker's *Steinbeck and His Critics*, a collection of articles and studies from many people who had known him and his work.[4] In 1963, J. E. Fontenrose produced *John Steinbeck: An Introduction and Interpretation*, an important contribution in the widening field of scholarship.[5] Many articles began to appear, and Steinbeck was starting to serve as subject for masters and doctors theses, not only in the United States but all over the world.

After Steinbeck's death in 1968, several people who knew of my friendship with him interviewed me on various aspects of that association and examined some of the letters, manuscripts, clippings, and other materials I had accumulated. Among these writers was

Jackson J. Benson,[6] working on a critical biography, and Nelson Valjean.[7] Valjean was preparing a biography of Steinbeck's California years and was the only one to see the loose documentary I had prepared twenty years earlier. I also supplied Elaine Steinbeck with copies of most of the letters for use in a compilation she was editing for publication in 1975.[8]

With such books and the intensive scholarship appearing in the *Quarterly*, I realized I knew things about Steinbeck that were available nowhere else and decided that it might be a good idea to rework my haphazard reminiscences, correcting some of the errors and bringing the account up to date insofar as was possible, though much of my later data was from correspondence. Thus these Memoirs.

Some of the material is based upon things that John told me, and in view of his "bad memory" and his capacity for polishing and rearranging the facts of a good tale, these must often be mildly suspect. I have tried to indicate at least some of the places where strict veracity may have suffered. I have done no research except where letters or printed material were handy—and not always then. Some of the dates and sequences may be out of place, especially during the years between 1925 and 1930, where correspondence was destroyed or lacking. We did see each other two or three times a year but my memory is inexact. Some of my accounts are of frivolous or regrettable episodes that have little relation to his writing, but they may contribute something to the picture of him as a man of diverse humors, talents, and faults.

As for the accuracy and dependability of his facts, a quotation from a letter shows some of his own doubts:

> I have thought about writing an autobiography but a real one. Since after a passage of time I don't know what happened and what I made up, it would be nearer the truth to set both down. I'm sure this would include persons who never existed. Goethe wrote such an account but I have not read it . . . He called it Fiction and Fact. I didn't know about this when I got to thinking about such an account . . . But surely the fictionizing and day dreaming and self-aggrandizement as well as the self-

> attacks are as much a part of reality as far as the writing is concerned as the facts are. And even the facts have a chamelion [sic] tendency after a passage of time. [March 2, 1964]

His remarks may well apply to a few of my facts, though I lack his capacities for dramatizing events. In most cases, I am very sure of things that we did together and his account of those that he told me about, however accurately, even though he may later have disputed the correctness of my memory or said that certain episodes never happened. As he remarked in the quotation above, the dreams and fictions are a definite part of reality; and to leave them out would be to omit an important part of the John Steinbeck who often could not resist editing, rearranging, and transmuting facts that were not in accord with what he thought they should be. Without that quality, he would not have been the man or the writer that he was.

Some of the excerpts from letters and other writings by John Steinbeck have already been printed in *Steinbeck: A Life in Letters* and have been quoted in part in various books and articles. As most of these letters were originally written to me, I feel they are an integral part of these recollections, as are my versions of episodes quoted or paraphrased by people who have interviewed me or read portions of my text. In addition, selected parts of my manuscript have been taped commercially by Spyglass Productions, Inc., of Monterey, California, as a part of a series called "Friends of John Steinbeck," to which I and others who knew him contributed.

Letter to Jawn from Dook

"You were the best friend I ever had."

I wrote that to your wife Elaine Steinbeck when you died in December 1968. It was completely true, though I had seen you only at rare intervals in the past thirty years or so, and most recently in 1964 when you brought Elaine to meet me for the first time.

It's hard to evaluate a friendship, especially when time has passed, draining warmth and immediacy from memories. I did not really know you until you moved into my dormitory room with me, though we had been acquainted since we entered Stanford three years earlier. We had even boxed together, and you told someone, *I like his getting up every time I knocked him down.* But only when we shared a room did I discover that you had literary interests and talents.

Do you remember when I had come to the university with $300 in the world? When that was gone by the middle of the second quarter, I had to find work, first as a printer's devil in the back shop of the *Palo Alto Times* and then in the University Press?

You recall, John, how my first roommate added to my feelings of alienation by subjecting me to almost constant ridicule for no reason other than a kind of sadistic pleasure that he seemed to find in deriding my interests, activities, and clothes? He was followed by several others, all engineers, who were pleasant enough but with whom I had little intellectual interest. By the time that you came to share my quarters I had almost no confidence in my self and very few friends—except in the print shop.

"They stuck me in with some Jew," you said. "I don't mind him being a Jew, but already he's got all the walls plastered with pictures of naked women. I don't think I'm going to like him and I'm damned if I want to live in a place decorated like that."

"From his name, my roommate may be a Jew, too," I said.

"If they'd be willing to move in together, how would it be with you and me?" you asked.

I said, "Fine," though I was still a bit dubious about you, John.

Our friendship developed rapidly when our feelings for literature and our mutual ambitions to write were established. You had already made progress, and although my efforts had produced almost nothing, you listened with apparent respect when I expressed my ideas. You even asked my advice on occasion. We like many of the same books, laughed at the same things, enjoyed nonsense games that we invented with words. You initiated discussions about life, morals, religion, and literature that let me express ideas in fields never touched on by previous roommates—or by the printers. When we argued, which we did frequently, it was largely for the joy of fencing with words, and we often changed sides in such exchanges.

When we enrolled together in a class in verse writing, we found new pleasure in the complex process of weaving meters, rhythms, and rhymes into disciplined expression. On occasion, inspiration failed us and we went out into the night to walk and look to the moon and stars for help. We wrote some very bad verse, but the creating of it brought satisfaction along with a new awareness of the intricacy of language and its delicious potentials. Once in a while, one of us produced a fine line and both of us were proud.

For the first time in my college career I had the feeling of sharing, not only of living arrangements but of ideas and sympathy. With it came a rebirth of my flagging self-respect, an intellectual blossoming, and a feeling of gratitude and affection that has never disappeared.

In the years that followed, there were long separations and even periods of estrangement over misunderstandings. But there were also many extended interludes in which we quickly resumed the old intimacy. I visited your home in Salinas a number of times, meeting your parents and sisters. I spent parts of summers with you in your Pacific Grove cottage. There, against your own background, you revealed qualities and enthusiasms that I had not known before. The pine forests behind the town, the bay below, the rugged hills seemed to strengthen him and become a part of his thought and feeling in a way that you later embodied in parts of *To a God Unknown.* Some of those feelings you transmitted to me, giving me a sense of perfect rapport with you and the terrain.

By no means were those visits all on such a plane. We drank and whored and did foolish things, but there was an air of camaraderie that I had never known before. It was strong the summer that we went to work in the Manteca sugar-beet factory where it was we against the people we worked with—not as an enmity or hostility but as a secret awareness that the hard work and the harsh hours were a kind of game and a stop-gap toward glorious things to come. We fraternized with our fellow workers and got along well with them, but there was an understanding between us that this was an adventure, almost a big joke, that we would appreciate later.

There were other periods of close association. When you and Carol came south to get married, you stayed with me and my wife. The house teemed with people and there were constant distractions. We went with others into the High Sierra, and often by choice stayed behind in camp as our companions ranged up and down the Kings River. We made a miserable attempt at laying a foundation for a cabin in Trabuco Canyon and shared the ignominy of our failure. You visited me in Marysville while gathering material for *The Grapes of Wrath* and were wounded and angry, misunderstanding me completely when I refused your enthusiastic offer to subsidize my further education in Europe. That led to our estrangement of a year or more.

With the beginning of your real success, you moved to New York, and with occasional exceptions, correspondence became the bond that remained of our friendship. We wrote not infrequently and with warmth, though you were often distracted by the teeming effects of your new life, new acquaintances, and the new fame that genuinely disturbed you, while I, somewhat awed not by you but by the eminence that had been thrust upon you, was hesitant to add to your letter-writing obligations. We lost track of each other during the war, and when we resumed writing, the old amity remained, but slightly shadowed by the passage of time, by distance, and by the diversity of experience.

How did you feel about me? I never doubted your strong affection as evidenced by your long and close association, by your confidences, and by the tone of your letters, which you often signed with "Love." You shocked me in 1979 when [Pat] Covici's published letters included one from 1948 in which you made some painfully derogatory remarks about me.[1] I have no explanation beyond the fact that it was a period in which your letters showed a deep depression bordering on despair, and that I may have intruded at an unfortunate time or with an air that did not meet your mood.

I would still feel stunned by those remarks were it not for the subsequent letters to me, which, up to the last one before your death, showed no signs of anything but sincere trust and affection, together with your final visit in 1964 when you drove a hundred miles to see me and introduce me to Elaine. I had no doubt then that we were friends and always had been.

Love,
C. A. S.

John Steinbeck, the Good Companion

HIS FRIEND DOOK'S MEMOIR

There are beautiful things ahead. I wonder if you know why I address this manuscript to you. You are the only person in the world who believes I can do what I set out to do. Not even I believe that all the time. And so, in a kind of gratitude I address all my writings to you, whether or not you know it.

—John Steinbeck to Carlton ("Dook") Sheffield
Dedication of *To a God Unknown* from Dook's *Ledger*, 1933

Part 1:

Roommates at Stanford

Sometime in the late fall of 1919, during the beginning of my freshman year at Stanford University, I became aware of a large, quiet freshman classmate. We were enrolled in a class in elementary French, and beyond the fact that I knew his name was Steinbeck and that he seemed unhappy when called upon to recite, I knew nothing about him. We nodded when we met, and once in a while exchanged pungent views on the absurdities of French grammar and pronunciation, but that was about the extent of our acquaintanceship, though we both lived in Encina Hall, the huge old dormitory now almost exclusively occupied by administration.

He was seventeen years old, almost eighteen, then, and looked a little older. His hair was dark and curly, and the way it was clipped high and close around his temples emphasized the height of his forehead, the breadth of this face at the cheekbones and its length down to the heavy, bluntly tapering chin. He had thick lips; his ears seemed to stick out at a slight angle; his nose was large, broad, and rather shapeless. In general, his expression was serious and dignified, but when he laughed, as he often did, one suddenly noticed how blue his eyes were and what an intense sparkle they had. They seemed to dance with merriment and delight when something pleased him.

Apparently he was eager to try everything. He went out for freshman football and was tried at various positions in the line, but in spite of his six feet and 180 pounds, he soon gave up the idea, perhaps because he could not work up the required spirit during a mere scrimmage, and perhaps because he had never taken kindly to being ordered around. Also, having for some time been larger than most of his schoolmates, he had early developed an instinctive gentleness in games requiring physical contact, lest his size and weight bring injury to his opponents or give him unfair advantage.

Within the next several months he also tried his hand at crew and while straining at the oars damaged the blood vessels of his legs, an injury from which he never fully recovered. He played polo, too, probably as a member of the ROTC unit, and that contributed a badly cracked kneecap that gave him periodic trouble for the rest of his life. It is possible that he tried still other sports. If so, he did not distinguish himself in any of them.

For a time he worked in the evenings as a waiter at the City Café in Palo Alto, a Chinese restaurant much patronized by students who wanted plenty of fair-quality food at reasonable prices. A $5.50 meal ticket cost $5 and lasted quite a while, what with the cost of the average meal ranging from 25 cents to 45 cents. The job, however, was a short one. After a couple of months, a minor feud developed between John and one of the Chinese cooks—John professed to forget the basis of it. One evening the disagreement reached a climax and the cook brandished a butcher knife, screaming insults. Steinbeck could not understand the words but their import was clear. Still wearing his apron, he dashed judiciously for the swinging door to the main restaurant. He and the knife got there simultaneously, but it remained sticking in the wood while he kept on going past the startled diners and out through the front door. There he paused long enough to tear off his apron and throw it inside the entry way. Except as a customer he never came back.

Stanford used to have several traditional interclass battles, especially between freshmen and sophomores, though one by one these games have been abandoned, largely because of the frequent resultant casualties. The Tie-Up, held a few days after autumn registration, was a good-natured gang fight in which the two lower classes, armed with short lengths of rope, faced each other on the football field. At a signal the contest began, to see which class could tie up the greatest number of the other, dragging each prisoner behind the lines, where he was slapped in the face with a large paintbrush dripping with the class color. Then the captive was liberated but forbidden to return to the fray.

An old photograph taken in 1920 of the sophomore class just before the Tie-Up shows that John had no fear of innovations. He and his roommate, George More, stand in the center of the very front row, ropes dangling from their belts and elbows locked. But whereas the rest of the 200 or so youths behind them are fully, though disreputably, dressed, John and George are bare from the waist up, a gross immodesty in that generation. Both were, moreover, thoroughly greased to make their capture more difficult. The faces of their companions plainly show the boldness of such unconventionality; every surrounding face is turned toward the pair with laughing astonishment, admiration, or amused disapproval. (Stripping for action was one thing, but being *photographed* that way was going almost too far.)

Just how they made out in the battle is not recorded, but they emerged without any notable damage. And from that year on until the contest was discontinued, the greased, bare torso was *de rigueur* for all contestants, a few of whom even went so far as to appear in nothing but swimming jocks.

In his freshman year, John had also set another precedent in inter-class rivalry, though this one was neither generally adopted nor condoned. A group of marauding sophomores hunting for frosh to bedevil shouldered their way into his room (the locking of doors was forbidden) and summarily demanded that he come with them. He had been expecting such an incursion and was prepared. From his desk drawer he pulled a long-barreled .45-caliber

Smith and Wesson revolver, snapped off the safety, and invited them to come and get him. After a brief conference they decided not to and retired, muttering threats about what future actions they would take to punish such a lack of sportsmanship. As far as I can learn, he was never troubled again, though the incident did nothing to increase his popularity.

Another photograph, taken about the same time, shows him again as a non-conformist. On the broad stone steps in front of Encina most of the residents of the hall were gathered for the start of the annual Pajamarino, a mildly Rabelaisian tradition in which everyone put on his loudest pajamas or nightshirt and toured the campus in shrieking serpentine, making special point of running through the ten-existent sororities and women's halls. Instead of pajamas, John wears a violently striped shirt, a turban, and a bath towel that is several inches short of his bare knees. It is held in place by something that looks like a Sam Browns belt from which hangs a whiskbroom. Dangling from the rear is a University of California pennant. His face bears an elaborate burnt-cork moustache.

Early photographs of him, however, are extremely rare, for he consistently refused to pose before the camera. A woman to whose house I had taken him about 1924 was unpleasantly insistent on taking a snapshot of him, even after he had at first courteously and then quite brusquely refused. When she continued to focus on him, he abruptly turned and walked away down the street, leaving his coat and hat behind. Later, in explanation of his attitude he said, "I have a superstitious feeling about being photographed as if the camera took away a part of me I can never get back." During our college period I did manage to get two or three bad pictures of him with a Brownie, but over his protests.

His early publishers had trouble with him on the same score, and for some years the only publicity picture of him they had was a black-and-white sketch. (He liked that, he said, because it did not look a bit like him, and therefore nobody could recognize him.) Eventually, in 1935, in Pacific Grove just after *Tortilla Flat* had come out, he reluctantly permitted one "official" photograph to be taken for general use. Another, taken about the same time by Sonya Noskourak, was published in a lush interview:

> Down out of the hills he came, he said; he felt as if he had somehow always lived in them. And John Steinbeck looks as if he might have; of giant height, sunburned, with fair hair and fair moustache and eyes the blue of the Pacific on a sunny day and a deep, quiet, slow voice. He belongs to this Coast, the Monterey bay, the ranges and cliffs of the Big Sur country. . . .[1]

The article first gave currency to the erroneous statement that he was born in Florida. He was really born on February 27, 1902, in the family home on Central Avenue in Salinas, California. Not for several years did he permit other photographs, and then only because his growing fame made it inescapable.

In the spring of 1920, or about the middle of his sophomore year, I had come to know him better, and from time to time we put on boxing gloves and sparred a few rounds in my room or the larger one which he shared with George Mors. Invariably I got the worst of it, for John had height, reach, weight, speed, and skill plus a catlike movement which made his blows unexpected and blurringly fast. On the other hand, he fought considerately, usually trying to keep his punches from being too punishing and never taking unfair advantage, though I regularly ended on the floor.

One Saturday morning early in 1921 I had agreed to bring my gloves to his room for a workout. When I opened the door, he was not there. George, his roommate, was sitting on the edge of his own bed, still dressed in pajamas and staring in sleepy puzzlement at a piece of paper as if it said something he didn't understand. There was something peculiar about the looks of the room too, though I didn't know quite what.

"Where's John?" I asked.

"Damned if I know," George said; "Read this," and he held out the sheet of paper.

It said, in essence: "Gone to China—see you again sometime.

Please look after the chipmunks." It also asked that George send to John's home in Salinas his trunk and a few bundles that were stacked on John's bed.

Together we looked around the room and quickly discovered what made the difference. Some of John's possessions were gone—clothes, typewriter, luggage, and other odds and ends. A cage which had contained a bird (I don't remember what kind) was open, but two chipmunks were still in another cage, and fish and turtles still swam in the small glass aquarium that stood on the window sill.

George was completely mystified and could offer no explanation. John had said nothing about going away nor had he given any hint that there might be reasons for his doing so. And why China, for God's sake? Neither of us had any answers. George said that all John's possessions seemed to be in place the night before, though John hadn't come home by the time George went to sleep. John must have come in during the night and, moving silently, packed, written the note, and taken his things away, letting the bird go free.

~

Only once in the next two and a half years did I hear anything more about John Steinbeck—somebody reported seeing him at "Big Game" time in 1922, his coat lined with dozens of chemist's phials filled with grain alcohol, which he was sharing liberally with friends—and during that time I almost forgot him. In fact, when I next saw him on January 2, 1923, I could barely recall his name and made the monumental mistake of calling him "Steiny." (He had always resented nicknames and viewed that one with even more distaste than "Jack" or "Johnny.") I never did it again.

Nor did I ever succeed in getting a full or coherent story of the reasons for his disappearance or of all his activities during his absence, and I have lost some of the details of what he did tell me. In brief, the reasons he gave involved an unidentified girl he had been seeing in San Francisco—one who had wounded him very deeply, and who, he felt, had intolerably abused his confidence and trust; how I can't recall. (There were other and less-romantic reasons.)

Anyway, he decided to run away to sea, and China sounded like a good place. He returned to his dormitory room, collected his most essential possessions, and departed without waking George.

In San Francisco, he looked around for a ship, but none of the shipping companies was hiring inexperienced seamen or even cabin boys. For several weeks he covered the waterfront, hunting for a sea-going job of any kind and meeting with nothing but refusals and discouragements. He may have communicated with his family, perhaps with one of his two older sisters, but I don't think he gave them any details about his plans or how to reach him.

Finally, his money gave out, and with it, temporarily at least, him maritime ambitions. During the next few months, he apparently picked up anything in the way of work that he could find.

One of this jobs was as a haberdashery clerk in Capwell's, the Oakland department store, during the Christmas holidays, according to a friend. Robert Bennett, at whose home he was staying, relates that when his mother inveigled both young men into accompanying her to church, John disrupted the sermon with audible comments on the minister's advocacy about food for the soul as opposed to food for the body.[2] Bennett's account is convincing, but such behavior was highly uncharacteristic of John, who avoided any public actions that would call attention to himself.

Eventually, skirting Stanford, he made his way down into the Salinas valley, where he had been born and reared, working at jobs as a laborer and ranch hand. At length he hired out on a big ranch above King City, which is about 50 miles south of Salinas, and there he remained, gaining the status of a straw boss or overseer but living in the bunkhouse with the men, many of whom were Mexicans. His experiences there furnished the background for *Of Mice and Men*, published in 1937. As he later told it, he worked very hard and didn't think at all. The first point may be true; the second is highly debatable. He never told me how he decided to come back to school in January, 1923.

~

I hardly recognized him when we met in the Journalism building on registration day, but he called me by name and asked me whom I was rooming with. It happened that my previous roommate had left school and I had not yet seen the new one who had been assigned to my quarters. I explained that to John while trying to put together what I could remember of him, which wasn't very much.

Somehow I had the idea he was studying engineering, and I had found little community of interest with the engineer who had shared , my room earlier, but this would be better than going in with someone sight unseen.

The plan worked out perfectly. The lad with the interest in nude pictures hit it off well with the one assigned to me and they both liked the other room, which was larger than mine, so John and I moved in together, to remain till I was graduated in June.

Quickly I was disillusioned about his being an engineer of any sort. On the contrary, like me, he was majoring in English, perhaps with a minor in journalism. (The English-Journalism major at the time enabled one to evade all courses in formal grammar and composition.) On our first or second evening in our room, he brought out a little pile of manuscripts, some of them written on the King City ranch, and stated without qualification or embarrassment, "I'm going to be a writer."

That was fine, I said. I wanted to be a writer too, though privately I was a little bit skeptical about the chances of either of us. Some of the stories he read me seemed to be pretty fair, though they were certainly not polished work. What fascinated me most was his method of reading them, for he seemed to be struggling between self-consciousness and emotion over what he had written. His voice went higher than was normal for him and read rapidly, with words quickly pronounced but tending to blur at the ends as if he were embarrassed at uttering them. His tone in general was flat, but it was the flatness of carefully restrained excitement. He kept good control of his face while reading, except for one eyebrow, which arched high as he reached something that he liked, that moved him, or that he was dubious about. He was inclined to hurry at the ends of sentences, underemphasizing the final word or two and rushing into the next one as if afraid of being interrupted. When he finished, he never looked at his auditor but grimaced depreciatingly, the single eyebrow as high as it would go and his hands fumbling busily at arranging the sheets or putting them away while he made some off-hand comment about the piece he had been reading or, as often as not, abruptly changed the subject. As the years passed and he became successful, he showed increased sureness and satisfaction when he knew something was good, but his method of reading did not materially change, and the eyebrow still arched skeptically.

Our room was a small one, originally intended to lodge a single student before it became necessary, with increased enrollment, to double and then almost triple the number of residents in the dormitory. With two cots, four chairs, two dressers, a big study table, books, two trunks, and a variety of miscellaneous equipment, space was at a premium and the two small closets were barely adequate for our major items of clothing. The walls were dead-white plaster, badly scarred from the decorative activities of generations of students. Even worse scarred was the heavy composition floor covering, in which every chair, table, and bed leg had left an ineradicable indentation, as had a number of pairs of hob-nail boots. The woodwork was painted an uninspiring grey. It was not a cheerful or colorful place.

When Steinbeck moved in, my decorative scheme was amorphous and haphazard. The pennants and home-town photographs with which I had adorned the walls in my first year were gone, and so were most of the more sophomoric "trophies" that had followed them, though some, like a long braid of blonde hair, some stolen signs, and a variety of more-or-less glamorous magazine pictures of females remained. Also, there were some of my amateurish experiments in art, in emulation of cardboard "paintings" created by a campus artist as part of the decor for a dormitory dance. Having stolen one of his winged scarabs, I bought heavy cardboard and show-card ink, made a couple of imitations of it, and then branched out into other pseudo-Egyptian inventions—clumps of palm trees, an out-of-perspective pyramid, a sphinx, and an oasis. After that, sometimes with the aid of a home-made pantograph, I had produced a Japanese-type mountain, some animals, an Indian head (Stanford teams were The Indians then), a lighted bomb with a pertinent inscription, a menacing skull on a saffron background, and an assortment of humorous posters. The outline of most of the figures had been laboriously carved with a jack knife. They were scattered profusely around the walls and doors, and to my uncritical eye they didn't look half bad. At any rate, they served to break up the dead white glare of the plaster.

John made no comment, but soon he appeared with a roll of soft brown patternless wallpaper which we affixed as an unbroken panel from the floor to a height of about four feet. That in itself did much to take the curse off the white walls, and in addition, it left far less space for my monstrosities. Eventually, most of those were thrown or given away, but a few of the best ones remained, properly spaced to set them off to what advantage was possible. The improvement in the room was remarkable, and it even gained us frequent compliments from other residents of the dormitory, who lived, for the most part, in quarters where every inch of wall space was cluttered with everything that could be glued, taped, or nailed to it.

Steinbeck's next contribution was less conventional and decidedly more startling. Taking up part of our meager floor space was a large wooden packing box holding articles for which there was no other place, and on top of it was a small steamer trunk, shorter and narrower than the box. The edifice was unbeautiful and usually was loaded with a junk heap of odds and ends. John produced part of a roll of turkey-red broadcloth and experimented with it as a cover for the eyesore. What resulted was largely accidental, but when it was finished, we had probably the only altar in the whole dormitory—certainly the only one of its kind. The box and trunk became a stepped dais of which the rich red covering continued up the wall behind it for three feet and then extended out over it in a graceful canopy with the corners held by almost invisible threads. Two long strips of wide white gauze bandage near the sides of the back drape broke the solidness of the color and helped to focus attention on the top step of the altar, in the rear center of which stood an eight-inch kewpie doll, fully swathed in a very white handkerchief except for the face and very blonde hair. She, John announced, was the Goddess of Chastity.

As an afterthought we constructed a smaller sacrificial altar on the lower step, made by covering a folding Sterno stove with a white cloth. Across it, diagonally, lay a gleaming Mexican dagger that John had picked up somewhere. The arrangement was highly effective, but it brought us some dubious and speculative glances from visitors to the room, especially those whose sense of humor was conventional.

~

Experimenting with the concept of the altar, we tried removing the dagger and cloth and lighting a can of Sterno before the goddess, discovering to our delight that in an otherwise darkened room, Sterno burns with an eerie flame that virtually decolorizes everything, illuminating all surroundings with a ghastly greenish flicker. The possibilities were too good to waste. On two or three occasions when friends were expected, we lit the spectral flame at their approach, extinguishing all other lights, and let our visitors come in to find us kneeling before our luridly lit shrine, as if in adoration. Most of them quickly understood the joke, but a few regarded us afterward with an uneasy suspicion.

~

John never spoke at any length about his earlier life, and I gathered only bits and pieces of it, disconnected episodes and reminiscences at school, and later, from visits to Salinas and Pacific Grove.

He did not mention his high-school athletic career or his literary work on school papers and year books or his having been president of his graduating class. He told me about having a pony as a boy and falling off it when sexually stimulated to his first ejaculation while riding it. He also said that in teaching his younger sister, Mary, to ride it, he had tied her feet together under the pony's stomach to keep her safe in the saddle but that she had slipped sideways and been dragged some distance before he could rescue her.

He mentioned his first seduction, which he said came by a teenage baby sitter with only one leg, who introduced him to erotic delights while he was in her care during the absence of his parents. He spoke of driving down to Pacific Grove on summer weekends and for vacations with the family in the tiny cottage that they had built there. It was a day-long trip in the horse-drawn buggy, and the twenty-mile road, which carried them past the Corral de Tierra (prototype of Las Pasturas del Cielo, his later *Pastures of Heaven*) was long and dusty. But there were very few such fragments. I learned more about his youth from his writings than from him, and he often insisted that his memory was poor and unreliable, although is writings show impressively how excellent his memory was for people, places, and living and growing things. He was less dependable about things he had done and experiences he had undergone. In many cases he strongly contradicted my vivid memories of events and exploits, some of which were even documented in letters he had written. On occasion he professed complete forgetfulness of activities we had shared, and more than once referred questioners to me to supply details about himself that he said he could no longer recall.

~

During the six months that we lived in Room 32 Encina, John brought in a number of friends and acquaintances, with some of whom he kept in touch for the rest of his life. One of the first was Carl Wilhelmson, a dour Finn, who later lived in San Francisco with his wife, Virginia, until his death in 1968. He also wrote two or three other novels which did not find a publisher and at least one which he decided was "not good enough" to send out. Late in life he published a book for boys—perhaps more than one—but was somewhat ashamed of doing so.

Carl, as I first remember him, was dark and morose, with a heavy accent. He loved abstruse arguments about philosophy and literature, and frequently would choke with rage when we opposed him too vehemently or became frivolous in our discourse. Occasionally he would divulge bits about his past, and pieced together they make a remarkable story, although the authenticity of some of these pieces may be doubtful. As I remember it, he ran away to sea from his home in Finland at the age of 13, but returned to get something of an education, including, I believe, a stint at the University of Paris. Going back to sea, he jumped ship on the west coast of South America and was subsequently jailed in Ecuador or Peru. After having served three months or so, he had ingratiated himself to a point where he was released and made a member of the police force. While a policeman for two years, he either learned English or polished his knowledge of it to a point that later demonstrated itself in a scholarly precision. His writing often tended to be complex and over-formal.

Thus equipped, Carl left the constabulary and came to the United States with the intention of continuing his education, but apparently just in time to get into the army for World War I. Of his service I have learned nothing, but he contracted tuberculosis and was discharged with a high-disability rating and allowance. Shortly afterward, he entered Stanford as a "Federal Student" and got an AB in English, granted about 1925. Following graduation he taught English in a school in Japan for a year. Until friends pointed it out, he had never seen any humor in the fact that a year's output of Japanese schoolboys should be speaking fractured English further tinctured with strong Finnish overtones. In fact, he was never quite convinced that he spoke anything but the purest of English, though his *w*'s always came out as *v*'s; and his *v*'s, as *f*'s.

Carl and John remained friends, though from about 1940 on they saw little of each other, and John more than once asked me for his current address. Earlier, however, they had lived together on several occasions and had often visited with other.

If Carl's story seems amusing (and there is much more of it), the alleged history of Pat Shannon (whose name may have been Patric Vaughan or half a dozen other variants) is preposterous. John found him in an English course where they were both enrolled and brought him to the room, starting a long succession of visits. There were probably elements of truth in the tales Pat told about himself, but there were so many tales and they were frequently so contradictory that we long ago gave up everything but wondering about him. He claimed to have been born in the north of Ireland, to have served in the British navy, to have been bombed while on a leave at home, to have deserted and come to the United States. Somewhere in the Southwest, he was persuaded to join a fine club where the members were paid for belonging, and when America joined the First World War, he discovered that the "club" was the National Guard and that he was in the army. Apparently his service history was highly unorthodox, for the certain facts are few. He, too, was discharged with a disability pension, but he told us that while drunk he reenlisted under another name and deserted when he sobered up and discovered what he'd done. Still later he was thrown off a freight train in Texas, and after wandering through the desert for miles was almost dead of hunger and thirst by the time he stumbled into an army camp. There he reenlisted under still another name, remained for two or three weeks to be well fed and rested from his ordeal, and then deserted again. During all this he was somehow still drawing his original disability pension and continued to do so for several years.

But the army finally caught up with him. He was ordered to make extensive repayments (you can't draw an army pension while you're a member of the army, even though you've deserted) and to serve a year in McNeil Island, Washington, a federal penitentiary. In any event, the night before he was to go into custody, he gathered all the money he could get his hands on and invited all his friends to a tremendous party. The next morning, according to report, a very drunken crew of merrymakers drove to the bridge leading to the prison and carried a comatose prisoner to the guards to begin serving his term.

More than a year later, Pat visited me and my wife in Eagle Rock for several days. He spun a new yarn of having spent his boyhood sailing a native boat around the Indonesian seas, and gave us further details of fantastic exploits. He had recently been working as a zoo keeper in San Francisco, he said, till he came back to his room and found a hanged Chinese dangling there. Pat disappeared with warning from our house in the middle of the night.

The last time we saw him was two years later when he phoned from San Pedro to ask if he could come and take a bath—a distance of 45 miles or so. He came, bringing with him a stolid Swedish girl who also wanted a bath. His story was that he had joined a party of strangers at an Italian restaurant in San Francisco, where he often ate, learned that the party was in celebration of the host's acquisition of a freight boat, and agreed enthusiastically when the alcoholically inspired host proposed that the whole group accompany him on his freighter, which was leaving that night for Guatemala to pick up a carload of tomatoes. So they all piled aboard just as they were (one girl was wearing only Japanese silk pajamas and Pat didn't have a coat), and the ship was half way down the California coast before anyone came out of his alcoholic haze.

There were many other acquaintances that John brought in. Gordon Bowers was often in trouble at Stanford, usually because of alcohol, and finally left to ship out. Once he returned with several cases of Scotch whiskey and Chinese absinthe, which he sold or gave away to friends in the dormitory before returning to sea. It was reported that eventually he committed suicide by jumping out of a high window, possibly in a hospital. He was said to have come from an excellent family and to have been brilliant.

There were Webster ("Toby") Street, who provided John with the basic plot for one of his books and became a leading maritime lawyer in Monterey; Frank CR, later also a lawyer in Palo Alto; and many others, some of whom remained friends for his lifetime.

~

In the spring of 1923, Steinbeck invited me to spend the Easter holidays at his Salinas home on Central Avenue, one block west of the main street of town. We drove down in my car.

His 1890s house was large, white, and formal. It had modified iron-and-wood gingerbread decorations, high roof with gables, a long, narrow front porch, and a relatively small but well-kept yard, where his father grew fine gladioluses. Everything emanated respectability. Several steps led up to the porch, and the glass in the front door was multi-colored.

Inside, the house was also eloquent of the turn of the century, its high ceilings and furnishings sound and well cared for. Opening from just to the left of the front door was John's mother's bedroom, and behind that was his father's. To the right was the traditional parlor with sliding doors, kept closed most of the time, rarely used by the family, which preferred the more informal living room behind it as the center of household activities. The parlor was usually kept darkened, dustless, and in perfect order, its heavy furniture carefully polished. The living room, although meticulously neat, had an air of greater comfort and appeared more lived in. Behind it was the large, somber dining room, top-heavy with massive furniture and precisely arranged glass and china cupboards. Beyond was the kitchen, large and fairly modern, with a narrow, closed-in porch for refrigerator and laundry at the rear. A utility room with mangle and pressing machine opened off the dining room. The small storage barn in the back yard had perhaps housed a horse in earlier days.

The upstairs, which had four or five bedrooms, was reached by a steep, narrow staircase that began opposite the front door. For the most part these rooms had been the exclusive domain of the four children, who used their own ideas about furnishing and decorating them. Beth and Esther, the two older sisters, were married and long gone, and their two rooms had lapsed into the impersonality of guest rooms. John's room, to the left of the head of the stairs, was small, and its space was further diminished on one side by the slant of the roof. A room farther down the hall belonged to Mary, the youngest sister, who had just started at Stanford as a freshman.

John had told me earlier of a series of experiments he had conducted with the decoration of his room. He had at one time covered the walls with zigzag zebra stripes of black and white, which soon threatened his sanity. He had also experimented with solid colors: with black, which sent him into profound depression; and red, which aroused murderous rages. He also claimed to have tried yellow, with resulting gaiety and happiness, but it is probably that while he may have considered such experiments, most of them were never actually put into execution as other than characteristic conversational gambits. When I saw the room, it was quiet and unspectacular in every respect.

John Ernst Steinbeck, Sr., usually called Ernst, gave the immediate impression of kindness, tolerance, and sweetness of character. His voice was low and soft, nor did he often raise it—never in my experience—and his smile was ready and sympathetic. He was a big man and rangy. Both his movements and his voice were slow, but it was the slowness of careful consideration and conserved energy. He was universally liked and respected, and he served for many years, perhaps until his death in the 1930s, as treasurer of Monterey County. His ancestry was mainly German, with perhaps some Swiss and Scotch. John told me that the name had originally been von Grosssteinbeck.

Although Olive Hamilton Steinbeck was dynamic, she expended much of her abundant energy on trivial things. About the house she pottered and bustled continuously, cleaning, dusting, moving furniture, cooking, and performing all the other household tasks, talking insistently as she moved rapidly from room to room, sometimes seeming to forget why she was hurrying or what her conversation was about. John gave excellent descriptions of both his parents, and especially of her, in *East of Eden*.

Once, as I sat reading alone in the living room, she hastened in, talking firmly to no one. As she saw me she stopped, stared frowningly at me for a moment, and then said as if demolishing an annoying argument with a triumphant truth, "Peach ice cream and things like that are *very* nice!"The next minute she had bustled on into the dining room, having, I suspect, hardly been aware of who I was or that she had spoken to me.

She was short and stout and addicted to white dresses that emphasized the pouter-pigeon contours of her bust. Some of her commanding presence may have come from her early experiences in relatively primitive areas of Northern California, where she served as a school teacher. I believe that she was active in various women's clubs and civic organizations of the Salinas area, and I know that she made frequent trips to San Francisco for shopping and social and cultural activities.

John told me that when he was 15 or 16, he went with some friends for an evening along "Tijuana Street," the nearby stronghold of Mexican and Filipino field workers, where gambling, vice, and other illegal activities were rampant. There he drank considerable quantities of various beverages, including "green dragon," a brew involving marijuana and alcohol. By the time he finally stumbled home he had rolled in gutters, torn his clothes, and been sick all over himself. He managed to crawl up the porch steps, but the door was locked and so were the windows. Too unsteady and nauseated to try other possible means of entry, he rang the doorbell and collapsed on the porch, vomiting some more.

To the door came his mother in her long white nightgown. "What's the matter, John?" she asked with some apprehension.

"Mother, I'm drunk," he said.

She looked at him with tender indignation. "John, you're sick!"

"No, I'm drunk."

Already she was helping him to his feet. "You certainly are not. You're sick, and don't try to tell me anything else." So she took him in, gave him a bath, and put him to bed.

During my brief stay we wandered around the town, visiting his father's office in the courthouse, the houses of a few friends, favorite pools on the willow-lined Salinas river, and other points of interest. We talked with a few people and had a pleasant but quiet time, which included the covert drinking of a bottle of bootleg gin in company with his sister Mary, who was home from Stanford for a part of the vacation. We felt very worldly.

On a later occasion, I visited during "Big Week," the period when the whole valley, along with much of Northern California, centers its attention on the annual Rodeo, held in a huge circular bowl north of the city. Before and during the contests and spectacles there, a festive spirit grips the community with parades, parties, and celebrations. We joined some of the activities, during which liquor flowed freely as if Prohibition were not the law of the land. Western costumes were everywhere. It was all joyous and exciting, with horses ridden into buildings, bands playing deafeningly in crowded rooms, and people singing stridently as they passed bottles around. Somehow, John and I never went to the rodeo itself, though I understood that the family, like all good Salinas people, had annual tickets.

~

After the death of both elder Steinbecks, the house passed into the possession of the Catholic diocese of Monterey, and during the 1960s and early '70s was used by the Newman Club of Hartnell Community College. Some of its student residents even insisted in 1972 that they had seen the ghost of John Steinbeck appearing there on several occasions with no evidence of hostile intent. In 1973, the house was listed for sale and a fund was raised to keep it from being demolished and to preserve it as a historical monument. The Valley Guild, a charitable organization, now owns the building and operates a restaurant in it. Whether that has discouraged the "ghost," there is no way of knowing. John himself alleged that the house had a resident poltergeist when he lived there. He never saw it but often heard it at night climbing the stairs and striking a certain squeaking step in just the right sequence.

~

Back at Stanford, we found our friendship getting closer as we uncovered a community of tastes and interests. One of those interests, to my disapproval, was a blonde Palo Alto girl with whom I had been going desultorily for much of my college career. During that period I had timidly and ineffectively been trying to seduce her. She steadfastly demurred, though yielding enough to keep me hoping.

Then one evening I introduced her to John, and in a very brief time he had made a date with her for a few nights later. The night came, and while he carefully shaved and dressed, I pretended to study but found time for insulting remarks about treacherous friends, love pirates, rattlesnakes, and the like, all of which he took in high good spirits as was intended. I think the charge of duplicity in stealing my girl did bother him a little bit, but not enough to keep him home.

A considerable number of hours later, I was awakened from my deep and peaceful sleep by screams of agony. Thumps and crashes were mingled with the howls. As I sat up in bed, I could see by the light of a small student lamp turned against the wall that it was John. Stark naked, he was dancing around the room holding tightly to his penis with one hand and clutching a small hard-rubber syringe in the other, obviously in excruciating pain, and flopping his member about in his fist, was both startling and hilarious.

I didn't understand why he was yelling, but the syringe made one thing very clear. The girl's virtue had not been impregnable and John was not one to let sentiment prevail over practical considerations. Coming in very quietly so as not to waken me and give me evidence of his perfidy, he had given himself a prophylactic, using part of the contents of a bottle of potassium-permanganate solution which stood in the window with his other medical supplies. That was when he started dancing, and it wasn't hard to figure out the reason. Originally the solution had been suitable weak, say 5 to 10 percent. But over many weeks, daily hours of sun striking the bottle on the windowsill had evaporated much of the contents, leaving a fluid strong enough to burn tough outer skin, let alone the delicate mucous membrane to which he had applied it. That there had ever been any danger of infection was highly improbable, and it is certain, indeed, that he had contracted no infection from the evening. Nor was I ever able to reproach him properly for betraying me. Every time I started, I saw again the wildly capering figure with hands desperately clutching, and the accusations drowned themselves in uncontrollable laughter.

That was not the only time that John woke me at night. Deafening gunfire almost broke my eardrums on one occasion—a series of explosions that were unbearably loud in the little room. It was Steinbeck home from a trip to San Francisco and gaily drunk. It would be a fine joke to wake me, he thought, so he got his long-barreled 45-caliber Smith & Wesson revolver and fired at the solid wall at the end of the room facing the court, emptying the whole cylinder. For several years afterward, that wall had a three-inch hole which penetrated two layers of bricks and continued into dark obscurity. More than once in the remaining period of the quarter he showed his marksmanship by firing other bullets through the same aperture.

Then there was the time when I woke to find him sitting cross-legged on my chest, cradling a bottle in his arms like a baby and crooning soft songs to it—but that starts further back and may have fallen just short of being fatal to him. I had spent Saturday night in San Francisco with some friends from the print shop where I worked in the afternoons, and Sunday afternoon I crawled home to the room, weak and pale in the aftermath of too much bootleg gin. John was in a similar state after a party of his own. With an exchange of commiserations we swore off drinking and solemnly shook hands on it.

A little later Carl Wilhelmson came in, looked at us silently, and without comment placed a pint bottle of Canadian Club whiskey on the table against which we were leaning with heads in hands. We stared at it and then at each other. Genuine whiskey was very rare in those days.

"Come to think of it, it was gin I swore off drinking," John said, and I agreed that gin must have been what I too had been thinking of. Anyway, we opened the bottle. Even good whiskey didn't sit well on my battered stomach, so I stopped after a couple of drinks, but it seemed to pick John up very satisfactorily. Soon he and Carl had gone in search of Gordon Bower, who had brought the liquor back from one of his sea trips to the Orient. They returned not only with him, and not only with some of his whiskey but with a couple of pints of Chinese absinthe as well, for Gordon had smuggled in a considerable assortment of potables, both as a token of affection for his friends and as an investment. I tasted the absinthe—it was a nasty yellowish-green color—but it didn't do anything for my viscera either, so I lay down and watched as John and Carl drank it with gusto. For some reason, probably to impress Gordon, John produced a little can of marijuana he had brought from Salinas, and they tried one or two puffs.

Dinner didn't remove the fine edge of intoxication John had achieved, and neither did further shots of the absinthe. He was definitely high when he went off about 8:00 to keep a date with a sorority girl he had just met. That was the night when I woke almost suffocated to find him sitting on my breastbone. He was drunker than I had ever seen him, and he kept drinking from the yellow contents of the bottle that he nursed tenderly in his arms. The girl, he said, with tears rolling down his cheeks, was wonderful, but she had led a sad, sad life. They had been walking around the lake while she told him about it, and it was so sad that he wept. Then he had told her about *his* sad life, and she found it so sad that she wept too, so they just sat there in the cold moonlight, holding each other tight and shedding copious tears.

"Was very very sad and she cried and cried and cried," he told me between sobs, "but she's wonderful." Eventually I got him off my chest and into his bed.

The next morning I was better. He felt bad and didn't go to classes. He was still unhappy when I got back in the late afternoon. Except for milk and sandwiches that he got at Jack Myers' cigar store down the hall, he had not eaten all day and didn't want to eat, though I tried to persuade him to go to dinner with me.

In the evening while I studied, he lay fully dressed on his cot, half-facing me. After a long period of quiet, I said something to him, but he didn't answer, though his eyes were looking straight at me. I repeated the remark a couple of times and when he continued to stare without replying, I said, "All right, the hell with you," and went down to the cigar store for a bottle of pop. Ten or fifteen minutes later I came back to the room. John was in exactly the same position and he did not move as I entered.

I said, "So you're still being comical?" He didn't answer or look at me and I began to feel that something was wrong. Stepping to the side of his cot I grasped his shoulder. It was like taking hold of a piece of wood. The flesh was rigid and unyielding and his posture did not change. I felt his arms and legs. They too were stiff and hard.

Thoroughly alarmed, I said, "What in hell's the matter with you?" and started shaking him, though no part of his body bent or gave. But after a few seconds, when I was wondering where I could find a doctor, the rigidity suddenly went out of his muscles and he collapsed, breathing heavily and moaning. He didn't speak for two or three minutes, and then he said, "That was close," in a very weak voice. It may well have been.

Eventually he explained that the seizure had come upon him without warning as he watched me studying. Every muscle in his body had abruptly tensed and extended to its utmost. The pain was excruciating. He couldn't speak or move and his only hope was to convey a message to me with his eyes, which he was able to roll very slightly though he could not close them. He said it seemed a very long time before I looked up and spoke to him but failed to understand what he was trying to tell me. When I spoke the second time and then went out of room in disgust, he despaired. The distension of the muscles was agonizing and he was having trouble in breathing. During my absence the pain became unbearable but there was nothing he could do about it. By the time I came back, he was convinced that he was gong to die and that it would happen without my even suspecting that anything was wrong.

I don't know whether such muscle catalepsy is the characteristic result of too much absinthe or whether the attack was the cumulative result of assorted indulgences; but thereafter, both of us viewed the stuff with extreme distrust—especially the Chinese variety.

Our previous experiences with absinthe, the Swiss variety, had been both cautious and pleasant. We had found it in San Francisco at the genteel bootlegging establishment of one Madame Torelli, a refined, elderly Italian woman with white hair and an elegant wardrobe about twenty years out of date. The darling of her heart was a huge white Persian cat which she said weighed 18 pounds and was 14 years old. Anyone who was nice to the cat became a welcome and honored guest in the apartment, which was upstairs at the corner of San Francisco's Greenwich and Powell Streets. We were nice to the animal and the Madame took us to her ample bosom, figuratively speaking.

A visit to the Torelli establishment, richly furnished in the Victorian tradition, was like a social call in which all the proprieties must be strictly observed. No vulgarities, no raised voices, no boisterous actions were tolerated, and any offender was promptly asked to leave. The Madame was the cultured, charming, and well-bred hostess at all times, and only those who were willing to enter on such terms were admitted. She preferred, too, that her guests be properly attired. Part of the favor that John and I found in her eyes may have been based upon the fact that at our first visit we were, for some reason or other, wearing dinner jackets ("tuxes" then), and our manners were in keeping with our clothes. We were an instant success and continued to be, even when we subsequently appeared in mere street garb.

The price of a tiny glass of straight absinthe was 75 cents—very high in those days when straight whiskey (bootleg) went for 25 cents in the average place—but because she liked us, she charged us only 50 cents after our first visit. The glasses were served with ceremony, and she sometimes sat at the table with us to discuss the quality of the liquor and watch us enjoy it. But there was a strict rule: two half-ounce glasses were the limit. After that we could drink other things if we chose, but the tall green bottle stayed tightly corked. Once John purchased an entire fifth of absinthe at the formidable price of $20, but with it she exacted a solemn promise that it was to be drunk only a very little at a time, and we kept our word.

According to John, there was a later occasion when Carl Wilhelmson, in one of his periods of deep depression, decided to commit suicide, and after extended meditation came to the conclusion that the most pleasant way of doing it would be by steady drinking of absinthe. He had a room in San Francisco and $200 to spend on the project. Day after day he consumed the stuff to capacity, growing more and more morose. Eventually, however, the $200 was gone, and annoyingly, he was still alive. So, philosophically, he reoriented himself toward living for a while longer—and started saving money for a new attempt. I don't believe he tried suicide again, but it *had* been a pleasant way to try to go. He was about 75 when he died of a stroke in 1968.

When John and I started rooming together, I was a member of the Los Arcos eating club, one of several which had semi-private rooms in the Stanford Union. On four or five occasions I invited him to meals with me there, and while he knew several of the members and was unfailingly courteous to the rest, he obviously withheld his congeniality. Some of the boys mistook his aloofness for condescension. Truly, he did not like the pretensions of some of the members, especially a little group that sat together, discoursed partially in French, and was quick to deplore or correct the table manners of the others. (One of them tried to get the University to institute a course in dining etiquette with him as instructor, although his own manners, of the little-finger-crooking school, were far from exemplary.)

I sounded John out about becoming a member of the club and he turned me down with derogatory remarks about some of the members and with a general denunciation of the snobbish, restrictive, and obnoxious qualities of all such pseudo-fraternal organizations, regardless of their professed purposes.

Two or three years later I thought of that lecture when he admitted that, to please his father, he had permitted himself to be initiated into the Salinas chapter of the Masonic Lodge, though it was against all his convictions and made him very unhappy indeed. As far as I was able to learn, he never attended another meeting of that lodge. If he did, he was probably ashamed to admit it to me. Certainly he did not include that affiliation in his *Who's Who in America* entry, which left out almost everything except vital statistics.

It is doubtless just as well that he didn't want to join the eating club, for after he had been a guest there a few times, one of the boys frankly told me that if John were put up for membership, he would be blackballed.

One of the classes in which both John and I enrolled was Verse Writing (English 35), taught by William Herbert Carruth. He was grey haired, elderly—to our eyes—and delightfully informal. When the weather permitted, we met on the Quadrangle lawn in the shade of a huge oak tree, sitting or sprawling as he read and criticized the contributions of the group. His criticisms were kind, and I can appreciate what restraint he used when I review his written comments on some of the inept rhymes that I turned in.

On the nights before the class, John and I used to face each other across our study table, searching for inspiration or even a phrase that we could build on to fit the metrical or structural assignment. Often, after long periods of nail-biting and trading suggestions, we would go for long walks, hoping for ideas which sometimes came. For one of the meetings John produced a verse that started:

> So we manned the brigantine
> With Chinks and yellow Malays,
> Couldn't speak the language of the Irish and the Dutch;
> Had to feed them rice and things,
> They wouldn't eat with faylays;*
> Take them as a people and they don't amount to much.

**Faylays* is a Beche-de-Mer corruption of a native term meaning "knives and forks."

Professor Carruth wasn't taken in by so palpable an evasion—actually John had despaired of finding a rhyme (neither of us knew that Malay should be accented on the last syllable) and didn't want to spoil the fine sound of the lines—and merely read the word with skeptical emphasis, commenting dryly that the use of unusual foreign terms, especially in stressed position, was better avoided.

Very few examples of John's lyric talents have survived, and those that do rarely mirror the quality of his prose.[3] The final assignment of Carruth's course was a sonnet, and John's followed a classic format, at least in its rhyme scheme.

Now and then in the next few years he lapsed into verse, usually of a lighter variety and motivated by something he had read or done. From Lake Tahoe in November, 1926, came a letter with the following disquisitions on aspects of the amusement world:

> In a recent article written by the estimable Mr. Hearst, a certain chorus girl, in suing a certain Hobokenite for seventy-five thousand dollars declares that she is not interested in the money. She merely wants to show that class of men who make a practice of playing on the trustfullness [sic] of her sisters, that they can't get away with it any more. "Chorus girls," she says, "are the most trusting and naive creatures in the world, and I am sick of seeing them so shamefully mistreated and lead [sic] astray" Of course an event like this can have only one effect on me. I must break into verse.

1.

Now here is a girl who can stand
On the steps of the law and demand,
That justice be gave
To the trustful and brave
Little theatre slave
For the way men behave—
Along with some seventy grand.

2.

Some call it trustfulness and some
Would say that these chorines were not so dumb,
Who take the cash and let the credit go.
This one takes credit but the cash will come.

3.

Sonnet to a chorus girl, who, rising veiled with the dignity of a virtuous mission, demands that her woeful sisters so long maligned in fiendish hearsay; so often palpibly [sic] penetrated by the pricks of pariahs; so mercilessly misread by the minds of morons; so degraded in the public prints, deluded by dangerous danmcgrews, denuded by strictured stagejohns, decimated by dilirium [sic] tremens, discarded by dilletants [sic], disgraced in divorces, deflorated by degenerates and denied by the Deity, shall have a hearing by the great discriminating public and their fame lifted above the level of street walkers, at which altitude they now stroll unconcernedly and even happily. (To be read with a good sonorous voice, which breaks into passionate woe in the third line, recovers itself, and finishes in a fever of outraged virtue.)

Oh! Wistful miss, whose tiny painted mole
Slays like a knife the first five rows of eggs,
I wonder of the figure of thy soul
Is one fourteenth as pretty as thy legs.
    Thy face is questing and thy being begs
For home and children and the things that will
Benumb the craving of a woman's heart.
These items lacking, then thou wilt in part
Accept a check or yet a little bill.
What may be given also may be sold
For little papers with their backs of gold.

Note: This sonnet has certain poetic features entirely distinct in the history of sonnets. j.s.

Also from Tahoe came a long and bawdy mock epic entitled "Ballad of Quid Pro Quo," a free-wheeling twenty-three verse narrative of a romance (fictitious) with a girl of questionable background who was summering at the lake. While it contained some brilliant characterizations and phrases in its 136 lines, a good deal of basic Anglo-Saxon crept in, and the denouement was very frank:

Flash back! The erring goil and I
Have copulated, if you will recall.
And did I send her lonely on the fly?
And did she boot me giftless to the wall?
Oh no! It was a trade; I played the sap,
Exchanged a baby for a dose of clap.

Epilogue

A THING THAT EVERY FARMER OUGHT TO KNOW:
COITUS IS A FORM OF QUID PRO QUO.

Then there was the later fragment, composed when he was surrounded by our cats, some of whom were in heat and vocal about it:

I love little pussy, his fur is so warm,
But his love-making tactics are wrong;
For it's not at all sporting and hardly good taste
To have prickers and thorns on his dong.

~

Conversation was one of our continuing entertainments, with lengthy and involved arguments for the joy of playing with words and ideas. Sometimes, indeed, we played a game of putting words together in alternate sequences that might sound like sense to an inattentive ear but actually were nonsense, except that they must conform to the terms and superficial meaning of the statements or theses they followed. Such exchanges required logic, alertness, ingenuity, and a facile vocabulary, and they were excellent training for the expression of more serious ideas.

John liked to involve visitors in arguments by championing an improbable point of view, and then, often with my help, slowly working the discussion around until the guest suddenly found himself passionately upholding the exact opposite of his original contention, while John too had reversed sides. He loved, also, to talk with such deep seriousness that an unsuspecting innocent would be convinced of an allegation or explanation that was ridiculous on the face of it. When a lad wondered why iced tea cost 15 cents in the Union, John went into an elaborate explanation that because of peculiar legal restrictions, it had to be brought over the border from Nevada in a pipe line, and for a time, at least, the young man believed him implicitly. There were many more-subtle cases of verbal mesmerism, sometimes practiced on me.

From my freshman year on, small-time gambling had consistently gone on in my room or the next one—hearts, fan tan, bridge, and poker—though the games usually were held next door because of the smallness of No. 32. John had no interest in any of the games, but on one occasion found me playing with a set of dice and challenged me. First he stripped me of my small amount of cash, then of the booklet of postage stamps I had in my wallet, and finally of all the remaining punches on my meal ticket and two sacks of Bull Durham. Happily, he returned the tobacco, so I could at least smoke till I got my next check from the University Press, where I was working.

John went home as soon as he had finished his final examinations in June, 1923, but I had to remain for the graduation ceremony because my family was coming up from Long Beach to see it happen to me; otherwise I would have taken the degree *in absentia*. But I had already accepted John's invitation to visit him in Pacific Grove, where both he and his sister Mary were to attend the summer session of the Hopkins Marine Station, an adjunct of Stanford.

Thus, when my mother and sister had returned happy to the south, I packed my car with a four-years' accumulation of possessions and headed for Pacific Grove, a little town between Monterey and Carmel. It was dark before I found the tiny house used by the family as a vacation cottage for many years. Mary hadn't arrived yet, so John and I went into Monterey for a dinner of magnificent enchiladas, then started looking for a place to get something to drink. John had beaten me to the peninsula by only a day or two and had not yet lined up sources of supply. I questioned a taxi driver on the main street and over his reluctance to give a non-fare any information learned that the Spanish Hotel might be the answer. On a dark back street, the building was ancient and somber with only a glimmering light showing through the door. I approached the place alone, for bootleggers regarded with suspicion the approach of strangers in pairs or larger groups. Even so, I had to do some fast talking when the proprietress finally answered my ring. At length, she decided that I wasn't a raiding party and took me back to the kitchen, where two Mexican types and a drunken soldier sat around the table. The padrone proved less trustful of me than his wife had been. Eventually I convinced him of my probity, aided by the soldier, who said he liked my face and insisted on buying me a drink. It was almost half an hour before I managed to get away from the soldier and his proposal that I team up with him in running a crooked crap game with some trick dice he showed me. In the end, with two well-wrapped gallon jugs of red wine, I got back to John in the car. (Anyone could have guessed what the packages contained.) The hotel was a formidable-looking place, but with my entree established, it became our main supply base for the next two weeks.

A couple of days later, John's parents brought Mary down in readiness for the summer session, and during the day came a Salinas girl named Phyllis, who had a nearby cottage and who also would be attending school at the Station. After the family had gone home, the four of us had a fine party, since we had thoughtfully augmented with wine supply the night before.

The cottage consisted of three rooms, a long living room across the front, and behind it, side by side, the kitchen and the bedroom. Back of those was a narrow enclosed porch, at one end of which was the toilet and at the other the bath. I got the bedroom, as John and Mary were accustomed to sleeping on the front porch, which was curtained by heavy screens of mattress vine completely hiding the two beds, one at each end. There was also a large couch in the front room to care for emergencies, which not infrequently arose.

Years later, John made some renovations of the house, tearing out the front wall so that the porch could become a part of the living room, almost doubling it. He also sacrificed a rear part of the tiny garden to accommodate a bunk house for guests.

The garden was screened from the street by a high hedge overgrown with vines, and was intensively planted with a variety of flowers plus rows of vegetables. It contained a small rock pool with a few goldfish and a cobble-stone barbecue pit bearing a Latin inscription testifying that it had been built by Steinbecks, father and son. The fogs and high humidity of the Grove are ideal for growing things in profusion, and the lush greenery also encouraged the proliferation of snails, among other plant pests. We all assisted in a daily snail hunt, plucking them from stems and leaves and executing them by the canful with liberal applications of table salt. Later that summer, John told me, the French proprietors of the local bakery passed by and found him hunting snails. With excitement, they identified the snails as a delightfully edible variety and for a time, at least, enthusiastically took over the task.

Many of the cottages in Pacific Grove, especially in the central residential district, lacked room for even so small a garden. The Steinbeck lot measured not much more than 50 by 50 feet—perhaps less. Actually it was two lots. The town got its start as a Methodist camp-meeting center, and the lots were originally sold more as camp sites than as residential property. When the annual evangelical campaigns were announced, people came from miles around, and entrepreneurs soon found profit in selling small plots—20 or 20 feet square—on which the faithful could set up a tent or a covered wagon to live in while the spirit was moving. Many of the visitors erected more or less temporary cabins or shacks on their camp sites, and these were the foundations of the village, especially when the owners began using them as week-end cottages or places to spend a vacation. Within a few years, most of the lots were occupied by somewhat permanent structures, and the transition to a year-round settlement was inescapable, though some of the original makeshifts, only thinly disguised, are still distinguishable.

In the old ledger which contained the first draft of two of his novels, *Pastures of Heaven* and *To a God Unknown*. John started a short story about the days of the camp meetings. The protagonist, a sensitive, small boy named Mizpah, plays games with himself in the forest. He picks up pine cones to use as fuel, smells the sweet yerba buena, and yearns for adventure, as enticingly set forth in a coverless copy of *Marco Polo*, which, with the Bible and *Pilgrim's Progress* constitutes the family library. In the distance he can hear hammering, as the preparations for the camp meeting are being made. He trudges an erratic path toward home, pausing with a pointed finger to shoot a bear and to decapitate enemies with a sweep of his stick, and finally arrives to find a strange van outside and portentous evangelical voices coming from within the house. Only about 500 words of the story were written, ending with a large and emphatic *OUT* in the middle of the page, but the brief start to the tale recreates very convincingly not only the religious miasma of the occasion but the very feel and scent of the air, the trees, and the sea. In that brief beginning are phrases, ideas, and points of view that are echoed or developed in later writing, but Mizpah and the untitled fragment died aborning.

Things were pretty alcoholic for the remainder of my visit, but we had a fine time. School occupied only part of the day, and while the others were in classes, I did the housekeeping and much of the cooking. Not much studying was necessary, or at least John, Mary, and Phyllis managed with very little of it. I'm not even sure what courses they were taking, except that their curriculum involved marine biology and English. John wrote a fine song in which the words consisted exclusively of the names of the phyla of marine life: Echinodermata, Rotifera, Platyhelminthes, etc. I've often regretted that I can't remember that song.

We took frequent walks through the winding streets of the little town and through the pine forests. We danced and sang, and we went fishing and crabbing. We had a fine trick of tying a piece of red rag on the end of the line, lowering it into the water so that a crab might seize it and be jerked out of the water before he had sense enough to let go. Some of the crabs were smarter than we were. We picnicked at Point Lobos, one of John's favorite spots, where the jagged rocks, the crashing waves, and the wind-blown pines seemed to have a hypnotic effect upon him. It was at Point Lobos after his death in 1968 that his sisters arranged a little service, just the family, on a cliff overlooking Whaler's Bay—a spot that he and Mary had especially loved. As Elaine, his widow, recounted it, an otter was playing in the bay and the gulls were flying overhead.

Like Mizpah, we gathered huge pine cones from the forest to use in the little fireplace, where they burned with fury and gave out much heat, augmented by the big half-cone of copper which John had designed and installed with pride of craftsmanship. We walked the streets of Monterey, where progress for the most part had yet to come. And of course we strolled on Fisherman's Wharf, watching boats as they brought in their cargoes of fish and smelling the mingled aromas of the harbor. We didn't go to any moving pictures. Oh yes, and we drank quite a bit of wine, usually at 50 cents a gallon.

Shortly after the girls arrived we took them with us to get some wine at the Spanish Hotel, but felt it injudicious to expose them to its potentially sinister *habitués*. Instead, we left the car around a corner a quarter-block away, and since that neighborhood was anything but respectable, John armed Mary with his loaded 45-caliber revolver. Getting wine at the hotel always involved the protocol of drinking a glass or two with the proprietors and engaging them in a certain amount of conversation, with the result that we were gone at least fifteen minutes. When we did return, heavy laden with gallon jugs, we walked furtively, having no desire to draw the attention of policemen or highjackers.

Our furtiveness proved ill-advised. As we quietly neared the murky spot where we had left the car, there was a quick gasp and then Mary's voice, shaky but menacing. "Don't come a step closer or I'll shoot!" She almost did, at that, before we could identify ourselves. Both girls were scared stiff. As they had waited silently for us to come back, a couple of tough-looking men had seen the car, and, after looking cautiously around, had tiptoed over to investigate it, not noticing the rigid girls in the back seat. Then Mary had reached for the gun, and the men, startled at the movement, ran. Mary had thought that John and I were the men returning, and this time she was ready.

Eating was largely informal. The first one up ground coffee beans in a huge, old-fashioned grinder and made coffee in a granite pot that held at least half a gallon and that often had to be replenished on days when there was no school. Somebody usually made toast on which we smeared things (John was partial to toast with lemon juice squeezed on it) and sometimes there was mush or eggs. When time permitted, the coffee drinking lasted well through the morning, and the favorite place for it, if the weather was suitable, was the wooden curb in front of the house with our feet in the gutter. They'd always drunk coffee there. A couple of times, especially on mornings following wine drinking, no one woke in time, and I had to rush them down to the marine Station breakfastless and still reeking of the night before. On one such morning, Mary blackened an eye by bumping into a door while trying to get to a class that had already started.

On the Saturday night before I was to leave for home, we made a tour of various dances in Pacific Grove and Monterey, and managed to get kicked out of three of them. Our offense was not drunkenness but "indecent dancing." Mary and I were the chief offenders, though John and Phyllis got called too. In the public dances of the area it was the custom for the elder women of the community to line the benches along the sides of the hall, from which vantage point they watched alertly—almost hopefully—for any impropriety. Some of the dancing was indecent: the currently popular jiggle, for instance, although it had the local stamp of approval. We, on the other hand, were in the first place strangers; and in the second, we had imported the latest collegiate glide, involving long, smooth, and graceful sliding steps. The grim matrons on the sidelines didn't like it and ordered the master of ceremonies to oust us. That he did apologetically, telling us privately that while he thought we were the best dancers on the floor, the matrons had decreed that we were "twining legs" and had to go. And their word was law. Another place requested us to leave for cheek-to-cheek dancing. Going home we found another dance in down-town Pacific Grove, but we had circled the floor not more than a couple of times when we were again evicted. The dance, it developed, was being given by a private club and our presence was dispensable. After that, we did go home.

~

It is for the period between June 1923 and 1933 that I deeply regret the loss of John's letters. Without exactly believing that John was on his way to greatness, I started saving whatever he wrote me, at first merely throwing envelopes and all into a large shopping bag but later arranging them in approximate order (he rarely dated them and postmarks were often illegible) in a capacious folder. When my wife and I separated in 1933, she remaining in Eagle Rock while I came north to do graduate work at Stanford, I forgot about the folder, which was stored in an old trunk. Shortly afterward I remembered and wrote her asking that she mail it to me. She was preparing to do that when John dropped by on his way home from a business trip to Los Angeles. Since we would obviously be seeing each other, she turned the whole thing over to him to deliver to me, congratulating herself on having saved the postage.

A few weeks later I drove down to visit him in the little Pacific Grove house and to retrieve the folder, aware by this time that it contained the record of the beginnings of a promising literary career as well as the archives of a treasured friendship. John, however, refused to surrender the letters. He had looked them over, he said, and was shocked at the bad writing many of them contained. In addition, they gave too many names and damaging facts to be permitted to survive, even in my care. So, after letting me salvage a very few pieces which I particularly admired, he burned the rest sheet by sheet, in the fireplace while I watched and mourned. They contained—particularly the earlier ones—much about an inadequately documented period of his life.

Later there were many letters. During the summer and fall of 1923 we wrote almost every day. I was handling the want-ad and circulation department of a Long Beach newspaper in the evenings and he was on the night shift of the Spreckles sugar-beet factory near Salinas, presiding over the chemical laboratory and providing first aid when necessary. Both of us had little to do and gladly turned to letter writing. In a way they were less letters than exercises in writing, and they took the form of essays, short stories, fantasies, verses, and satires, along with accounts of our daily lives, often exaggerated. In general we let our thoughts wander and tried to follow them with the typewriter, or often in his case, with pen or pencil. A little of John's writing was first rate, much of it was superior, and some just silly. No matter how inconsequential his subjects, the letters always had a spark, a zest, a feeling for the savoring of words and the things they could be made to do. Often he took up an idea that I had toyed with in a previous letter and reexamined it, changed the focus, and returned it, polished and hardly recognizable. Sometimes the daily letters ran to two or three thousand words.

Along with the literary experiments, he sent me entertaining tales of his nocturnal experiences in the big factory: descriptions of people who worked there, amusing episodes, bits of conversation, and meditations upon life as seen from a sugar laboratory after midnight.

There was the affair of the disappearing grain alcohol, a precious commodity during prohibition. Someone had been stealing it from the lab; only one chemist was on duty and he often had to go out into the plant. John laid a trap. He loaded the alcohol carboy with a strong dose of phenolpthalien, the chief ingredient in a number of commercial cathartics. Within a few hours the Mexican culprits were unmistakable, and almost intolerable. They were, moreover, very sick, for the drug had been used liberally but not to a dangerous degree. There were no more alcohol thefts, particularly since John had firmly impressed upon the beet workers not only that the chemical was a deadly poison but that it could deprive a man of this sexual power—a fate worse than death to the macho. It was a miracle, he added, that the men had survived with their lives, and time would tell about the other possibility.

There were stories about the Mexican and Filipino boys employed chiefly for cutting beets. They used heavy, murderous knives armed with an additional spike hear the tip, and most of the youths gained an amazing dexterity in handling them, not only for their proper purposes but as throwing-knives and weapons. John quickly achieved popularity in this group and learned some of the fine points of throwing and fighting with knives. The boys regarded him as a very learned person and brought him their problems for adjudication—problems of love, sex, economics, and social relationship. He also performed first-aid services for minor injuries, gave them medicine (chiefly cathartics) when they were ill, and supplied sage advice for almost any emergency. He even gained limited immortality among the Spanish speaking segment of the plant with an inspired phrase. When one of the boys became angry and abusive during a lunch-hour argument, John brought instant ignominy upon him by saying scornfully, "Pone un condo sobre la cabeza" [Put a condom on your head].

The auditors screamed with laughter and the truculent one wilted. As much as year later, and probably after that, "Pone un condo. . . ." continued to be the supreme and favorite insult among the beet boys.

There was the fragile old Ortiz, who never seemed to have any money and always cadged food and tobacco from fellow workers, though he earned as much as any of them and was unmarried besides. John learned the reason when Ortiz came in to ask if John could test him for venereal disease. (The Mexicans never doubted the omniscience of the laboratory man in any field.) Ortiz, it developed, having no wife, had to pay for his sexual delights in the houses along "Tiajuana" Street. Immediately upon getting his pay, he lit out for the fleshpots and stayed till his pay envelope was empty. But there was a further complication. Someone had told him a sure method of detecting disease in a woman. All he had to do was squeeze the juice of a lemon on the vagina of the girl in question, and if the juice turned cloudy, infection was present. The trouble was, the girls didn't like it, for the juice both stung and insulted them. Some refused to submit to such an indignity and threw him out. Some, being tested and failing to pass, would not return the money they had already demanded. And some extorted extra money for the additional service. Some of the establishments just wouldn't let him in when, he came carrying his little sack of lemons. Along with the expense, the arguments and unpleasantness were having a bad effect on him: sometimes, having examined and approved a candidate for his amours, he found he was no longer *fuerte*, and left in a storm of ridicule. The whole thing was breaking him up, John shocked him by discrediting lemon juice as a revealer of gonococci and sent him away pondering on whether to try to find someone who would marry him or to use rubber goods, of which the girls in the houses were also unreasonably scornful.

There were innumerable such stories, many of them showing the sympathy and humor which later characterized the treatment of paisanos and other simple folk in books which were to follow.

~

In October, 1923, John returned to Stanford. By that time he had come to certain conclusions about what he wanted out of college. He knew that he wanted to make writing his life work, and he was impatient with anything that distracted him from that objective or seemed to have little bearing upon achieving it. The trouble was that the University had a number of basic requirements for each course of study, and some of them, economics, for instance, did not appeal to him. About this time, then, he decided to have nothing to do with the formal requirements of the curriculum and announced to the authorities that he did not want a degree—he wanted to take the courses that would be useful to his writing career, and nothing more. The administration did not like it, but he was permitted to attend school under those terms, or perhaps on the proposition that he could defer completion of the requirements until a later day.

Chiefly, he enrolled for writing courses, and later was able to boast that, with one exception, he had taken every writing course in the University, along with many in literature. He also took classes in philosophy, sociology, Greek and Latin classics, while continuing some of his investigations into marine biology. On more than one occasion he enrolled in a class, attended long enough to decide that he didn't like the professor, his methods, or his subject and dropped out permanently. There was also the time when he sat for four weeks in a class taught by Professor Sam Seward, then recognized a joke the professor told, and realized that he had already taken the course. For the most part, he did not take final examinations. He succeeded in persuading some instructors that his sole concern was the content of the course, that he had no interest in the grade save as it related to his remaining in college, and that the teachers should by this time be aware of his sincere desire for learning and of his having made adequate progress toward accomplishment of that desire. Apparently he got away with it, for he stayed in the University till June, 1925, and by that time had accumulated some 95 units, or just over half the 180 required for graduation. No doubt, he lost several units by failing to take examinations.

He alleged—although Professor Henry David Grey said he didn't remember it—that he wanted to enroll in Dr. Grey's course in playwriting, but that Dr. Grey refused to let him enter on the grounds that he did not have the right kind of talent for the work.

Part 2:

Apprenticeship from *Cup of Gold* through *Pastures of Heaven*

In the summer of 1924, I was out of a job. The owners of the *Long Beach Telegram*, for which I had been working, bought a little weekly paper at Laguna Beach, and with extraordinary bad judgment sent me down as circulation manager and assistant to the advertising manager. Or maybe I was business manager—I forget. At any rate, after I had been three weeks in the position and was still suffering agonies every time I tried to solicit an advertisement, my Long Beach boss discovered that I had not even thought to start a set of books on receipts and disbursals, having thus far placed all incoming cash in a drawer of my desk, together with bits of paper from which I hoped to be able to straighten out the accounts when I got around to it. He was amazed and incredulous (and I was shocked and embarrassed to learn that I should have been keeping books) but was kind enough to permit me to resign—immediately.

So, early in June, I again climbed into my car and drove north to join John in the cottage at Pacific Grove. This time we had it almost exclusively to ourselves, though there were occasional visits from the elder members of the family, and Mary was frequently present, for Bill Dekker, to whom she was engaged, had enrolled at the Marine Station for the summer.

Bill, who became a fighter pilot and was lost over Sicily in the early part of World War II, was responsible for an episode which almost certainly provided the idea for the frog hunt in *Cannery Row.*[4] The instructor of his zoology class had suggested that members bring in toads for laboratory dissection the next day, and after a few drinks, Bill enlisted John and me in the search. Somehow, the party grew to six or eight, each armed with a burlap sack and a flashlight or plenty of matches. Led by John, we headed for the upper reaches of Pacific Grove, and in the concrete gutters, as John had promised, toads teemed. Light stupefied them and it was easy to seize them and plop them into our bags. When the hunt ended an hour or two later, we had hundreds of toads in the dripping bags as we congregated at the cottage that Bill had rented, and the problem was what to do with them till morning. Bill solved that by emptying out an old dresser and filling its five drawers with protesting *buffi*, chirping indignantly all night long. In the morning, Bill and his cabin mate carried the entire dresser in their car to the Marine Station. The seat of the car was drenched with toad juice, and more of the same sloshed over on steps and floors as the students pridefully carried the whole thing to the instructor. He, they reported later, was dismayed and overwhelmed, having hoped for a dozen or so specimens at most; and eventually he made Bill and his friend carry the dresser, still laden and sloshing worse than ever, away from the school to some point where they could release their irate captives. John deplored the initial inexplicitness of the instructor and the waste of good, hard-come-by toads, but he glowed in the awareness of a difficult mission fulfilled and of a good party, for once we had assembled the beasts the night before and stowed them away safely, we had toasted our successful safari in considerable quantities of fine, raw, red wine.

Generally, John and I spent our time in reading, writing, talking, and taking long walks, some as far as Carmel. John always had a feeling for the night and for walking, and often would set off by himself—sometimes in the middle of the night—to spend hours on the hills, along the shore, or in the pine forests of the Monterey peninsula. For that matter, he walked at night wherever I have known him to be, even along the silent streets of Los Angeles and San Francisco—presumably of New York too. Such walks seemed to be an aid to his thinking, and on innumerable occasions when he was in low spirits or wrestling with some writing problem, I have known him to rise and walk silently out of the door, often not returning for many hours. After he was well launched into serious writing, he usually reappeared with an air of deep abstraction and immediately busied himself with pen and paper, saying no word, as if any conversation would shatter his mood or interfere with the setting down of ideas that he had formulated during his solitary wandering. Nor was it wise to speak to him at such times. If he answered at all it was with grunts or ungracious monosyllables.

On one of our walks together, we saw middle-aged women entering a residence, on the lawn of which was a black-and-gold sign notifying the public that meetings of the Theosophical Society were held there at specified times, one of which coincided with that very day and hour.

"Let's go in and find what it's about," John suggested, and we did, though I felt some timidity. But John deferentially greeted the aging matron who welcomed us at the door, explaining that we were students of philosophy and religion and that we had a burning desire to learn and understand about the tenets of theosophy. He was 22 to my 23, and that could have aroused some skepticism in the more astute, but the several women present fluttered and smirked flatteringly as we were introduced. Then, not too comfortably, we sat through the reading of a paper which dealt rather confusingly with various aspects of Hindu mysticism in an esoteric vocabulary that was largely over our heads. The woman who read the paper was obviously intelligent and sincere, and she had a journeyman grasp of her subject, at least as set forth in the publications of the Theosophical Society and some of its recommended reference books. When she had concluded her address and thrown the meeting open to questions, it became apparent that she was not equally versed in speculative thought.

As questions were called for, the speaker and all the nice ladies beamed at the polite and interested young men who had seemed to understand everything so well and would probably have questions or comments. John took over the situation masterfully by quoting one of the less-succinct statements in the paper and asking, "Isn't that point of view strikingly similar to the monad theory of Leibnitz?"

Our preceptor was visibly embarrassed, having quite apparently never heard of either Leibnitz or his monad (neither had I), but she rather skillfully admitted that such a similarity had never occurred to her before and that she would have to study the matter before accepting such a conclusion, although it was unquestionably a point meriting close investigation. Then, as the rest of the group sat with its collective mouth open, she suggested that John give a brief explanation of the monad and its relation to the subject at hand. That was really turning the heat on and proved that we had underestimated the forensic powers of the speaker. But John, summoning up his extremely vague memories of what he had heard about monadology in a philosophy class, frowned with concentration and then, with every evidence of striving for simplicity, delivered a five-minute "explanation" that Leibnitz would never have recognized, studded as it was with random bits of philosophical patois, plus tidbits from psychology, chemistry, and biology, creating a melange from which any intelligible meaning would have been almost impossible to draw. The ladies were entranced by all the nice words and nodded their heads in agreement whenever he paused. Then one of them whose gestures of concurrence had been most emphatic asked a question which showed that she had not the slightest comprehension of what John had been talking about—or for that matter, of the whole general body of Theosophy—and I came haltingly to the rescue with scattering references to Buddhism, the atomic theories of Democritus, Epicurus, and Lucretius, throwing in a bit about the supernaturalism of Flammerion and Arthur Conan Doyle, while John alternated with referrals to Kant's categorical imperative, the Arab invention of zero, and the gestalt theory.

We had a wonderful time, and so did all the ladies, but we were fortunate that apparently not one of them had ever taken an elementary course in philosophy or done any basic reading in the field. Otherwise, our inventions would have been quickly unmasked as the double talk that they were. (Perhaps, of course, our hostesses were only being kind.) But it was a game that we had often played with each other—a dead-pan argument which demanded neither sense nor continuity, so long as rhetoric continued to flow, embellished with impressive names, adroitly adduced theories or systems, and pseudo-facts to back them up.

The afternoon ended with the serving of coffee and cookies, and while we ate and drank, the dear ladies almost overwhelmed us with their gratitude for our visit and for all the fresh light we had cast upon their studies. In departing at last, we promised faithfully to attend another meeting very soon. But we didn't.

John always did have a strongly developed mystic sense, and that summer we tried a series of experiments at his suggestion. The odors of things, he said, affected him deeply, and with the aid of the right odor he could sometimes superinduce a kind of trance or self-hypnosis under which he could see and communicate with the person he associated with the odor.

One night we went out and sat in the dark at the corner of Eleventh Street and Lighthouse Avenue. At his request, a girl with whom he had had an affair had sent him a handkerchief tinctured with her favorite perfume and had promised to be looking at Arcturus and to be concentrating on him exactly at midnight to see if they could effect a telepathic communication. He told me they had done it before and even achieved a community of physical sensation. As midnight neared he smelled at the handkerchief and stared at the star, while I sat silently by. Fully a quarter of an hour passed before he sighed, put the handkerchief in his pocket, and got up. No, it hadn't worked this time, though he seemed to have a sense of the girl's nearness. Perhaps she had forgotten or something else like illness had interfered. The failure seemed to depress him, and we retired to our beds without further conversation.

We also tried hypnotism, but that wasn't too much of a success either. Once when I was trying to hypnotize him, his body stiffened, his voice answered me in a dead monotone, and he followed my simple directions that he lift one arm, scratch his nose, etc., but when I suggested that he unbutton his pants, he "awoke" and said that my frivolity had brought him out of it. I doubt that there had been an actual trance, though he doubtless tried to create one.

We did a good deal of reading, much of it from the little Pacific Grove library. One of John's discoveries was Jeffery Farnol, writer of innumerable picaresque romances about an England that never existed but is nonetheless delightful. John produced *The Broad Highway*, and with chuckles of pleasure and suppressed excitement read lengthy sections of it aloud to me. It was not the plot and action which charmed him but the whimsical rustic characters, the ancients and tinkers and peddlers and old fighters, all of whom spoke with a dialect only slightly related to normal colloquial English but vastly effective in helping to create the illusion of humor and quaintness. Their conversation was studded with barbarisms, tortured inversions, and catch phrases: ". . . as ever was . . ." ". . . as the feller says," ". . . that's all I hopes." One gaffer referred to all women as "Eves," and an old mariner used sea-going vocabulary to deal with land-bound phenomena.[5]

John loved it all, and for months adapted many of the Farnol tag lines to his own conversation, particularly when we were talking the type of nonsense with which we often amused ourselves. It was chiefly the quaintness of the characters, the sympathetic satire with which the author presented them, and the skill with which their synthetic language was created and handled that seemed to appeal to him. Certainly there are overtones of that admiration in the dialogue of some of John's own simple characters, though other influences tempered and refined the one-dimensional Farnol formula, which is often close to caricature. Thus the Steinbeck rustics rarely are characterized by a distinctive dialect. Rather, they gain their individuality by a pattern of word order without recourse to distinctive colloquialisms.

A stronger literary influence on John's developing style was the work of James Branch Cabell, whose delicate ironies and stylistic arabesques for a time hypnotized many of the would-be writers of the 1920s. We read and admired *Jurgen* together and in our letters and literary experiments, we strove to emulate its polished frivolities. The deplorable effect can be seen at its worst in an essay-article John wrote for the *Stanford Spectator* of June, 1924, entitled, "Adventures in Arcademy." It is also present in what I believe was his first commercial sale, a story called "The Gifts of Iban" published under the pseudonym of John Stern in the short-lived *Smoker's Companion* magazine for March 1927. The influence is still very apparent in his first book, *The Cup of Gold* (1929), but is partially obscured by the seductive dominance of another popular writer whose books gave John a romantic impetus in a slightly different direction.

The writer was Donn Byrne, whose *Messer Marco Polo* and *Blind Rafftery* charmed much of the reading world.[6] John's own part-Irish heritage embraced Byrne's overtones of brogue. It is this influence, only mildly tempered, that sets the tone of much of *The Cup of Gold*, though the submerged Cabellian touch is also discernible.

Many classics had been in the Steinbeck home as John grew up; he was well acquainted with Plutarch, Herodotus, Cicero, Seneca, Malory, Gibbon, and Dr. Johnson, to name only a few. He had constant recourse to such books, also maintaining an eager interest in contemporary writers, like Dreiser, Sherwood Anderson, and Sinclair Lewis, though John said he hesitated to read Hemingway and some of the newer stylists for fear they would influence his own style.[7]

~

For a while, we stayed out of Monterey and vicinity as the result of a rather ridiculous but potentially dangerous coincidence. On the day I arrived for my visit, John and I set out to find something stronger than wine to celebrate the reunion, and he led me to a stairway opening off the main street of Monterey. At the foot of it he mysteriously drew out a match and inserted it in a very small hole on the side wall, thereby operating some kind of signal in the drinking establishment on the second floor. At the top of the stairs we were admitted by a scowling ex-pugilist type, who didn't seem very cordial. The bar was not elaborate. It consisted of unpainted pine boards nailed together with all the finesse of a packing box. Whiskey was the only choice, and the bartender poured it from a white-enamel pitcher at twenty-five cents a slug. It tasted pretty raw, and when I asked what brand it was, he produced an empty Queen Anne bottle and said he used the pitcher only for greater ease in serving. I was skeptical but John had achieved a jovial mood, and, assuming the role of a connoisseur, contended that he was very fond of Queen Anne whiskey and that he'd never tasted any better. Of course it *could* have been genuine, and I caught the bartender looking at John with what might have been scorn.

My memories of the evening from then on are vague. I know that we picked up a man who took us to another drinking place, and that from there we went to several others, tossing down straight whiskey for the most part, but no more Queen Anne. Somehow we got home.

The next morning we were in terrible shape, and till past noon we sat with shaking hands lifting cups of black coffee that didn't seem to do any good and that would barely stay down. In the afternoon, one of John's male Pacific Grove friends came for a brief visit, and we explained the cause of our indisposition.

"Say," the visitor said, "you must have seen some of the raids."

"Raids?" we asked dully.

"Yeah, the Feds tipped over practically every speak in town. Just went down the street and took them one after one. Why, today there isn't a place in Monterey where you can get a drink."

We said we didn't want one at present, thank you.

Our informant went on. The bootleggers are all mad as hell, and they're looking for the guys that acted as tipoffs. They all got together and found that the same two guys had been in each place just before the raids. Looked like college students, they said. A big guy with dark hair and cords and a dark blue shirt, and a smaller guy in tweed pants and sweater. It'll be just too bad if they find them . . ."

For several days after that, John and I stayed out of Monterey and confined our drinking to wine purchased at places where John was well known. And we didn't go to any more speakeasies in town all that summer.

As the days went by, we continued to have a fine time, but there was one serious drawback—we were running out of money. I had brought very little when I came, and John had something like $25 a month from his parents to pay all expenses. Reluctantly we decided we ought to go to work and half-heartedly set about looking for something suited to our talents. The sense of virtue that came from even hunting for a job sustained us for a time, but eventually the state of our joint exchequer forced the issue.

Somehow, John found that a crew of laborers was being recruited to dig ditches near Carmel starting the next Monday morning, and we signed to appear then at the Pacific Grove office from which the gang was to be transported. Work started at 8:00 o'clock sharp, the foreman said.

So Monday morning we rose at dawn instead of our usual 8:00 or 9:00 o'clock and appeared at the jump-off point. Carrying hastily contrived lunches, we were dressed in old clothes and armed with canvas gloves which we hoped would avert blisters from pick and shovel handles. No crowd of workmen lounged around the office, nor were there any vehicles suitable for transporting a gang. That cheered us up. There had probably been a delay of some sort, so we sat down on the curb to wait. From inside the office a man kept looking at us, and in about fifteen minutes he came out to our curb.

"You fellows waiting for somebody?" he asked.

"Yeah," we said, "they told us to be here to go with that Carmel ditch-digging gang, but we don't see anybody. Something wrong?"

The man looked at us with pity, or maybe it was something else. "You fellows come too late. That gang left here at 7:00, and the boss wondered where you was but he couldn't wait."

"But he said we started at 8:00," I objected.

"Work starts at 8:00 over in Carmel, but the truck starts from here at 7:00." He spat on the ground and went back into the office.

We walked slowly back to the cottage, and when we got there we ate our sandwiches, for we'd rushed away without much breakfast and we'd been up a long time. That evening, over a few glasses of red wine, we agreed that there must be better jobs available, and we'd probably been fired anyway for not showing up. We never did try to meet the truck again.

A friend of John's father found us the next job opportunity. Deer were becoming a nuisance in some of the better residential districts of Carmel. They were breaking down or jumping fences and were doing extensive damage to fruit trees, gardens, flowers, and vegetables. Since by law they couldn't be shot, the property owners wanted a couple of men who would patrol the area on horseback, scaring off the deer and driving them back into the hills. It would be an easy job but a lonely one, since each of us would have his own beat to cover.

The one major drawback was that I had never ridden a horse. But John, who had ridden since he was six years old, thought he could take me out to a friend's ranch and teach me in plenty of time. It took a couple of days to get hold of the friend, and when we finally went out to the ranch for the first lesson, our host produced some excellent wine made by one of his neighbors, and nobody ever got around to climbing aboard a horse, nor was I in good condition for learning. The next day we had visitors and the day after that was Sunday, when we ought to be home in case John's family decided to come down. The family didn't, but John's father's friend did. He told us that the property owners were tired of waiting and had found someone else for the job a couple of days ago. John and I were just a bit relieved. There were more pleasant ways of spending nights than riding alone over dark roads, and we sympathized somewhat with the deer, especially since most of the people who were complaining were filthy rich. I've still never learned to ride a horse.

Eventually we did get a job. John ran into a friend who was a foreman in the Spreckles sugar-beet factory near Salinas, where John had spent some vacations working night shift in the chemical laboratory. Bill, the foreman, said that the company was about to open up their smaller factory at Manteca, in the San Joaquin valley, to handle the short, pre-season run. He was being sent there and would be glad to take us with him if we could come right away and were willing to work.

We were, could, and did, though we used our last nickels and dimes on food and gasoline to get there. Normally, workers of our class would have had to find our own lodgings and feed ourselves, but because John knew Bill and a couple of other members of the supervisory staff, we were permitted to stay at the Officers' Club, where the foremen, superintendents, and some of the executives lived. Fortunately, the charge for our board and room would be deducted from our paychecks. Otherwise we would have been forced to borrow the money for our first week of food and housing.

The club was immaculate and well managed, and the charge for a comfortable furnished room and three meals was, if I remember correctly, something like $1.50 a day. There was a large, pleasant general room with books, magazines, a piano, and phonograph, not to mention over stuffed chairs and divans with plenty of reading lights, and equipment for cards, checkers, dominoes, chess, and other games. Meals were well cooked and plentiful. Breakfasts usually included huge platters of fried eggs and either ham or bacon. They were sometimes replenished twice or more, for each man ate all he wanted and often that was half a dozen eggs and three or four large pieces of ham or ten or twelve slices of bacon, along with hot biscuits and jam or honey.

John, as befitted his previous experience, expected to go into the laboratory, where his chief responsibility would be to test and to check the beet juice as it moved from the presses to the crystallization vats and centrifugals. The laboratory staff was already full, however, and John's foreman friends apologized for assigning him to a lesser job, though it was a good one from factory standards. Exactly what it was, I am no longer sure, but it had something to do with the department where sacks were filled with the completed sugar and made ready for shipment or storage. His duties included examining 100-pound sacks as they moved past him on a belt.

Totally unacquainted with any of the processes of sugar manufacture, I was put in charge of the first carbonation process. The assignment, more formidable than it sounds, consisted of keeping five eight-foot-high tanks full of the raw beet juice as it was squeezed by the presses from the shredded beets, and "cooking" it to the proper point by admitting calculated quantities of boiling milk of lime into the tanks. The specific gravity of the lime had to be tested for each batch as a basis for finding how much should be used; the gauges had to be watched carefully so that the tanks could be emptied as soon as the contents had been cooked to the precisely proper point (otherwise the solution would "burn"), and discreet use had to be made occasionally of a vegetable oil to keep down excessive foaming. Chiefly my job required me to spend much of my time straining to open and close big wheel valves, burning my glove-clad fingers on the hot lime as I gave it the "Brix test," and trying to avoid slipping in the spilled lime and oil that usually covered the concrete floor.

Apart from the labor, which was less in John's case, two factors made the job hard. One was the heat. Although it normally was delightfully cool in the early mornings and we wore jackets to breakfast as a protection against the almost frosty air, by 10:00 the sun had gone to work, and during many days the temperature in the shade outside reached 110 degrees or better. Inside the factory there were no available thermometers, but in the part of it where I worked, the beet juice and lime were kept at the boiling point, and directly across from my vats were the evaporation ovens, with the result that the air was not only hot but thick with a sweet, sticky steam.

On one of the hottest days, the old Yugoslav who ran the first filters came past my station, his overalls dripping, the sweat running down his exposed torso, and his shoes squishing as he walked. Pausing before me, he wiped his face with his drenched bandana, scattering a shower of perspiration from his face, and said, "If yesterday is as hot like tomorrow, I'm a son of a bitch, that's what I hope!" Then he splashed on toward his filters.

Even worse then the heat was the fact that the plant was being run on a 12-hour shift. We went to work at 7:00 in the morning and quit at 7:00 in the evening—not just during the normal work week but all seven days, for the Manteca plant was operating under pressure of time. It took care of the early beets until the volume of harvest required the opening of the big Salinas plant—once the largest in the world—and then, after the Salinas plant closed down, it cared for the late-season crop. Even without the high temperatures of the San Joaquin valley, eight hours would have been a good work day, but half as much again with no chance for a Sunday rest left most of us in a constant state of semi-exhaustion. By the time we got back to the clubhouse, bathed, dressed, and ate dinner, we had small energy for anything but going to bed, though we generally spent an hour or so in the recreation room conversing, reading, listening to other people's choices of music, or looking through magazines.

Among the residents of the club was a Russian woman chemist who was studying American methods of production, and John soon struck up a friendship with her. They conducted lively discussions about literature, music, art, and even a bit of politics, but there was little time or opportunity for anything more intimate, though he seemed to charm her quite effectively and she gave him an attractive set of color prints showing scenes from various Russian ballets.

John and I did have one great advantage over most of the plant workers by virtue of our special position as friends of the supervisors and our residence in the sacrosanct "bosses" club, both of which gained us some suspicion and animosity from the less fortunate men who labored beside us. Like the foremen, we were permitted to leave our stations and go to the clubhouse for a large, well-cooked mid-day dinner, while all the rest of the non-supervisory staff had to eat "on the hoof" from lunch pails or sacks they brought with them, before continuing their regular duties. John, I think, gained the right of leaving the plant for lunch right from the beginning, and I spent several days munching sandwiches from one hand while I twisted oily valves with the other, but somehow it was arranged that I eat in the dining room too. Thus, daily I had to delegate someone to watch my tanks for half an hour while I departed to eat with clean hands from a linen-covered table loaded with good hot food. Every time I went to lunch I could feel scowls beating against my back, and no wonder.

Only once during our Manteca stretch did we summon up energy enough to go out in the evening for a tour of the fleshpots. Our friend Bill and another foreman organized the party and asked John and me to join them. It was almost 9:00 by the time we got dressed and started, and our first stop was on a dark dirt road behind the nearby town of Escalon, where Bill went into secluded farmhouse and emerged with two bottles of something he called wine. It was effervescent and had a taste not unlike cider. Because prohibition-enforcement agents were reported to be very active in the area, we drank most of it parked on a bridge separating San Joaquin from Stanislaus County. It was John's idea: he said if we saw anyone approaching we could move to the other side of the bridge and be in a new jurisdiction where we couldn't be touched. No one came.

The wine was very potent, though perhaps our weariness from the succession of long working days made it seem to. My memories of the rest of the evening are spotty. I know that we went to Stockton and had a drink or two of something else in a shabby dive, and that we went to a whorehouse with an electric sign designating it as the Elite (pronounced E-light). It had a working staff of three girls, one of whom was completely flat chested. John went with her—the bosses had first choice—and I waited in the front room, amusing myself with a litter of very young puppies till he came out. Then I went with the bustless Venus but earned her biting scorn by being completely impotent—as much from shocked esthetics as from alcohol, I suspect. Anyway, we ate somewhere and I slept all the way home. We got in about 2:00 A.M., leaving only four hours for sleep. The twelve hours of the ensuing shift were among the longest I have ever experienced, especially since the Escalon wine had left me with a virulent hangover. Even John admitted that the day had been a bad one, and it may have led to our eventual resignation not too long afterward.

We had signed for the whole run, which was expected to last a month and a half or more. Soon after we started, John came up with a fine idea on how to spend our sudden wealth. We were earning something like 65 cents an hour—a good wage for that era, but $1.50 a day went to the club. When the run was finished, he suggested, we could drive to Long Beach, leave my car (it was really my mother's), buy an old but dependable Model T Ford, and drive down to Mexico, which neither of us had seen.

Before the end of the first month, however, and not too long after our night on the town, John began to get restless and bitter. His job was monotonous and his working mate was an ignoramus who talked constantly and was always picking at him. John kept telling him to shut up—politely, no doubt—and trying to teach him to be reasonable, but the man yammered on and John wasn't going to stand it much longer. Besides, John wanted to write and there was no time for it.

I was beginning to get somewhat accustomed to the long daily work period and to the exhausting regimen; moreover, I knew we didn't yet have enough money for the trip as we had planned it. But John's irritation, which was more against the plant and the monotony and the unbroken work schedule than against his working partner, kept growing, and eventually, over my objections, he said he was going to start a fight with the man the next day, and then quit.

He did it, all right. He let a full sugar sack fall against the man a couple of times, told him off when he protested, and then engaged in minor fisticuffs. After that John went to Bill and said, "I'm quitting. I won't work any longer with that son of a bitch." But it wasn't that easy. Bill agreed that the partner was a difficult man to get along with and said that he'd shift him somewhere else. When John said no, Bill said that now there was a place for John in the laboratory—the most aristocratic place in the whole plant to work. John wasn't having any. He said he didn't want to stay where he was, even with the man gone. He didn't want to be shifted to the laboratory. He was sick of the factory and everybody and everything in it. He was quitting, and that was all there was to it.

Hurt and a bit aggrieved, Bill came up to where I was twisting my valves and told me that my pal had quit, but that he hoped I'd stay with them, for I was a good carbonation man and he didn't want to have to break in somebody else. He even hinted that there might be a better job for me coming up if I stuck. Of course I had to say that if John was going, I would too. I didn't like doing it, for Bill had taken us on as a favor and given us a good many breaks, but John was counting on me, and I wouldn't like staying on at the plant alone. So I quit too, and Bill went away with a look of mingled anger and reproach. Unquestionably we hadn't played fair with him, and he was accustomed to playing fair with people and expecting the same from them.

So, when I had finished out the day, we were freed from a long ordeal and ready to step forth into a new world of shining adventure. There was one little setback. The woman who managed the Officer's Club frowned at us, perhaps reflecting the attitude of our former friends among the foremen, and crisply told us that the room-and-board rate which had been granted us was based on the assumption that we would stay for at least a month. Since we were leaving before a month was up, we would have to pay the transient rate, or a dollar more a day each. We offered to pay for the remaining four or five days of the month at the original rate, which would have saved us a considerable amount, but she stiffly refused even to consider any such unprofitable compromise. Reluctantly we handed over about $50 of our inadequate hoard and departed glumly. Both of us felt guilty at having betrayed the trust of the people who had hired us, and we were indignant at having done it in a way which permitted the manager of the club to victimize us. We were further saddened by the suspicion that the $80 or so which remained wasn't going to carry us very far into Mexico, or for very long.

Our depression, however, was more than balanced by the feeling of liberation from the killing routine of the factory, from the long grinding hours and the weariness that followed them, from the heat and the sticky steam, from the boarding-house ritual of the big dinner table, and from the lack of time or energy for meditation, conversation, reading, and our other accustomed types of recreation.

Naturally, we headed immediately for San Francisco, where we could celebrate our escape from bondage. Judiciously, the first thing I did was to put the car into a public garage to be held till called for. Then, with John leading, we went out on the town, starting with a visit to Madame Torelli for a couple of absinthe frappes and a take-out bottle of gin. From that point on, the picture is dim but roseate. We ate some fine meals in various parts of town (at Herbert's Men's Grill you could then get a two-inch rib steak tender enough to cut with a fork, along with a baked potato, salad, and coffee for 45 cents), visited a number of dives, drank a lot of unclassified intoxicants, saw a show, and talked to all sorts of people.

During a fairly lucid interval, we were having dinner at Il Trovatore, with drinks from a bottle I was carrying, and John had brought a couple of girls to the table. Suddenly the front door burst open, and in trotted a long line of policemen in uniform. From all over the big dining room we could hear the frightened word "Raid!" and instantly from all sides bottles began sliding to the center of the dance floor, since possession of even a teaspoonful of liquor was a felony. Our bottle was hidden in the pocket of my overcoat and I was too frightened to do anything about it, but John was quicker on the trigger. He instantly rose and walked away from the table, ready, as he said later, to swear that he'd never seen me before if the bottle were discovered in my possession. It would have been better, he explained unselfishly, that he remain free, because if I had been put in jail, he would still have been at liberty and able to take steps to get me out. How, he didn't say. I was taking care of all our money.

But the police weren't raiding. Ignoring the collection of bottles, they headed directly for the band platform, where one of them announced that they were selling tickets for the forthcoming Police

Widows and Orphans Benefit Ball. Then they circulated among the tables offering tickets to the diners. We didn't buy any but a lot of people did. As they were filing out the door, John used his head and redeemed himself by kicking a couple of fine full flasks under our table, where we easily rescued them when the coast was clear.

On another occasion we were in a small restaurant late at night and John made the acquaintance of a nice-looking girl by telling her he was an artist and asking that she let him sketch her. She moved to our booth to facilitate the process—and let us pay her check—and John, who couldn't draw the simplest thing, made squiggles which he convinced her were a kind of artistic shorthand from which he would later develop a full and flattering picture. He also introduced me as a visiting English journalist, and I did a miserable job of trying to assume an English accent without letting it slip into burlesque Irish. The girl had a drink with us and was very kind about everything, regretting that her husband would worry if she went with us to see the bay from the top of Telegraph Hill, so we escorted her to her street car line and kissed her hand as the car came to a stop for her.

Once we went to the famous "Stanford" whorehouse at 717 Van Ness, but the madam apparently decided we were too drunk and wouldn't let us in, explaining that the girls were all busy and that she wasn't taking any more customers that night. As we walked away we were indignant to see three men enter and the door close behind them. John thought we should go back and argue the matter, but we magnanimously decided to forgive her.

On the last of our three nights in town I remember just one thing—Steinbeck weeping before a drugstore window because I wouldn't part with our dwindling cash to let him buy some of the delightful jointed wooden animals that were displayed in it. So we went to our hotel room, where he bitterly accused me of miserliness till we both went to sleep.

The next morning was a bad one. Both of us had painful heads and stomachs. Liquor had no appeal for us, and neither did the prospect of further high life. In the drabness of the hangover, another thought came to me, and with forebodings I took out the bankroll which was to take us to Mexico. It contained just about $20, the remnant of what we had toiled and suffered for during our long, hot days as sugar-makers. After that revelation we had no thoughts of staying longer in San Francisco.

Retrieving the car from the garage, we drove sadly to John's home in Salinas, where his mother recognized the marks of dissipation upon us and greeted us coolly. She clearly considered me as chiefly instrumental in her son's fall from grace. John, in one of the black moods which usually followed his excesses, didn't want to stay at home anyway, and readily agreed that we probably wouldn't have any trouble finding jobs in the South, and that when we'd saved up some money again, we could continue our projected Mexican trip. So, without much conversation, we drove down Highway 101 to Long Beach.

My mother had heard a great deal about John and was anxious to meet the boy of whom her son was so fond, though she had a strong feeling that he was a bad influence on me and was responsible for many of my lapses from virtue, real and imagined. But the welcome was cordial, and while John sensed the slightly disapproving attitude, he settled gracefully into our family life, though he obviously felt the restricting influence of our five-room flat.

Almost immediately we started looking for work. Unfortunately, neither of us was knowledgeable in that enterprise. Asking for a job seemed a shameful thing, and we tended to mumble and hang our heads, at least figuratively, while being painfully aware of stares from people not involved in the interviews. We answered many ads in Long Beach and Los Angeles and we didn't even get a nibble, perhaps because we had no firm convictions that we could fill the posts we were applying for. In the meantime we were almost penniless, for the journey south had used up most of our reserves. Mother kept the car in gasoline and contributed enough for Bull Durham and minor necessities—even an occasional movie.

One day I happened to notice in the paper a little item about the presence in Long Beach of a Senora de Balyeat, acting as commercial consul for the state of Nicaragua. The idea struck me that perhaps John and I might find employment and adventure in foreign lands to the south—rather a refurbishing of our original dream about Mexico. John liked the idea. So, after I phoned for an appointment, we put on our best clothes and drove to the house which served as the lady's home and office.

Our reception was encouraging. Sra. Balyeat was a handsome woman in the best Latin tradition, and she greeted us with warmth, the more so after John revealed his modest abilities with the Spanish language. She served us tea and cakes in her parlor while we tried to impress her with our talents and training. They might fit us, we thought for some post in the Nicaraguan department of education or a related cultural field. There might even be a liaison position in which our skills in writing (we didn't elaborate or substantiate) and linguistics (I could speak a *little* Spanish) could be of value to her country. She appeared charmed and impressed and was even discretely flirtatious as she described the beauties of Nicaragua and the broad opportunities there for ambitious young men. No children were illegitimate there, she said—such ones were "naturals" and regarded without prejudice. She assured us that all political troubles were over, internal and external, and that peach would prevail forever. (A year later, the U.S. marines landed there again.) It all sounded wonderful, and she seemed to like us—particularly John, who was at his most charming. As we parted after a long visit, he kissed the lady's hand to her apparent delight.

We realized later that there had been no commitments and hardly any specifics. Nor did we ever hear from the Senora again, though we continued to hope.

Eventually we did land a job—of a sort. Urged by a friend, we reluctantly invaded the small Long Beach radio station, KFON, and were, somewhat to our horror, enrolled as salesmen of the Echophone, a primitive oblong radio set with three protruding peanut tubes, a separate horn of classic design, and jacks for earphones, extra equipment not included in the $100 retail price. For every one we sold, we were to receive a princely commission of $5. It was a cinch, the fat, balding manager said, providing us with a list of "Prospects," which he assured us were all red hot.

So we started out with a demonstrator set, a reel of "talking tape" for setting up temporary indoor aerials, and some wire for making ground connections. It was the first radio that either of us had ever been near, and apart from the superficial instructions provided us, we knew almost nothing of how it worked, except that a battery made the tubes light up most of the time, and if they didn't, we would have to go back to the station and find out why.

John, moreover, regarded the device with deep suspicion and would have nothing to do with it. Nor for that matter would he take any part in the sales talk, although he would accompany me into the houses of the prospects and occasionally converse politely with them about almost anything but radio. Once in a while he would help me string the metalized tape around the picture molding (we had gained the fixed impression that it wouldn't work anywhere else) or to run a ground wire to the nearest water faucet. Everything else he left to me.

Most of the red-hot prospects turned out to be far from that. Usually they were people who had dropped into the showroom on the Long Beach Pike out of curiosity about this new marvel of science and indiscreetly permitted their names and addresses to be wrested from them. Some of them denied having done so and refused us entry. There were other difficulties. Only a few stations were broadcasting, most of them were of limited range, and programs tended to be awful. When we had finally climbed on chairs to place the tape, with the housewife watching disapprovingly, and run ugly wires out the window or through doors to the nearest water pipe, there was the problem of tuning in and finding a program that we hoped would enchant the listener into buying a set. We had been told that a saxophone sounded well over the air, but saxophones were rarely available, and we often had to settle for tinny music from a pre-electronic record or a tired live ensemble. Besides, $100 was a big price for a box 14 inches long, especially in view of the ineptitude with which we (I) demonstrated it and tried to answer questions. If the questioning became too intense and technical, John would often excuse himself and slip out to wait for me in the car.

I don't remember how many prospects we visited during the next month, painfully jerry-rigging our set in strange parlors while trying not to scratch furniture, disarrange pictures, or knock over bric-a-brac—all of which we did do from time to time. Probably it wasn't very many, for the strain of conducting a demonstration was so great that after the ordeal was over, we often tacitly agreed it was enough for the day, and with sighs of relief took off for the beach or went for a ride at the end of which there it took us two or three days to recover from an unhappy selling attempt. And I'm sure that our skepticism, our awkwardness, and our embarrassing ignorance about everything electrical convinced more than one of our reluctant hosts that the Echophone was the set they did *not* want.

But we were not complete failures. No sir! We did sell a set and collected the $100 and delivered the money to the man at KFON and received our $5 commission. We also quit the job. The purchaser who had not been able to resist our powers of salesmanship was my elderly aunt. She couldn't really afford it and didn't actually want it very much, but she felt sorry for us and wanted to do something to make us feel better. After that, we had lots of fun with the set and ran it almost constantly, wearing out several sets of A, B, and C batteries, which she, of course, replaced. What with hair-line adjustments of three dials and other gadgets, she never completely mastered the technique of tuning in stations.

~

Once when the entire family was in Los Angeles for the day and boredom lay heavy upon us, partly because we had no money, John voiced a plaintive wish:

"God, if we only had some whiskey!"

Then I remembered. Buried in a back corner of a closet in the upstairs apartment inhabited by my aunt and family was a quart of pre-Prohibition bond, purchased years before and hidden against an emergency. I had discovered it earlier while aimlessly prowling.

In a spirit of bravado I conducted John to the priceless cache, intending only to let him feast his eyes on it. He was impressed, all right, and easily persuaded me that we could take a couple of drinks from it and fill it up with water so that no one would ever know the difference. The first drink was so good that we each had another, leaving an alarming deficit in the bottle.

Then John had another idea. "It's a shame to have liquor like this going to waste," he said. "Especially when we need it so. This bottle has been here for years and nobody has ever touched it. Probably nobody ever will. Why don't we take out the whiskey and fill it up with something that looks like whiskey? Then if anybody looks at it, he won't even guess that it's been opened."

At the moment it sounded like a fine idea. We each had another shot, then poured all but half an ounce or so into a couple of clean medicine bottles. We grudged the half-inch but sacrificed it so that the bottle would "still have the whiskey smell" in case anyone sniffed at it. Then, improvising, we refilled it with tea of the proper color and John ingeniously added an injection of Tabasco sauce "to give it more of a bite." Maybe the color wasn't exactly right, but we were sure there was little chance of discovery, and we restored the bottle to the dark corner from which we had taken it.

By the next day we were less convinced of the wisdom of what we had done, though conscience troubled us more than fear of being caught. The pilfered liquor was in the very bottom of John's suitcase, which, with another suitcase on top of it, lay in the rear of a closet in our bedroom.

In the afternoon we returned from the beach to find Mother waiting for us. The look on her face chilled me. A lifelong crusader against alcohol, she had an incredible sensitivity to its presence—along with something I always suspected was second sight. Some taint of whiskey must have clung to the air, and her nose carried her unerringly to the bottom of the buried bag. Then she had grimly visited her sister upstairs and checked on the secret bottle (obviously not so secret as I had thought), easily discovering the imposture.

Reproachfully she told us that she had discovered our stolen liquor and found where we got it. If my aunt were to have a sudden heart attack and tried to use what we had left as a stimulant, we might readily be guilty of her death, she said. Then she lectured us on the evils and dangers of drink. Liquor (pronounced "likker") was like a fearful disease whose victims couldn't escape, and it could strike you down at any time. We might, she said, even wind up in drunkards' graves, if we went on the way we were going.

Under his breath, John said to me. "What'll the poor drunkard do?" and I think she heard him, for the lecture ended and she turned sadly away. During the rest of her life she was never completely comfortable about our continued friendship, although upon the whole, she liked John and his writing.

Mother was of the school which feels that "in a world where there is so much ugliness it is a shame to write about it instead of the beautiful things." More than once she tried to convince John of that idea, and it always made him uncomfortable. Me, too, for we were both dedicated to realism in art. We knew that you had to look life straight in its ugly face and report what you saw, including warts. Until her death Mother faithfully read all of John's books, but after each her face registered distaste—as if she smelled an impolite odor or had forced herself to go through an unpleasant and vulgar experience. She praised his powers of description, particularly of Nature, and the dramatic qualities of his style, but she deplored the people and situations he depicted. Even *Tortilla Flat* struck her as a series of sordid incidents about people devoid of moral sense. They drank, too—and she could see nothing humorous about them.

Almost her sole criticism of *Of Mice and Men* was: "I wish John didn't have to use 'gut' so often—it's such an unpleasant word."

It was apparent at times that Mother's air of Christian morality was a bit oppressive to John, as to a lesser degree—through habituation—it was to me. Not that she enforced a Puritan ethic. Her concepts of behavior were, in a way, Victorian. She had led a relatively sheltered life, free from many contacts with the less-than-genteel world. Rarely did she offer a reproof for unseemly acts or speech, but her disapproval was always evident in her silence. It floated in the atmosphere of the house when we had said or done something that she felt was disappointing—or even when she suspected that our thoughts violated good taste.

Thus John was usually glad of any opportunity to get away from her silent scrutiny that gave him a sense of guilt at times. And a fine opportunity offered itself when I remembered that by law I was required to make material improvement on a cabin site in the Cleveland National Forest on which I had at some time earlier paid the nominal leasehold fee. Otherwise it would revert to the Federal government. With enthusiasm, and neither plans nor experience, we loaded up the car, packing assorted tools and two bags of cement, and set out for Trabuco Canyon, a few miles into the mountains from El Toro, not yet a wartime Marine base, happy to emerge into a world where our consciences would at least temporarily be our own.

It was a totally ridiculous project. We had no plans for a cabin and no idea of what would be required to build one. Our main purpose was to show that work was being done on the site so that the lease would not be canceled. And it was delightful to get out into the world of wild growing things and away from the physical and moral miasmas of urban apartment dwelling. We had never seen the lot and we spent much of the first day in locating it and pitching an elementary camp where we found it.

We had brought along two folding cots, and after exploring the surrounding area and settling on the best spot for the tentative structure, we cooked a good meal on a grill positioned over a semicircle of rocks, sang a while to my ineptly played ukulele, and went to sleep under the stars. We slept magnificently and woke with the crisp dawn. As I opened my eyes and peered out from under the mosquito netting with which I had covered myself, I looked at the boulder beside which I had pitched my bed, and on its tip, eighteen inches from my head, sat a tarantula the size of my hand, staring at me with all its eight eyes. I yelled to John, who was already sitting on the side of his cot several yards away, and he picked up an axe handle as he came, while I slipped out the other side of my cot. But he didn't attack the spider. Instead, with an expression of malicious delight he attacked the alarm clock which also sat on the boulder—my contribution to an orderly world in which knowing the time of day was of vital importance. The tarantula fled as John battered the clock into submission, continuing to pour on blows until it was a flattened mass of metal, making it the scapegoat for all the repressions he had been suffering. And over my protests he delivered a diatribe on the evils that clocks imposed on mankind, governing and restricting the free range of life and thought. He continued while I rose and got breakfast—his enthusiasms rarely included cooking though he later contributed to a "celebrity" cook book. For the rest of our stay we remained timeless, a condition which he more than once referred to with approval.

Then we got down to the business of building a foundation for a cabin of unknown dimensions and shape. There were plenty of rounded rocks available, and at first we began distributing those of a suitable size and shape around an area that looked level, after tentatively marking off a large square. Then we discovered varying depth would be necessary. That involved a lot of work including removal of buried rocks, but the round-point shovel we'd brought along wasn't really suited to the job. We didn't have a carpenter's level and John devised one from a wooden triangle with a drop line from the apex. It wasn't very accurate but it showed us that the excavations would have to be surprisingly deep. The work went very slowly, as we had to sit down and think things over with progressive frequency. Moreover, we drank much coffee after breakfast, delaying our start; we halted for an hour or two at lunch time; and when the high ridges around us cut off the sun in mid-afternoon, we took Nature's hint that the work day was over and happily turned to more cultural occupations like smoking, talking, playing the ukulele, and preparing for as good a dinner as our supplies permitted. We never got around to making even a rough plan of the cabin.

We skimped on the trenches. Digging in the rocky soil was hard and there were tough roots to remove by hand. In the lowest corner of the site we decided that a large boulder would be all that was necessary, thereby cutting down on the required labor. Then came the matter of mixing the mortar and we weren't sure of the best proportions of sand and cement but decided to be economical since the bag we had brought along seemed inadequate for the job. In fact, we had to drive down to the nearest town and get two more bags, once our suspicions had proved to be true. So we piled stones on stones, seating them precariously in a paste that often let them slip right down again, but we toiled at the task with a growing awareness that the narrow, pyramidal walls we were building looked neither strong nor adequate.

On about our fifth day, we woke to find that about half the foundation-to-be had collapsed, partly because of its structural defects, which often had small rocks largely balanced on larger ones, and partly because we had mixed too much creek sand and pebbles with too little cement. We also noticed that our hands were developing red patches that itched—many of the roots we had been grubbing out manually turned out to have been poison oak, and as we surveyed the ruins, two men drove up and stopped to see what we were accomplishing. They tried to be kind in their criticisms of our methods and achievements, but the facts were apparent even to us. And then one of them, a resident of the upper canyon, gently told us that in the spring, the site we had chosen was generally under a few feet of water. We could see it when he pointed out the evidence.

That was the final blow. When the men had gone we didn't even discuss what to do next. We ate most of our remaining food, packed our belongings—all except the martyred alarm clock and the empty cement sacks—and headed for home,, not without a certain relief. I never went back. Presumably the spring torrents tumbled the remnants of our humiliation and the land reverted to the government and became a training ground for Marines.

By November, the supervision and enforced respectability of my household, together with our dependence on Mother for every cent of our spending money, began to wear on both of us, particularly upon John, in whom it produced long, brooding silences and an increasing gloom. He even thought of bumming his way home to Salinas, though he probably would have walked most of the 400 miles rather than lift a thumb to beg transportation from motoring strangers. Even our favorite pastime of parking on a downtown street and evaluating the passing girls palled upon him. We smoked some marijuana and it made him more morose. We went calling on some girls and he insulted them. He went for long, nighttime walks without inviting me. He was not happy.

Then we had a windfall. Through the influence of a woman who had one of the other apartments in the building and was an officer of the Tuberculosis Society, we were given the contract for addressing, stuffing, and mailing Christmas seals for the entire 1924 Long Beach campaign—perhaps three-quarters of a million stamps, usually in sheets of one hundred to the envelope. Each of us had a portable typewriter—the old three-row, double-shift Coronas—and for the next few weeks we worked at the job almost constantly, using the local telephone book as a source. Even as we listened to the Stanford-California Big Game over my aunt's (Echophone) radio, we continued to type addresses and fill envelopes with stamps and covering letters, though occasionally we rose to cheer and urge our team on against the invincible "Wonder Team" of UC's Andy Smith.

Eventually the big job was done and the last box of envelopes delivered to the post office. John took his half of the money we had earned and almost immediately left for home. After the Christmas vacation he re-entered Stanford to remain until June 1925.

About this period of his life, my information is sparse and spotty. We did exchange letters, but his were among those he later insisted on burning. I did see him on a trip I made to Stanford, but for the most part he was fully occupied with a variety of activities, academic and otherwise, in company with a diverse circle of student and faculty friends. Harold Chapman Brown, head of the Philosophy department, often invited him to his home, and John saw a good deal of Samuel Seward, an English professor. Also in the English department was Dr. Margery Bailey, an 18th-century scholar and authority on Dr. Johnson. Their friendship was an explosive one, with frequent periods of hostility. Earlier, John had taken courses from her at the Hopkins Marine Station during the Pacific Grove summers, but he never fitted into the little coterie of males with whom she habitually surrounded herself for soirees and salons, so that social relations, when they did exist, resembled an armistice.

Among the strong influences upon Steinbeck was that of Dr. Edith Mirrielees, under whom he studied the writing of the short story and from whom he learned a great deal in art and technique. Their association continued for many years, during which she criticized a number of his manuscripts before they went out to publishers. He held her assistance in high esteem. I believe it was in one of her classes that he wrote the short story, "A Lady in Infra-Red," which he developed, some three years later, into his first book, *The Cup of Gold*.

Whether or not John was a formal member of the English Club, then a dynamic literary force on the campus, I do not know, but he attended many of its meetings and associated closely with many of its active members, including Dr. Bailey. Among them were Katherine Beswick, who wrote excellent poetry; Milton Rosenfeld, who had lost a leg in World War I; Frank Fenton, who later served as acting president of San Francisco State College; Vernon Givan, the only engineering student ever admitted as a member; Dean Storey, who became a highly regarded physician and diagnostician: and Serge Eremievsky, a White Russian who later changed his name to Dagver and became a Hollywood producer. Others were Carl Wilhelmson, whom we had known earlier; Toby Street, who provided the idea which became *To a God Unknown*; Howard Pease, subsequently a prolific writer of boys' books; Charles "Mike" McNichols, also a war veteran who became a movie-script writer; John Murphy, with whom he had grown up in Salinas; and a number of others including some he told me about but whom I never met.

With Montgomery Winn, who became attorney, he engaged in a number of exploits, some of them sensational, though I have to rely on Steinbeck accounts, and those are not always completely dependable. As a protest against the campus caste system, they brought two beautiful Chinese girls in full Oriental costume to the formal junior prom, one of the three important social events of the year. Explaining nothing more than that their dates were from San Francisco, John arranged with his sister Mary, who was president of the Alpha Phi house, to let the girls use the sorority facilities in making final preparations for the dance, such as putting on last-minute parts of the costume, combing hair, adjusting makeup and corsage, and the like.

Lacking a car, Winn and Steinbeck brought their guests to Palo Alto on the train, expecting to transport them to the campus in a taxi. They overlooked the fact, however, that on the nights of cotillions and proms and balls, every available taxicab has been reserved for days ahead, most of them with reservations in a tight time sequence. Thus when they arrived at the station, no transportation for the campus was available and time was growing short. So, while one of the lads stayed with the girls, the other dashed out in search of a vehicle—any kind of vehicle. He found one, too-a Model-T Ford laundry wagon with doors at the rear. It was battered and noisy but it ran and was clean.

Now formal dances at Stanford were display events. In front of every fraternity and sorority house stood the shiniest big cars (some of them borrowed for the occasion) that the members could assemble. The driveway of the Alpha Phi house in particular was resplendent with Cadillacs, Packards, and even a Pierce Arrow. Mary Steinbeck was proud of the way it looked, all smaller and dingier cars having been moved to other locations or parked in the outer darkness.

The procession to the ballroom in Encina hall was starting. Distinguished alumnae visitors were being shepherded toward the front porch, already filled with nervously or suavely immaculate young men and their female partners, adjusting an evening wrap, giving a final pat to an expensive permanent, or making sure that the orchids or gardenias were not being crushed.

It was then, of course, that John and Monty arrived. With a terrific clatter, their ancient laundry wagon lurched dizzily into the driveway and skidded to a squealing stop on the freshly raked gravel. The sorority sisters gasped in horror. Out of the driver's seat leaped Steinbeck and dashed to the rear of the shameless vehicle, flinging wide the creaking doors. Out jumped Winn, and with exquisite, though slightly alcoholic aplomb, they assisted the Chinese girls down to the driveway, where they stood smiling with no apparent self-consciousness in spite of the staring eyes. And leaving the humiliating truck where it was, the young men picked up the girls' dressing cases and conducted their partners into the house to search out its almost apoplectic president. It was years before Mary forgave her brother.

At the prom, the exotically dressed Chinese girls were a sensation and their partners were besieged with requests for dances with them, also for introductions. Even the chaperones were fascinated. Steinbeck and Winn, both of whom carried flasks in the accepted collegiate fashion of the day, had a fine time and told progressively elaborate stories about the identity of the girls, who, by the end of the evening, had turned into direct descendants of the Dowager Empress. Everyone was envious except perhaps Mary and some of her sorority sisters.

Who the girls actually were, I never learned, though their escorts later hinted that they were prostitutes. It could have been true, but Chinese prostitutes have been rare in San Francisco since early in the century, and the girls were both young and beautiful. Whatever the truth was, the exploit brought fame of a sort to the perpetrators and added to Steinbeck's reputation for inspired unconventionality.

Then there is the highly dubious story that John told me about a behind-the-scenes fling at campus politics. I suspect its veracity although he related it with embellishments as a genuine conspiracy.

Nor do I believe that a search of campus records would give any substantiation. As he confided it (with an expanding complexity of detail—but no names) a notably competent young man was a candidate for the student-body presidency and had an excellent chance of being elected. His ability was amply proved, his character was unimpeachable, and his record was spotless. In addition, he was very popular. Unfortunately for him, his uncompromising virtue got under the skins of John and some of his associates to whom openly professed clean living and Christian morality seemed an affront. It wasn't that goodness was objectionable, but an aggressive evangelical goodness was definitely in bad taste. The lad, they felt, was something of a prig and verged on being a horse's ass, so they conspired toward his political downfall.

The opposing candidate had a reputation as a rounder. He had no marked fitness for office other than a polished social manner and a fair academic record, but there was no prudishness about him. The conspirators did not openly support him—particularly since their only objective was to defeat the paragon. In fact, to the best of their abilities, they kept their interest in the election a complete secret, outwardly maintaining a bored indifference to the contest and the issues involved in privacy, they were making their preparations. And in the dark hours preceding the opening of the polls they were mysteriously very busy in all parts of the campus.

Daylight revealed that the campaign had been enriched by a spate of new posters, lavishly affixed to strategic trees, posts, and buildings where they could not be missed by any prospective voter. The paragon must have been pleased and surprised when he caught sight of the first one. In large, black, compelling letters it urged a vote for him, and there was a mass of printed text apparently supporting that appeal. Clearly, someone had paid a sizeable printing bill. But when he started reading the body of the poster, he was doubtless not quite so happy.

The campus, however, after the first indifferent examination that befits all election literature, did a collective double-take and began reading very carefully, with a rising chorus of chuckles that grew into a university-wide belly laugh. For the poster consisted of a series of Delphic endorsements. Leading off was a statement professing to come from the boy's mother, cataloguing many of his virtues and endearing qualities. Following was an encomium from someone who seemed to be his hometown minister, remarking proudly upon his spiritual attainments and leadership among the church-related organizations. A Scout leader attested his clean character and high ideals; a grammar-school teacher mentioned the inspiration of having had him as a pupil; and a YMCA secretary gushed over the fine type of young American manhood that he represented. A leading University official said flatly that his election would greatly raise the moral status of the campus and work toward the elimination of hypocrisy, poor sportsmanship, and opium smoking. And the Palo Alto police chief said gruffly, "We don't know him down here and don't want to."

It was character assassination, of course, and the rival candidate was elected in a landslide of votes and snickers, for flagrant virtue is rarely admired by the collegiate mind; and the poster had been so skillfully done that its spuriousness could have been open to doubt. The university conducted an investigation, but since care had been taken to have the poster printed out of town at a shop which intentionally left off its identification, the conspirators retained their pleased anonymity and were never apprehended.

Well, that's the way he told it, and with so artistic a set of details and such a convincing manner that I never doubted any of the story. Until later, that is. And I prefer to avoid totally a grubby search of the records, which might bring complete disillusionment about a machination that could—and should—have happened.

Part 3:

Living in the The Sphincter

At some time in 1924 or 1925, John deserted the dormitory and moved into a shack at the rear of a big house next to San Francisquito Creek in Palo Alto. "Shack" is really too elegant a word, for his quarters actually consisted of half of a very small woodshed. The room was barely six and a half feet square and was tightly furnished with a steel cot, a table, and a chair. There was a water faucet in the yard outside his door, but for further toilet facilities he had to go to the big house, where he also was permitted to do a little cooking, though he sometimes prepared coffee and simple foods on a small open-air grill set up on rocks. His friends were delighted with the place, and four or five of them often jammed into it for bull sessions or drinking parties. Appropriately, they named it "The Anal Sphincter" and professed to be raising a fund to buy a commemorative brass plate for the door so that the world would know it as a shrine when John had reached the literary immortality for which he was so determinedly bound. (It would have been futile.

Where the shack once stood, along with the large late-Victorian house to which it belonged, now rises a huge apartment house—Palo Alto's first multi-story building, and the hovel in which genius was germinating is long gone.)

While he was living there, a girl came down from San Francisco to spend the weekend with him, heedless of the cramped quarters. But, as they were lustily fornicating during the second afternoon, a knock sounded at the door. Quickly, John peered through a crack and then hurried his scantily clad visitor into the dust and cobwebs beneath the cot, tossing her clothes and other signs of her presence after her. Then he opened the door.

The caller was Mrs. Price of Palo Alto, owner and operator of Fallen Leaf Lodge near Lake Tahoe, for whom John had worked during a previous summer. She wanted to discuss his possible employment there during the coming vacation, as well as certain personal matters relating to the prospective marriage of her daughter Frances to John's friend, Toby Street. Mrs. Price liked Toby, as did everyone, but she was not quite sure that he was possessed of the high moral character that she would have wished, and that Frances, with her careful training, would expect and deserve. He was frequently very unconventional in behavior and attitudes, his language was often unrestrained, and there was reason to believe that he sometimes drank. What did John think about it?

John had quite a few things to think about as he sat on his chair and she on the cot, beneath which lay the half-dressed Girl, shrinking from the spider webs and covering her nose to keep herself from sneezing as dust showered down with every movement above her. It was warm, and perspiration trickled down her face and shoulders. John was perspiring too, for Mrs. Price was a rigid moralist, particularly with regard to relationships between young men and women. Almost as many employees had been discharged from the Lodge for sexual reasons as for liquor, which, beside being wrong, was illegal. Even a suspicion of the hidden guest might have permanently eliminated John as a future worker at Mrs. Price's pleasant summer resort. It might also have constituted another black mark against Toby, whose contamination by association would have been held against him.

The discussion went on for almost an hour, and by the time Mrs. Price had gathered her skirts and gone, the girl was almost dead. Streaked with the mud of dust plus perspiration, wreathed in cobwebs, and matted with dirt and floor debris where she had lain prone for so long, she emerged painfully from her hiding place. She was a spirited lass who was proud of the way she had gone through the ordeal without a revealing sneeze or cough, without a gasp at the heat or the crawling things, and her chief indignation was at Mrs. Price, at whose conversation and questions she had been hard put to restrain chuckles. The most painful part, was that every time Mrs. Price changed position, the weight of her posterior pressed the springs into the tender back below.

Mrs. Price never learned that she had perched for an hour only an inch or two over the body of an abandoned woman—*flagrante interruptu*—though she later came to the unhappy conclusion that Steinbeck was not a person of the highest moral standards.

I have no accurate information about the number of summers that John spent at Fallen leaf and nearby Tahoe. He worked at the Lodge during parts of one or two years, and at other times for several other people in the lake area—mending fences, cutting wood, making roads, clearing brush, performing minor carpentry and painting, and such other tasks as are requisite to summer resorts and mountain estates. One of his principal employers was Mrs. Alice Brigham, who owned a huge area with a long stretch of Tahoe lake front at the south end, and a mountain acreage which included at least two smaller lakes. It was here that John came to spend the winter of 1927-28 as custodian and to start serious writing on his first published book, *The Cup of Gold.*

Nor do I remember the steps that led up to his decision in 1925 to go to New York. An uncle, Joe Hamilton, had an advertising business in Chicago but often visited the larger city, and Beth (Elizabeth Ainsworth), one of his older sisters, had a position with a metropolitan department store. John had been writing determinedly for several years, though he had sold nothing. Still in my possession is an envelope inscribed in his cramped printing, "The Literary Adventures of Dook and Me," in which repose a number of rejection slips from various magazines, *The Atlantic*, *Harpers*, *The American Mercury*, and others of the better class, for we set our sights high. Most of those were collected during the summer of 1924 when we were in penniless bondage at Long Beach.

When he did make up his mind in the fall of 1925 to try the big city, I was in my first year of teaching English and Journalism at Occidental College in the northeastern or Eagle Rock section of Los Angeles. He had arranged to travel on a freighter, the *Katrina* from Luckenbach, and managed his arrival so that he would have several days with me, sharing my furnished room across from the college. He brought a bottle with him, and when that was gone—soon—we got more from an ex-hotel clerk with whom I had worked until he was fired for bootlegging to the guests of the Beverly Hills Hotel. He offered a choice of gin, whiskey, or apricot cordial, all of which he made with alcohol and various syrups and flavorings in his apartment on Lake Street near Westlake Park. For his high-class clientele, he actually used to take cases of his product to the beach and dip them in the ocean to substantiate his claim that they had been smuggled in from boats. For the most part, we selected the cordial as the least unpalatable of the lot. We did our adventuring at night and as far away from the little presbyterian college (about 600 students then) as possible.

In the daytime while I was teaching, he read or wrote or called on other friends in the area. He attended a few of my classes to evaluate the quality of my teaching, and once I persuaded him, using all the arguments, pleas, and pressure I could think of, to appear as a practicing writer before a very small class in Advanced Journalism and lay bare some of the secrets of literary success. I almost had to fight him into the room where five students waited his message. He had made no notes, and on stepping to the lectern he froze. For some ten agonizing minutes he mumbled brokenly with long waits between unfinished sentences which said very little, and then suddenly, he who could charm an intimate group and spin delightful stories without pause, chokingly said, "That's all," and went out the door. During all the rest of his life, he shunned public appearances and refused to make speeches, often angrily. Photographs taken of him when he was accepting the Nobel Prize for Literature in 1962 show a facial expression that betrays an intense discomfort.

And he looked up Yvonne, who by that time was working in Los Angeles and sharing a room in Inglewood with a girl friend. From his first visit there he returned disheartened, for the roommate had refused to leave John and Yvonne alone. So he proposed that I go along a couple of nights later and syphon the other girl away with the aid of liquor and a professedly uncontrollable desire to dance, an activity for which he and Yvonne would display a strong distaste. I had no automobile at the time, and Inglewood is a long fifteen miles or more across the city from Eagle Rock, but the York Boulevard trolley line made the whole trip without a change, though it took almost an hour.

The girls had dinner prepared by the time we arrived, and when we had eaten, I went into my act. After some argument and with marked misgivings, Yvonne's roommate finally yielded to my importunities and the apricot cordial. As she went to get her coat, John whispered, "Keep her away just as long as you can."

We were already well primed with the nectar, and I had a full pint of it in my pocket. We nipped from it as we rode on the street car toward the bright lights. Later, when we had found and entered the Roseroom, a huge dance hall in downtown Los Angeles, we managed to have more nips in the darkness of the balcony between cavortings on the floor. By the time the pleasure palace closed, we were feeling the effects rather strongly.

Happily we went to the nearest corner to wait for the proper street car—and wait and wait and wait. Many cars came along but none was the right one, to our mystification, and we caught a few more drinks from the almost empty bottle. Finally, in a burst of inspiration, I asked a news vender what was the matter with the E car, and learned that the line to Inglewood ran on the *next* street, not the one where we had been standing so long. It seemed very funny to us at the moment, but not when we got to the proper corner and found out, after another wait, that the last Inglewood car had already gone.

By that time it was 2:00 o'clock and the few dollars in my pocket were not nearly enough for a taxi ride to the suburb. Even if they had been I would still have wanted to give John all the time he requested. I was proud of my unselfish success in that direction so far, and this seemed a fine opportunity to dower the lovers with an entire night together. Thus inspired—as well as with an inability to think up an alternative—I told the girl we would have to go to a hotel. She demurred violently, but followed when I started walking. Eventually we ended up at a medium-grade establishment near Third and Hill Streets, where, hatless and without luggage, we registered under the names of Mr. And Mrs. Lynn C. Doyle, and for $2 in advance were shown to a comfortable room with a double bed. In spite of the remaining cordial, the inforced intimacy of the bed, and my arguments, the girl remained stubbornly chaste and we simply slept. In the morning, after a pleasant breakfast in the hotel dining room, she phoned Yvonne to explain her absence and to promise that we would soon be there. Yvonne was not pleased. She was furious. No, John was not there. He had left on the last street car to Eagle Rock after an uneasy evening during which they nervously listened to every trolley as it stopped by their corner, thereby failing miserably in their attempts to reestablish their old rapport.

So I phoned Eagle Rock and got a similar and even more bitter blast from John. I had expected praise for my efforts to provide them with opportunity for an uninterrupted period of love making. Instead, I got a blistering denunciation. Yvonne had been too worried about the safety of her roommate and the danger of interruption to pay proper attention to romance, and she had refused to let him stay in the apartment. In addition, the expressman was coming to deliver John's trunk to the ship and John had no money to prepay it, nor could the landlady.

Saddened by the ingratitude, I put the girl on a car heading toward Inglewood and took another in the opposite direction. By the time I got home, the landlady had borrowed the money for the trunk from a passing student and it was on its way, but John was still furious and totally unsympathetic with the good deed I had tried to do for him.

Later in the day we went into Los Angeles and took the big red interurban to Long Beach. The next morning I used my mother's car to get him to the pier in Wilmington, from which the *Katrina* was to sail. It had accommodations for the customary twelve passengers in addition to the crew, and I went aboard with him to examine the freshly painted quarters that he would inhabit during the long voyage through the Canal to New York, his Mecca of the moment. A little later, I stood on the dock as the ropes were cast off and with a finger traced an imaginary *ave atque vale* in a burst of cultural sentimentalist on a nearby wall while trying to keep down the lump in my throat. He didn't understand what I was trying to say except that it probably was something suited to the occasion, and we both wished that the ship would move faster as it edged into the channel. Farewells can last too long.

I had a letter from him that had been mailed in Colon. It was long and done in sections and somewhat frayed. He wrote of the barren coast of Baja California—which he was later to know much better—of the many sea turtles that the ship passed as it headed south, and of the incredible lettuce green of the foliage as they neared the tropical regions. He had made friends aboard and described some of them, making them sound more colorful than they doubtless were, and he had observations on the new and strange sensations of being on the water in an area he had never seen before. Everything delighted him, the blueness of the ocean, the sun on the waves, the birds, the languorous air, and the lush vegetation. That part of the letter throbbed with excitement.

The remainder was less exuberant. There had been a layover in Panama, and in company with a shipmate or two he had toward the less-reputable part of the town, entering native establishments, drinking a good deal, spending much of his money getting into a fight, and acquiring a sizeable hangover. He was not very clear about some of the details and the handwriting was a bit shaky, but he assured me that he had been having a wonderful time.

I next heard from him in New York. The ship had paused at some of the West Indies ports, bringing new adventures only vaguely hinted at. When he landed in New York, he said, there was exactly five cents in his pocket. Presumably Joe Hamilton or his sister Beth and her husband kept him from going hungry, and within a few days, Ainsworth had got him a job loading bricks at the base of the New Madison Square Garden, then under construction. He had even been provided with a laborer's card, filled with the necessary union stamps. He held the job only briefly. A week after he started, a workman several stories up missed his footing and landed in a splash of bloody jelly within ten feet of him. John became violently ill and quit the job.

A week or two later, however, he was hired as a reporter on the *New York-American* through his uncle's influence. In spite of his strong aversion for Mr. Hearst and everything he represented, John did general assignments for a couple of months, with a growing distaste for the ethics of the job and the paper, and for the drastic editing to which his copy was invariably subjected. In the traditional manner, his every adjective was removed and often his stories were scornfully turned over to rewrite men. Apparently, too, there was a fairly consistent criticism of his accuracy in gathering and presenting facts. He occasionally clashed with his superiors about such strictures and complained about his assignments. I don't know whether he quit or was fired, but both may have happened simultaneously. During that period I heard from him only irregularly, and sometimes on postal cards.

So for a time he became what he called a journalistic freelance. He was proud of discovering the former pugilist, Kid McCoy, wearing a blue smock (men didn't *wear* smocks in those days) and taking care of the quotations board in a big bond office—and his story made the wire services. He sold stories now and then to various newspapers and worked at home on short stories, some with a New York background. It is doubtful that he made enough to cover all his living expenses; and his parents may have continued to send occasional contributions or a monthly allowance such as he had received in college. The presence of his sister Beth in the city could have been a help at times.

By this time he had taken a small apartment on Gramercy Park, where he lived for the remainder of his stay in New York. He was meeting people, among them Mahlon Blaine, an established illustrator with multiple but undisciplined talents. According to Blaine's account of himself, he was born in a small Oregon town, and in his enthusiastic study of art had paid great attention to the protective coloring of birds and animals, a fact which resulted in his being requisitioned at the start of World War I by the government group which developed the theory and practice of camouflage for uniforms, trains, and other transport vehicles. During the war he lost one eye in France, but his other eye remained remarkably keen. He was aware that his monocular vision often resulted in a lack of depth in his art work, but professed to find that a virtue in many respects.

Blaine helped Steinbeck to make a few contacts with writers and publishers, though the artist was usually at swords' points with the people who commissioned him; he often refused to follow the suggestions of editors, preferring to substitute ideas and treatments of his own and consequently had been thrown out of several offices and refused admission to others. Blaine may have shared John's apartment for a while. He was a very stimulating companion, not only because he had a widespread acquaintance in the literary and artistic circles of New York but because of his dynamic interest in ideas as well as every kind of art, and he had accumulated a tremendous mass of assorted information in a surprising number of fields. He was aided by a photographic memory, and I have seen him humiliate "experts" on Communism by quoting page, paragraph, and line from *Das Kapital* to prove that they had been misquoting or misunderstanding Marx. (He was liberal but took no political partisanship, and had read the book, he said, merely to find what it contained and why people got so excited about it.) Blaine was later to do the dust cover for *Cup of Gold*, published four years later.

Among other friends, John met a talented young concert pianist, Mary Ardath. She lived in a neighboring building, and in the best O. Henry tradition, the affair developed through their seeing each other regularly at their windows. Soon they were spending much of their time together and she was widening his circle of acquaintances. He accompanied her to several of her public recitals, held in major halls, but wasn't very happy at some of the salon parties to which she took him. The friendship lasted for two or three years till she married, and she visited him at least once in California. At his suggestion, she came to see me in Long Beach and played Bach on our old upright piano.[8]

In June 1926, I was married to Ruth Carpenter just before leaving for the summer session at Stanford, and I duly notified John of the step. It resulted in a mock-serious letter to my new wife, affirming our friendship, which he hoped could be extended to her, and making dire but humorously intended threats. At least, they probably started out to be half-humorous, but as often happened, the theme dramatized itself and ran away with him. His loneliness and lack of success in the big city may have helped to guide his expression. When he and Ruth met later there was no evidence of hostility and they quickly became good friends.[9] Viewed objectively, the letter is formidable and even frightened her:

Dear Ruth,

I received notice of your marriage to my friend with the same spurting flame of hostility that you will doubtless feel on reading this communication. Naturally I can conceive. Pictures of the jealousies of normal women for their husbands' friends grew up in my mind. But after a time I resolved to write you a letter containing a threat, an appeal and an explanation. On your reception of these three I must base my esteem of you. I agree that my esteem may seem of little consequence.

1. I love this person so much that I would cut your charming throat should you interfere seriously with his happiness or his manifest future. And I assure you that I possess the subtlety, the cleverness, and the ability quite to ruin you if only punishment seemed expedient. Thus I threaten you very openly.

2. I appeal to you to allow my memory, if it must remain such, to rest in status quo. In the power which is given you simply by being a woman and a chosen woman from among many, do not injure the very beautiful thing which has grown up between us. That would be very difficult for you would have to circumvent an iron loyalty and castellated memories, but it is not unthinkable. You have in your hands the seeds of a very great genius, be careful how you nourish them. Many a woman has thrown acid in the eyes of the future. If Duke loves you, then you have qualities which are impeccable, and to which I must bow. But since you are a woman, you have attributes which I, in some measure, understand, and fear. Distraction has before now battered to powder the forts of brilliance. How I wish I could be assured that you understand these things. Do you think that I am intimate with things that do not concern me? If so you are not only foolish but foolhardy and boastful. For you cannot tear in a day the cloth which was long and careful in the making. Thus I appeal to you, since you were given the honor of being the victim, to sacrifice yourself, not to this person's person, but to the children of his brain. If you are big enough you will have understood this before now, if not, all of my telling will only make you angry.

3. I have promised some explanation of my position. Neither this person nor myself had a brother. Both of us were rather abnormally constructed. Because of these things, we went through our very young years lonely and seeking. We had no intimates, practically no friends. We made enemies readily because we were far above our immediate associates. In college we met, and at every point the one seemed to supplement and

strengthen the other. We are not alike, rather we are opposites, but also we are equals. The combination was put to severe tests. We took the same girl to dances and things, and the friendship grew. We fought bloodily and the matter was strengthened. We worked in a vicious heat and emerged to find a wonderful comradeship. The outcome was a structure of glorious dream. We builded tall rocks in the sea and perched lovely castles with sky piercing capped turrets on top of them, and up the steep path we manoeuvered a pageant of green and gold. Are you understanding me at all? He was the cathode and I the annode. We laughed, quarreled, drank, were sad, considered life, ethics, philosophies. We did not always agree. More often we openly disagreed. But always in the back of the mind of each there was the thought that the one was not complete without the other and never could be. The one supplied a blind appetite in the other. It would have been, from our constant attendance, to draw obscene conclusions, but our fists quite precluded any such feeling. We were constantly together. Do you wish to interfere in this so that you may have him more surely to yourself, or would you rather attempt to come into the circle? Perhaps you can. I do not know you. Undoubtedly each of us supplies a great need in him, take care that you do not overstep your need and your usefulness.

I offer you my friendship, if you are worthy of the circle, and my vindictive, active hatred if you are not. You may possess a part of him, but no woman who has ever lived is big enough to have all.

Meanwhile I congratulate you as one who has found a very precious thing. I give you my utmost respect and allegiance as long as you are worthy of it. I shall regard any attempt at alienation as an act harmful to him, because I know that I am necessary to him as he is necessary to me.

May I not hear your attitude?

[Signed: "sincerely john steinbeck"]

In the mean time, John was devoting more and more effort toward the serious writing of short stories, chiefly with a metropolitan background and of fair quality, in spite of a tendency toward restrained sentimentality and pathos, which occasionally became bathos. When he had eight or ten of them finished, he showed them to Guy Holt, then editor for McBride (Robert M. & Co.). Holt liked them for the most part, and after suggesting a few revisions told John that if he could write half a dozen more, equally as good, his house would publish the book.

Success seemed assured at last, and although he had practically no money, he dropped all attempts to make a living and started to write furiously, working night and day and hardly stopping for the scanty meals he could afford. Bread, cheese, and sardines were his staples. Friends now and then supplemented his diet, but he still didn't get enough to eat, and the fires of creation were burning hotly within him as he wrote, rewrote, discarded, and polished.

Finally, six new stories were done to his satisfaction, and with stomach fluttering he set out to deliver them to Holt. But when he climbed the stairs to the editorial office, there was a new name on the door. He described the new editor as a "a smart young Jew," and when he was finally admitted to the presence, the presence was not impressed or even particularly polite. Holt, he explained, had left a couple of days earlier to become the top man in the new house of John Day, and he had taken his publishing policies with him. He shuffled disparagingly through John's manuscript, carefully typed by Mary Ardath, and after a cursory examination tossed it back at John. No, he said, McBride wasn't interested in that sort of thing. Sure, maybe Holt *had* said he liked it, maybe he'd even made promises, but Holt wasn't editor any more and the new editor felt himself in no way bound by any dubious commitments that his predecessor may have seen fit to make.

It was probably the young man's scornful air and his casual rejection without even the pretext of a reading, as much as the undernourishment, mental strain, and deep disappointment, but John blew his top. He shouted insults and may have even threatened physical violence. As a result, he was hustled down the stairs and ejected with his manuscript from the building. Blind with rage, frustration, and perhaps undernourishment, according to his account to me, he fainted on the sidewalk. He was, he told me, taken to Bellevue

Hospital, where he was found to be in a state of utter collapse and remained there regaining strength for several days. (The hospital episode has been vigorously denied by his sister, Beth, who presumably should have known about it at the time, and no one else has given it any verification. My memory of his telling me is very strong, and it does not seem the kind of literary elaboration that he would have been likely to make, particularly with the name of the hospital.)

I have no further information about the brief remaining part of the New York adventure. It is probably that he looked up Holt and found him unwilling or unable to undertake any fresh—or questionable—commitments for the new publishing company. As far as I know, none of the stories has ever been printed. He gave me the carbon of one of them, "The White Sister of Fourteenth Street," and four others that may have been part of the group were given to Wilbur Needham, a book reviewer for the *Los Angeles Times*, who turned them over to Lawrence Clark Powell, then Librarian for UCLA, and he sold them to the Houghton Library at Harvard. Holt did offer to introduce him to James Branch Cabell, then at the height of his literary popularity and visiting in New York. John refused, saying that although he admired Mr. Cabell's work tremendously, he didn't want to run the risk of being disillusioned by meeting the man. Holt reported this to the novelist when they lunched together, and the great man sent a hand-written note to his young admirer. "Dear Mr. Steinbeck," it read, "Sometimes I wish that I too did not know James Branch Cabell."

John treasured the note for years, or at least until he began to lose enthusiasm for the delicate traceries and the involved, leering allegories of Cabell's style.

Still weak from his illness and bitter from his disappointment, John was homesick for the brown hills and scattered oaks of the Salinas valley, and he had no stomach for further efforts to make a living in the big city, whose inherent hostility to the newcomer was by this time very apparent to him. Eventually, through certain pulling of strings by Amasa ("Ted") Miller, a former Stanford friend, he was signed on as a deck hand for another Luckenbach ship which was westward bound. Certain is that representations, even minor bribery, must have been involved, for he was provided with proper working papers as an able-bodied seaman.

On his first night at sea, as he told the story, he was chosen by the crew as the most likely candidate to fight the ship's bully, a huge and tough Irishman who had already knocked out every previous contender. Seasick and still not in the best of health, John reluctantly faced the champion and managed, through his speed and knowledge of scientific boxing, to knock the sailor out cold. John thus gained a reputation that was never again challenged and he became popular among most of the men—even the Irishman. That's the way he told the story, at least, and with his normal modesty, the main outlines are doubtless reliable.

That the crew liked him is indisputable. For several years he got letters from some of them, and one or two came to visit him. Within a few days of sailing, he was writing letters for many of the men, giving them advice on personal affairs, including love, telling them stories during leisure hours, instructing them in various cultural fields, and serving as arbiter in disputes. One youth who had sailed all over the world read him selections from an interminable epic "poem" he had been writing for years. It was obscene and almost exclusively erotic, and the verse was execrable. In the whole thing, John reported, there was a single memorable passage:

> And there he saw a nigger with a trigger that was bigger
> Than an elephant's proboscis or the whanger of a whale.

The ship landed in San Francisco about the end of June, 1926, and John said goodbye to all his friends aboard and headed for Palo Alto. Unaware that he had left New York, I emerged from a classroom at Stanford, where I was spending the summer, and found him waiting for me outside the door. Delighted, I took him to the little cottage that my wife and I had rented in a rural area just outside Palo Alto, and we immediately started a party with a couple of bottles that he pulled from his suitcase. The party atmosphere continued for the two weeks that he stayed with us. One of his less-brilliant inspirations came when it was time to bottle some home-made fig wine that had been fermenting in the garage. Tests showed that it should be bottled promptly, but we discovered that we had neglected to provide corks, and as it was late in the evening, there was little chance that we could find any even if we drove to town. Then John had his idea. Taking some of my wife's Plasticene modeling clay, he fashioned corks of it and contrived harnesses to hold them in. He was very much pleased with himself—until several days later, that is, when we opened the first bottle for testing. The wine was undrinkable, of course, for the strong and pungent oil from the clay had permeated the contents of the bottle, making it very unpalatable. After one or two attempts, we sadly poured out the whole batch, into which had gone weeks of attention and anticipation. John's inspirations in non-literary lines occasionally turned out that way.

He left us after a while and may have put in another brief stretch in the laboratory of the Spreckles sugar-beet factory in Salinas, but for the next year or two he spent the major part of his time in the cottage at Pacific Grove. During some of the summers he worked at Fallen Leaf Lake. The letters which documented his various movements and activities were unfortunately among those which he later insisted on burning. I know that he stayed a few days with us in Eagle Rock late in 1926 but I do not recall the business which had brought him to Los Angeles at that time. And it was probably in the autumn of 1927 that he accepted the winter-long job of acting as caretaker for the Brigham estate at the south end of Lake Tahoe.

From the time of the first snows until the final spring thaws he was alone in his cottage beside the main house, though a few visitors found their way to the Tahoe Tavern at the upper end of the lake and then came down on the weekly mail boat, which also brought supplies to the little settlement of Tallac. John's mother mailed fresh eggs and other foods to him each week, and the Tallac store provided staples. A number of year-round residents were at scattered points nearby and accepted him into the community. Carl Wilhelmson visited for several days, almost driving John wild by idly ringing the bell on his typewriter as they both were attempting to write. Carl, ever the dour Finn, left in indignation after a storm blew away the privy in which he was sitting meditatively, leaving him exposed to the swirling snow. He had no patience with country like that.

There was work to be done—cutting wood, removing fallen trees, keeping the main road open, repairing windows and structures damaged by snow or storms. But there was also ample time for writing, much of which he devoted to what was later to be *Cup of Gold*.

Ever since he had written his story, "A Lady in Infra Red," for a Stanford course in 1924 or 1925, the idea for *Cup of Gold* had been working in his head, although the original story, far from a masterpiece, had brought pointed criticism from his instructor. In style, it was heavily influenced by Cabell and Donn Byrne, and the plot dealt with a mysterious woman known to the inhabitants of the Isthmus as La Santa Roja, or the Red Saint, whose beauty drove men mad, though she was unapproachable. Henry Morgan, hearing of her charms and her purity, vowed to win her—by force if necessary. To attain that end he fought and slaughtered and looted and burned until he had forced his way with a band of ruffians across the Isthmus into the city of Panama and the home of the lady. He stood face to face with her, seeing with his own eyes the inscrutable smile for which so many men had died screaming. But when he sought the culminating act of his conquest, he discovered that the beautiful face and the maddening smile hid the mind of a backward child, while the body was unsuited for love; the inference was that she was hermaphroditic. Irony was laid on with a trowel, and the text sparkled with ornate rhetoric and with dialogue that bore little resemblance to ordinary speech.

Steinbeck still liked the story, however, and he was excited by seeing with his own eyes the tropical jungle he had only imagined in the story. Now the memory of its unbelievable lush greenness and of the city of Panama clung in his mind, as did the paradoxical character of Henry Morgan, who metamorphosed from a merciless pirate to a British Knight and a colonial judge. During the preceding summer John had read everything on Wales and on pirates that the Stanford Library had to offer, which was not a great deal, including *Wild Wales*, a work probably contributed much of the material for the background of Morgan before he ran away from home to sea.[10] Now, fortified with his reading and with many notes he had taken, he was ready to begin serious work on a completely revised treatment of the story, in which Morgan himself would be the chief figure. Although he worked hard on it, the book was not to be published until 1929, and it was to go through what he said were six complete rewritings. (He told someone else that he had rewritten it nine times; he was often vague about such details.)

On February 25, 1928, he wrote me, again from Lake Tahoe, a sadly lyrical letter about what may or may not have been the final version of the book, and it said in part:

> My failure to work in the last three weeks is not far to find. I finished my novel and let it stand for a while, then read it over. And it was no good. The disappointment of that was bound to have some devastating, though probably momentary effect. You see, I thought it was going to be good. Even to the last page I thought it was going to be good. And it is not. . . .
>
> I am finishing the Henry mss out of duty, but I have no hope of it any more. I shall probably pack it in Limbo balls and place it among the lost hopes in the chest of the years. Good bye Henry. I thought you were heroic but you are only, as was said of you, a babbler of words and rather clumsy about it.
>
> I shall make an elegy to Henry Morgan.

A boy who had dreams, who captured his dreams and saw them die in his arms. Who struggled toward unbelievable beauty. Who found himself sick with a disease called mediocrity, who married boredom and was so convinced by his boredom, that he came to disbelieve in the old years, and who died with gratification. Who did not want to believe in heavy because he did not want them to disturb him once he was dead. To Henry Morgan whose name has lived because he destroyed churches. And last, an elegy to the death of his deathless romance. His romance had perfection because it never actually existed. And last again, an elegy to Henry Morgan, who is a monument to my own lack of ability. We will pack him in Limbo balls for an unending winter.

My soul is not a little white bird. I haven't any soul, nor much of agonized ambition any more. I shall go ahead but I wonder if that sharp agony of words will occur to me again. I wonder if I shall ever be drunken with rhythms any more. Duke has his Rosalind, but I have no Rosalind nor any Phryne. I am twenty-six and I am not young any more. My wings have dropped as Merlin's dropped and as Robert's dropped and as Henry's finally dropped. Like Merlin's voice, my voice is thick like a drover's voice, and my phrases are thick with plans and considerations. It is sad. I shall write good novels but hereafter I ride Pegasus with a saddle and bucking pads, and martingale, for I am afraid Pegasus will rear and kick, and I am not the sure steady horseman I once was. I do not take joy in the unmanageable horse any more. I want a hackney of tried steadiness.

It is sad when the snow is falling.

Only a few hardy residents braved the rigors of winter in the High Sierra around Tahoe in those years, and these people were well scattered over the area. Yet, though roads were generally impassable, there was social life of a sort. A few boats were available for occasional transportation to the major winter colony at Tahoe city and to other lake ports where parties or dances were held sporadically, and almost the whole population gathered to meet the mail boat and later to sit around the stove at the Tallac general store discussing the news of the week. John soon knew all the permanent residents of the lake and wrote long letters filled with vignettes of some of the amusing characters, or with their pungent dialogue and their racy tales.

He also produced the long and very bawdy "Byronic" epic dealing with the courting and winning of a wench—no doubt fictitious. It ends:

> Alas, it was a trade—I played the sap,
> Exchanged a baby for a dose of a clap.

The burned letters contained a vast amount of such diverting material, echoes of which continue to appear in various of his books—phrases which pleased him, quirks of character, sexual exploits, and points of view. There was also a running history of events in the snow-covered wilderness. Very little really happened, but a trip to town or a visit from a wandering woodsman formed the basis for entertaining tales which made the winter forest seem anything but lonely.

At one time he almost got into serious trouble at a spot several miles across the Nevada line. I recall few of the details, but he told of going to a dance where he engaged in a rough-and-tumble fight. John's opponent fouled from the start and was apparently quite unaverse to murder. It ended when John knocked him down and kicked him in the face with his heavy boot, knocking all his teeth inside his mouth and breaking his jaw. In the letter which described the brawl, John was genuinely apprehensive that the man might have died and that his friends might be seeking revenge or a murder warrant. He warned me that he might have to disappear for a while. As far as I know, there was no follow-up on the incident.

For the most part, Steinbeck was snug and happy in his comparative solitude. Bootleg liquor could be obtained for a price, and on a few special occasions he looted the cellar of the big Brigham house, where an assortment of fine wines and other potables was stored. Toward the end of the winter, a bad storm sent a huge tree crashing down on a part of the house, and when Mrs. Brigham came up to investigate the damage, their relationship terminated. John insisted he was fired because he let the tree crush the house, but existing members of the family say that had nothing to do with it.

At all events, he was soon working in the Tallac fish hatchery, one of two such government establishments on the lake, as an assistant to Lloyd Shebley. Although their temperaments were not compatible, they got along satisfactorily in their job of stripping mature female trout of eggs, taking care of the eggs till they hatched, and then feeding the fry on milk and ground pork liver until they were of a proper size for release in designated streams. Except for the necessity of punctuality and a degree of alertness to anything that could endanger the fish, it was not hard work, and there was plenty of time for writing—as well as for drinking and cultivating female friendships.

I am not sure how long he worked at Tallac, but I believe he spent at least part of one summer in his cottage at Pacific Grove, for I think I visited him there on my way to Stanford for the summer session. By the next spring, however, he and Lloyd were working at the other hatchery near Tahoe City at the north end of the lake. Possibly he spent the winter there.

Bob Cathcart, whom he had met while working at Fallen Leaf Lake, tells a story of a wild trip in an ancient Ford belonging to John. With them rode a fat and elderly Indian woman who was anxious to get down to the valley. The car developed a series of troubles, necessitating stops for repairs, and eventually collapsed, with the woman silent and rigid with fear in her seat. At that point, Bob deserted and went home by bus, while John somehow patched up the damage and completed the journey.

Work on *Cup of Gold* was progressing through a series of rewritings, and John's feeling for good music entered into the shaping of the final version. With him at the lake he had a phonograph and a number of fine recordings which he played frequently during the long, lonely evenings. Among them was Dvorak's "New World

Symphony." It was not illogical that this composition, written by a homesick man in an America that was strange and unlike his native land, should seem to have a certain parallelism with the story of the Welsh boy who ran away to the Indies to make his fortune, and having made it, found little satisfaction and no substantial meaning in his achievement; nor did he ever get back to the home for which he yearned. "The book follows the movements of the symphony," Steinbeck told me and went on to explain that he had carefully regulated the speed of the action, the tonal quality of the narrative, and the word sounds to conform to the major changes in tempo and mood of the music. He doubtless exaggerated the closeness of relationship between the story and the symphony, and it is improbable that the course of the action was materially influenced at any time, but the book parallels very neatly the general outline of the music.

Part 4:

Carol before She Was "Drunk and Formidable"

During the summer of 1928 I was again at Stanford and arranged to drive to the lake and visit him over the Fourth of July. He had mentioned no specific women in his letters, and on my arrival at the Tahoe City hatchery I was surprised to be introduced to Carol Henning, with whom he had obviously established a strong sexual and emotional bond. Both of them, completely wrapped up in each other, were unhappy because her two-week vacation was ending, and on the next day she would be returning to San Francisco where she worked as a secretary to the elderly owner of the Schilling Coffee and Spice Company. Carol was about 22 at the time, but she looked scarcely more than 16 as I first saw her. They had been attending a rodeo and parade in Truckee. She wore a light summer dress with a bandana at the neck and had a smudge of dirt on her nose. Both of them were covered with dust from the unpaved road.

With Carol on the vacation was her younger sister, Idell. Both girls were born at the old family home in San Jose. Their father, Wilbur Henning, had spent most of his life as an official of a building-and-loan association and served for several years as "Commissioner of the Port of San Jose" when the city was conducting an active campaign to have the south end of San Francisco bay dredged to enable the establishment of a deep-water harbor there. Their mother was a militantly religious woman who was often unhappy over the more frivolous interests of her daughters.

John and Carol met shortly after the girls had rented quarters in one of the numerous resorts which ring the lake, and soon she and John were spending most of their time together. He quickly put her stenographic abilities to work on the novel, and by the time she left, she had prepared a fair copy of much of the book, John always protested that he could not compose on the typewriter. Instead, he did his creative writing in minute longhand with a steel pen that had to be dipped into an inkwell. (Sometime later a friend gave him a carved walrus-tooth pen holder from Alaska and he used it for many years, producing several of his early works with its aid.) With Carol's cooperation, he adopted a system that he subsequently employed for a long time: he would read aloud from his manuscript and she would type, punctuating with particular attention to his cadences and stresses rather than by strictly formalized rules. John then made his corrections and revisions on the typed version (surprisingly few, for the most part) and the fair copy was prepared from that.

While I was there I did some cursory editing on the manuscript at his request and found very few mechanical difficulties. Carol had done an excellent job. John was quite amenable to most of the minor changes that I suggested, but on the matter of dashes he was obdurate; dashes spoiled the appearance of the page, he said. He was also reluctant to use hyphens, perhaps for the same reason. And in looking over some of the earlier work sheets I saw how carefully he had toiled with the text to achieve the rhythms and tonal effects he wanted, revising to eliminate undesirable alliterations and even scarcely noticeable sequences of vowel sounds in a sentence or series of sentences. All his work shows attention to such details, though stylistic fastidiousness of that type soon became instinctive to a point where long passages could often be transferred almost without change from his original manuscript to the printed page.

He finished *Cup of Gold* sometime that autumn or winter and sent it to Ted Miller, who placed it with McBride & Company in New York, where it was published in August, 1929, to the complete indifference of almost everyone. At John's suggestion, design of the dust cover was turned over to his New York Friend, Mahlon Blaine, who produced a picture of a flamboyantly dressed pirate, whose appearance was better suited to a boy's book of adventure on the high seas than to the taste of the discriminating adult, and insofar as the promotion department of McBride handled it, that is the way it was offered to the world. Checking over all available literary or semi-literary periodicals in the Stanford Library at the time, I found only two advertisements for the book: *The Saturday Review* and the *New York Times Book Review*, though there may have been others. The ads were little one-column, two-inch squares with the same ferocious pirate and a line or two of text indicating that here was a fine swashbuckling tale of derring-do. There were two or three reviews, not one of them more than ten or twelve lines and all perfunctory. It is little wonder that only a few hundreds copies were sold from the small edition of 2476, only part of those bound. Frank Fenton, later acting president of San Francisco State College, who had known Steinbeck at Stanford, made it required reading for one of his literature courses at a southern college, and other friends bought copies, but for the most part the literary world was supremely unimpressed by the birth of a new novelist. John received a $400 advance royalty, and it was several years before there was any further increment—only dribbles even then. In 1936 Covici-Friede put out a new edition from the unbound sheets of the original, but the sale of that was very modest and did little to help the Steinbeck finances.

One man, Ben Abramson, Chicago bookseller and critic, saw promise in the work, and after McBride had remaindered the unsold copies, he acquired them, reportedly from Max Salop of the

Harlem Book Company, storing them away until his belief in Steinbeck should make them collectors' items. Abrahamson was later to persuade Pascal ("Pat") Covici to take a chance on *Tortilla Flat*, which had been turned down by most of the leading publishers and which became the first commercially successful Steinbeck book.

At least one other person found inspiration in *Cup of Gold*. A year or so after its publication, John received a copy of a new book in verse by the well-known rhymster, Berton Braley, along with a letter of praise that included a strong disavowal of any borrowing from the Steinbeck story. The title of the work eludes me, but it dealt comprehensively with the life of Henry Morgan, not just as the history books have it. Included were all the major episodes of John's version, many of which were John's original inventions. The slanting of the verse, moreover, showing Henry as a bumbling quester after dreams that turned to dust when achieved, was almost identical with that of *Cup*. John was slightly indignant at what he considered the theft of material, though his book was mentioned in the preface, and he was amused by the difficulties into which Braley had been forced by the lack of suitable rhymes for "Morgan."

"The only legitimate ones in English are 'organ' and 'gorgon', neither of which fits very well into a pirate story," he laughed. Braley used both of them more than once, and not with felicity.

~

The affair between John and Carol was no summer romance. After her departure they corresponded voluminously and enthusiastically, and John's eagerness to see her led to his purchase of what was probably his second automobile—a 1922 Dodge for which he paid $50 or $100 at a garage in Placerville. According to his account, in filling out the contract form, he wrote "Piscatorial Obstetrician" in the space for occupation, thereby completely bewildering the salesman, who half-suspected he was being ridiculed, half-feared that there might be an honorable profession by that name, and hated to reveal his ignorance. But the car ran, and in it John made periodic visits to San Francisco until he finally gave up his hatchery job and, after a period spent writing in the Pacific Grove cottage, moved to San Francisco.

By the time he had finished writing *Cup of Gold* he was already toying with the idea for a new book. Actually, the idea belonged to his friend Toby Street, by then married to Frances Price, whose mother had earlier questioned John about Toby's suitability as a husband for her daughter. Some years before, Toby had started a play called "The Green Lady" in which the protagonist, always a lover of trees and growing things, developed an increasingly psychotic fixation for the forest and eventually immolated himself when fire was sweeping his beloved grove. John too loved trees, and doubtless his long sojourn among the giant evergreens of the Monterey and Tahoe regions had heightened his feeling that in the silences and shadowed wildernesses of the forest was a high mysticism, a Druidical sublimity, which dwarfed the soul of man and was beyond its full comprehension. The theme, moreover, appealed to his convictions that there is a vital relationship between man and the soil and the things that grow from it. There were elements, too, of the cruel and inescapable destiny which energies the Greek tragedies.

The idea of having John turn the play into a novel may have originated with Toby, but both of them were enthusiastic about the project, in which they agreed to share credit. But collaboration proved difficult, even with John doing all the writing. As he studied the plot he saw many changes that he thought must be made, and Toby by no means concurred with all of them. Nor did Toby's wife, who, according to John seemed to feel that he was trying to steal away the whole book for himself, and with it any possible glory that should accrue to the original author. Eventually their ideas of how the book should be written had become so divergent that Toby withdrew from the whole enterprise, generously granting rights to the title and to whatever portions of the plot John desired. "It isn't my story any more," he said.

Running to 107 pages and representing perhaps a quarter to a third of the projected book, an original typescript of *The Green Lady* still exists. It is written on yellow paper and prefaced by a carefully typed asterisk-outlined box serving as a title page reading:

The Green Lady
A Novel
by
John Steinbeck
and Webster Street

Internal evidence indicates that it was composed by John himself on the typewriter, or perhaps by a girl friend whom he had indoctrinated with some of the characteristics of his typing style: the dislike of hyphens, the division of unit words into components like "red wood," "horse back," "any one," "shot gun," and many others; and his misspelling of certain words like "carressing" and "occassionally." In many cases there is a double space where a comma should be as if he had hesitated about using one. A few brief passages have been X-ed out and there are rather rare penciled corrections and short marginal notes. Though it could have been copied from a hand-written version, awkward constructions, reuses of the same word, and the like, that would have been partially caught, at least, in a retyping.

Just when John gave it to me, presumably for reading and evaluation, I have no memory, but it may have been in 1929 or even before. As far as I can recall, I saw no further manuscript of the book, and I don't know whether there was a continuation of the story before it was abandoned for the rewriting into *To an Unknown God*, which he said was refused by his publishers because of a 40-year gap between the first and second parts and because of the current depression.

The story starts with a rapid summary. Young Joe Wayne, responding to the call of gold in California, sells his little herd of cows and abandons the ancestral Vermont farm to come west by way of Panama. For fifteen years he pans and tunnels and washes, accumulating enough to buy an enormous ranch at Jolon. He "stocked it, married a school teacher from San Francisco, and wrote his relatives in Vermont to come west if they wanted to. They did. A dozen of them arrived at Jolon, congratulated Joe on his marriage and his ranch and settled on the place."

His wife is delivered of a daughter and dies within two years of loneliness and overwork. He mourns her for sixty days and then marries another school teacher who gives him a son, Andy, whom she pets and spoils and protects, to Joe's dissatisfaction. When the boy is still very young, he goes on a picnic with his mother to a fern-filled spot in the hills. She slips, strikes her head on a rock, and dies. The boy is left with a mingled feeling of fear and love for the ferns and greenery that his mother had loved and that had killed her. His father marries for a third time, a timid, ineffectual woman whom Andy is unable to respect or regard as the mother he has lost.

As Andy grows up, he learns to conform outwardly to his father's requirements, but no rapport is ever established between them. He becomes inured to the endless, exhausting work of the ranch, holding his own with the others in management of the herds but retaining a feeling for the beauty of the hills, the trees, and the skies.

Then comes the drought, drying up streams and withering the grazing lands, while cattle die from lack of fodder. On a trip over the hills to the sea, he visits a rancher, Otto Seib, with a Mexican wife and a beautiful daughter, Julia, with whom he falls in love and soon marries. On the wedding night, Julia waits eagerly and with apprehension the nuptial consummation, yet her modesty makes her refuse Andy's demand to see her naked. Balked, he loses interest, does not even hold her as she begs him, and falls asleep.

At that point the manuscript ends, but there had been strong earlier leads that he would take his new wife and move northward from the dry and empty ranch to buy another in the moist and verdant area of Mendocino County.

One chapter deals almost incidentally with a small neighboring farm operated marginally by Rosa and Maria Lopez, who often are visited by men of the region bearing gifts of foodstuffs, wine, and other staples, receiving a compensating fleshly affection, all in a comradely spirit. Even Joe Wayne calls on them between marriages, while the women relatives of his own ranch deplore but half condone, knowing the nature of men. The Lopez sisters do not appear in *God Unknown*, but they become a delightful episode in *Pastures of Heaven* with characters brightened and their philosophy of synthesizing the moral with the economic rounded into an ironic comment on the social ethos.

Relatively little of this manuscript was transferred in recognizable form to the later versions of the story, apart from the fiesta attending the marriage, but the basic design of the mystic relationship between the man and the green, pregnant earth is apparent and predominate. The seeds of the ultimate story, including many of its episodes, are clearly discernable.

Just when the writing started on the early manuscript I have no clear idea. It is possible that Street wrote his play as early as 1925 or 1926, and John may have worked with him on it in his final year at Stanford. In his letter of February 25, 1928, John indicated that he had an idea for his next novel and that was almost certainly the present incomplete story, though there could have been a prior attempt which flowered into this.

Evidence is lacking whether *The Green Lady* went beyond the 107 pages that he gave me or whether, if so, it was ever submitted in any form to a publisher. As I recall, the first submission was under the title of *To an Unknown God* and it was roughly the story that eventually appeared in *God Unknown.* A long opening segment deals with the move of the Waynes—"a dozen relatives"—from Vermont to California and their establishment on a ranch in the Jolon area. After that, however, there is a gap of 40 years during which the father dies and the characters of the sons develop into their necessary forms for the denouement that John had planned. Presumably, McBride had a chance at it and wanted no part in its publication after the fiasco of *Cup of Gold*, wherever the blame lay. Other houses may have read it, and I believe that an unidentified publisher may have seriously considered it. John was hopeful for a time, but said that the ultimate refusal was based on the missing four decades, though there were doubtless other reservations. The financial crash of 1929 had rocked the economic basis of the nation by the time the manuscript started on the rounds, and publishers, like everyone else, were hard hit and tended to shy away from speculative propositions, especially those involving an almost unknown author whose first book had been so notable a trade failure. According to John, the house that made the last refusal—perhaps John Day or Brewer, Warren, & Putnam—indicated a willingness to consider it "in a year or two."

John might have finished *The Green Lady* in San Francisco if it was finished, but some of the work was done in the cottage on Monterey Bay. His move to the city was largely motivated by his desire to be near Carol, who shared an apartment with her sister Idell on or near Jackson Street. This may have been the time when he lived with Wilhelmson, who was finishing *Midsummernight*.[11] Both men were moody and temperamental, especially when working, and the arrangement did not last long.

In the summer of 1929 I again came to Stanford, this time with a new wife, Maryon, and we rented an amplified double garage in Palo Alto—small but with adequate room to care for visitors and overnight guests. John and Carol came down frequently over the weekends, usually in a venerable Buick roadster belonging to Carol. At such times there were gatherings of friends, including Toby Street, Carl Wilhelmson, Grove Day, Dean Storey, and others. After one of the parties during which quantities of local red wine had been consumed, Maryon took my car, an old Studebaker special six with bright-green disk wheels, and went for a post-midnight ride, during the course of which the car hit a chuckhole in the road between Belmont and Half Moon Bay. A semi-crystallized axle broke, the wheel went rolling off into the night, and the car stopped abruptly. Fortunately it had been traveling slowly and no real damage was done to it or the driver, who managed to relay a call to us through a neighbor in the mists of a hungover morning. I borrowed a car and rescued her; then John and Carol drove to the site of the accident, where John managed with superlative powers of persuasion to borrow the only towing dolly that a nearby service station owned—on a Sunday, too—and hauled the three-wheeled Studebaker back to Palo Alto. Then he had to take the dolly back. His comments on the situation were caustic. He didn't feel well, either.

When Carols' vacation came in August, they gathered equipment from friends and camped for two weeks near La Honda in the high hills near the coast, sleeping on cots in the open though they had a shelter tent stretched from the side of the Buick.

As usual, they were in a state of semi-impoverishment—John's income was still the $25 a month supplied him by his father—and their diet consisted largely of bread, bacon squares (then selling at 10 cents a pound), bacon gravy, beans, corn meal in various combinations, and hamburger, which often could be bought at three pounds for twenty-five cents. When we visited them for a couple of days, they were rejoicing at having purchased a whole gunny sack full of slightly wilted corn on the cob for a mere twenty-five cents from a nearby farmer. We discovered, also, that there were crayfish in the stream that ran through their camping place, and having caught and cooked a number of them, we prepared a magnificent salad, using miner's lettuce for the greens. John's dog, Omar Kiyi, participated merrily in all activities, roiling the water as we searched for the crayfish.

During this vacation, John devoted several hours a day to working on *The Pastures of Heaven*. Immediately after an early breakfast, he would set out from their camp into the towering redwood forest, carrying the old ledger, in which he did his writing, appropriated from his father's office, a five-cent bottle of ink, a carved walrus-tusk penholder, and a couple of extra nibs. The weather was warm and much of the time he wore only sandals and a pair of blue jeans; the upper part of his body soon acquired a magnificent mahogony color. He preferred to work in a little clearing he had discovered, where the sawed-off stump of a redwood tree served him as an excellent writing table. There, surrounded by the huge, ancient trees and the forest silence that even birds seemed reluctant to break, he wrote rapidly and intently, taking pride in the ridiculously small script which often crowded twenty or more words on a single line. I have suspected that the minuscule writing was in some way connected with a concept of fine craftsmanship, and with the idea that delicate and exact expression was not conformable to a large and scrawling hand. Perhaps, too, the tiny letters aided the illusion of secrecy, or at least the privacy with which a writer likes to enshroud himself when he is struggling with the problems and doubts of creation. Or maybe he just liked to write small, particularly as it permitted him to get many words on a single page. Paper cost money. At one time, several of us corresponded with each other on penny postal cards, trying to see how much text we could make a single one carry. John won that competition hands down with a card that contained 554 microscopic but legible words.

In the mornings when he was preparing for a session in his sylvan glade, his eyes had a distant look and he spoke hardly at all as he breakfasted. Then without a word he tucked his ledger under an arm and strode off into the forest, nor did we try to distract him. He might be gone for three or four hours, and when he returned he was a different young man. His eyes seemed bluer and they danced; his step was light and eager, and his face was free of the withdrawn expression that had marked his departure. Clearly he was pleased with the morning's accomplishment.

The entire text of *The Pastures* is written in less than 104 pages of the 12 by 7–inch ledger, including some lengthy deletions. The same ledger also contains all of *To a God Unknown*, a somewhat longer work, using 133 pages, and the start of an unfinished story about a boy living in the early days of Pacific Grove when it was a camp-meeting site. Toward the end of *Pastures* with the writing growing progressively smaller, perhaps with the fear that there wouldn't be room for the whole story, there are sometimes 800 words to a page.

He worked remarkably fast and often reported having produced three or four thousand words in a single sitting of a few hours (Carl Wilhelmson once said bitterly, "Yes, but vat *kind* of vords?"), and for the most part they were words which remained little changed in their transition to print. There were always changes, however, bringing subtle refinements of sound, movement, and impact to the text. Yet in all his work there are long sequences in which the hand-written original and the published volume are almost identical.

Part of this sureness and speed came from his habit of careful thought on the problems and essentials of the narrative before he picked up his pen, and in this he asked and wanted no advice. He claimed that if he concentrated carefully on a difficulty that was bothering him in the narrative before going to bed, his mind would work on it during the night and produce a solution by morning. After he had impregnated himself with the characters and mood of the work that lay ahead of him, sleep and dreams would often iron out all the complexities, he said, or even formulate the exact manner of the treatment so that all that remained was to set it down as fast as the pen could travel.

But having closed the ledger for the day, he could usually shed his abstraction and creative intentness, though sometimes, when engaged in episodes of high emotional content or significance, he remained withdrawn and contemplative heedless of much that was going on around him. Ordinarily, however, he was pleased with the feeling of work well done and was ready for recreation—light conversation, wine drinking, music, or parties.

~

With her vacation over in the fall of 1929, Carol returned to San Francisco, and shortly afterward, John went back to the Pacific Grove cottage to concentrate on his writing under conditions that would be as economical as possible. Other than the $400 advance on *Cup of Gold*, he had only the monthly remittance of $25 from his father, a surn which permitted few luxuries.

Toward the end of the year, Carol left her job and returned for a while to her family home in San Jose, 80 miles from Pacific Grove, and they were able to see each other frequently.

About that time, John and Carol became interested in some experiments with a plastic moulage process introduced to them by

Ritchie Lovejoy, a young man born in Mountain View, California, who was showing considerable talent in both art and literature. Lovejoy had found a Swiss product named Negocol that opened up new techniques in making casts from almost any type of surface with amazing ease and flexibility. It was a colloidal, rubbery substance, supplied by the manufacturers in the form of large, rough crumbs at a cost of $8 for a two-pound package. A relatively low heat—approximately 120–130°—would reduce the particles to a thick, fluid paste, which would maintain that condition until it cooled to about 100°, after which it set rapidly and dried to a glossy, elastic surface. Unlike plaster of Paris, it underwent no distortion during the period of cooling, nor did it cling to anything to which it had been applied, making unnecessary the customary heavy greasing required for plaster casts of the human face. Above all, it was so fine textured that it reproduced with complete fidelity any surface to which it was applied, showing the tiniest pores and finest hairs of the skin, the veining of leaves, and the grain of even polished wood, transmitting them perfectly to plaster when used as a mold. It was so delicate that it could be applied painlessly to the open eye, and its elasticity permitted it to be used in countless ways impossible to plaster, such as the interior of the ear and the inside of the lips to produce a cast of the teeth and gums. (A special variety of the material called Dentocol was reported to be in established use by dentists for many kinds of oral castings.) And, of importance to the meager pocketbook, it was capable of re-use for an indefinite number of times, apart from the small amounts inevitably lost in each process.

Ritchie had discovered the stuff and immediately saw artistic and commercial possibilities in it. Aiding him in his tentative experiments with it was his wife Tal, born Matalia Kashevernoff in Juneau, Alaska, one of six daughters of a Russian Orthodox bishop there. Excited over the results, they demonstrated some of the uses of Negocol to John, and he too was fired with excitement. To the uses Ritch and Tal had thought of, John added others, and together they had soon begun to formulate a project which seemed certain to bring fame and fortune, together with a lot of fun. The "fortune" aspects appealed to both of them. John told me of once going to the nearby Lovejoy house after having seen neither of them for several days, and finding them in their garden, lying flat on the ground watching bugs. When he asked for an explanation, Tal volunteered in a wisp of a voice, "We're starving to death," and said that they had no money and had had nothing to eat for two or three days. John, of course, fed them.

Just how they decided to bring their process and ideas to Los Angeles I don't remember, except that they believed the commercial possibilities of the project might be realized better in a metropolitan area. None of them had any money but that did not dim their optimism. John had written excitedly to me, and I had told him I would be delighted to have him and Carol stay with us while they set up their enterprise.

So that was the start of the Faster Master Plaster Casters, an organization with no capital and almost unlimited potential with a highly and diversely talented personnel but with no business sense or capabilities. It failed completely in the end, never having gained a single cent of income other than that I advanced, but we all had a tremendous amount of fun out of it, along with innumerable headaches.

John had written that the Lovejoys, whom I had never met, would be arriving but gave no date, and we offered to put them up for a day or two in our Eagle Rock (Los Angeles) home until they could get located. And then, several days before Steinbeck was due, a telegram addressed to Ritchie Lovejoy arrived at our house. Having heard nothing from them, we decided that we'd better open it. It was signed by someone named Nadja, unknown to us, and said merely that the sender was getting into the Los Angeles Union Station the next morning and expected to be met. At the proper time, Maryon and I drove the seven miles into Los Angeles proper and met not only the specified train but the next two without seeing anyone who looked like a frightened Russian girl traveling alone to a strange city and peering around for a welcoming party. Disgusted, we drove back to Eagle Rock and started to enter our house. We were met at the door by an apparently terrified young woman who tremblingly demanded to know who we were and what we wanted at her sister's home. It was Nadjezda ("Nadja") all right, who, seeing no one she recognized at the station, had accepted the offer of a Pasadena-bound fellow passenger to ride to the address that had been given her—our house.

Nadja, it developed, was one of Tal's sisters and had been notified by letter that the Lovejoys were moving to Los Angeles and could be found at our address if she cared to make a visit, though they had neglected to mention us or to state that the house belonged to someone else. Thus, Nadja, walking from the train with her companion and finding herself unmet, assumed that Ritch and Tal were temporarily away and did not hesitate to make herself at home—a few minutes before we returned—in what she never doubted was their house.

We welcomed her, of course, and allayed some of her nervousness while watching for the arrival of the Lovejoys, but they hadn't come by the time we all went to bed. In the morning, however, we found them soundly sleeping on a single cot in the front room, surrounded by their belongings. They had spent a good part of the night trying to locate our very secluded home, and having finally discovered it by a miracle of luck and persistence, they crept quietly in without even turning on a light and went to bed in the first available spot.

John and Carol got there a day or two later. Carol's antiquated Buick had suddenly succumbed near San Jose, and somehow, by trading it in and adding a bit from their scant store of cash, they had acquired a battered Marmon, purportedly the former property of Barney Oldfield and capable of great speed.

Our hillside house consisted of a thirty-foot front room, a small bedroom, a large kitchen, a bath, a large sleeping porch at the rear, a tiny utility porch, and a wide covered veranda extending across the front and looking out over the valley. There was also a dugout cellar with rough earth walls and floor where we brewed quantities of beer, and a sun-bathing "pavilion," consisting of a pair of old mattresses screened on two sides from out not-too-close neighbors by burlap sacking, and at the back by the hill, which extended upward for half a mile.

In spite of its limited number of rooms, the house was a fairly commodious place under normal conditions, but even people and three cats tended to strain its capacities. Tal and Nadja exemplified many of the proverbial qualities of Russians: they were volatilely emotional, they drank anything available, they loved singing and dancing and loud music and games, they were always developing new ideas for entertainment and carrying them out with an enthusiasm that was disruptive to household routine. Maryon was delighted to have company with whom to talk and play and sit up late at night, and frequently she wrestled with Carol, who, among other activities, was learning to play an old accordion that I had bought from Pierre Huss when he came with his father in 1920 as a refugee from Belgium. (He later became head of Hearst's United Nations news staff and died in 1966.) John was trying to write, and I had regular duties of preparing lectures and grading papers for my classes at Occidental—functions not at all aided by the fact that the Russian girls kept our aged player piano going for hours at a time, managing to upset many cans of beer into the keyboard in the process. And the cats, eager to be in the center of things, were always coming loudly to grief under the multiple and unpredictable feet.

Maryon and I retained our sleeping porch; John and Carol staked out a corner of the front porch and spread a mattress there as their homestead, coming, when it rained, into the big front room where Nadja occupied a couch; Ritch and Tal drew the small, dark bedroom with the wall bed; and the cats slept on all of us except John, who detested cats and hurled them away with imprecations.

As a further guarantee against the quiet life, our own friends were augmented by the friends of our resident guests and people who came with them to meet the group and to drink our beer. I stepped up my brewing quota to an average of 18 gallons every five days, and at that could barely keep up with consumption, though after a few days I sternly limited the amount that could be drunk while I was away at school, a move made necessary by the uninhibited thirst of the Russians, which became operative as soon as their eyes were open in the morning—they *loved* beer for breakfast—and was apparently unslakeable. When I returned from classes in the afternoons of the first two days of their visit, I found that three or four gallons of beer had already vanished and the enthusiasm for further drinking was unimpaired. John and Carol enjoyed participating when the party spirit was high but were less inclined to make life a continuous fiesta.

Under such circumstances, it was hardly surprising that the activities of the Faster Master Plaster Casters were launched in a less than scientific and businesslike manner. In our initial experimentations we found many minor difficulties that had to be surmounted, and many techniques that had to be perfected and mastered. When a Negacol mold had been taken of a face, we discovered, the weight of the plaster poured into it would spread the elastic material, resulting in a broadened or distorted cast. We solved that by applying bracings and cross-hatchings of cloth strips dipped in plaster to the outside of the mold as it dried on the face, thereby insuring that it would retain its original shape during casting. We learned to make an entire head in two casts, though the joining of them together demanded a great deal of sculptural care. We learned to paint the Negacol around the nostrils of the subject and then build it up by successive applications so that breathing was uninterfered with—an improvement over the plaster-cast method of inserting straws in the nose to supply air. We discovered dismayingly that a plaster head looks larger than the head it was taken from although it is identical in size. People told us that the heads of department-store dummies are smaller than real life would be. We discovered that a cast of a thin face may look thinner than the original, and a full face may seem fatter, so we often had to make careful adjustments before pouring the plaster.

Soon we had acquired two new members to the project, like the rest of us, unpaid. One was Mahlon Blaine, artist and illustrator, with whom John had lived briefly in New York who helped in perfecting some of the processes and particularly applied himself to the use of color on the finished casts—a difficult matter since the absorptive qualities of the plaster can materially change the quality of the colors applied to it unless the surface is first prepared.

The second was Arjuna ("Archie") Strayer of Pasadena, a former Occidental student of mine with whom I had shared a room at Stanford during the summer session of 1927. He had business abilities shared by none of the rest of us (at least we thought so), and we soon delegated to him the matter of making proper contacts and arranging for what we hoped would be the commercial development of our project. Ritchie and the girls became the chief technicians, Blaine the artist, John the idea man, and I the provider of funds—for wasn't I earning around $2000 a year?

Our agenda was vague but optimistic. We thought there should be a good market for personalized masks of individuals, made and finished to order like portraits or photographs, to hang on walls, be mounted into bookends or plaques, to be poised on pedestals, or to serve as paperweights. We could produce perfect casts of hands, arms, feet, or valued personal possessions. We could mass-produce conventionalized and artistic masks or plaques for general decoration. John bubbled with ideas. There should be a fertile field in young movie stars—or would-be stars—and perhaps we could work out a publicity tie-in by which heads of such hopefuls might be used in display windows to enhance the attractiveness of merchandise. In addition, the studios should welcome a process by which facsimile likenesses could be supplied without the dangers and discomforts of the standard plaster methods. We could supply lifelike heads with distinctively human features and expressions to replace the blank and artificial faces generally used in window dummies—perhaps using motion-picture actors and actresses. And there was a tremendous potential field in supplying schools, museums, laboratories, and novelty shops with perfect reproductions of flowers, fruits, insects (large), animals (small), and marine specimens. The possibilities were limitless. We were very naive.

But Negacol was expensive, and so, for that matter, was plaster of Paris in the quantities we used it. Nor had we quite perfected all our processes or brought them to the point where we were equipped to start full commercial production. We needed demonstration pieces to illustrate the various types of work we could supply, and our haphazard approach was not aided by the fact that everything was conducted in a general air of beery festivity and that no one succeeded in controlling the rest of the free spirits or in persuading them to work efficiently toward a limited and practical end. We made a fine mask of Tal, and by narrowing the mold, adding twisted horns, and touching up some of the features, produced a delightful conventionalized faun. We cast John's features and got a face which seemed gross, with a too-large nose and protruding ears. It emphasized the coarseness of some of his features and justified his earlier reluctance to serve as a model. Eventually we gilded it, but the lips looked heavy and had a semi-Negroid appearance. Although he was not pleased with it, he claimed it and probably destroyed it. One small photograph of him, taken from a bad angle, remains in my album.

Nadja also served rather unsatisfactorily as a subject, but none of the masks were as unappealing as the one they made of me. At the time I was wearing a short and hideous beard grown during a mountain trip, and from the point of view of demonstrating the fidelity with which Negacol would reproduce hair, the cast was highly successful. But the plastic mold split down the center of the nose when plaster was put in it and it also spread, making the face unduly flat and broad cheeked. The crack was repaired but the nose remained too wide and the forehead was distorted. In addition, the cast had been made with my eyes closed, and Blaine, in a subsequent attempt to carve them open, did a very bad job and the finished mask, even when painted, was a horror.

With Maryon we had much better luck, casting almost two-thirds of her head including all of both ears, thanks to the elasticity of the material. Blaine mounted it on a plaster slab about sixteen inches square, applying heavy lacquer paint to the head and making intricate multi-color designs on the slab. The result was startling and attractive, suggesting an exotic bit of handicraft rather than a life mask.

John by this time was losing both interest and faith in the project, as well as confidence in the free-wheeling staff. Archie, however, had been busy and brought the first (and only) movie "starlet" to the studio for a portrait mask. She was a round-cheeked lass named Marian Schilling (I think), and came accompanied by the brother of the well-known actor, Ricardo Cortez. He was obviously skeptical about the whole project and clearly suspicious of all of us. Taking of the mask went without a hitch, as did the subsequent casting, but from it we learned the painful lesson that people with plump faces are not good subjects, for in plaster the plumpness is exaggerated. Thus it was with the Schilling girl. Her well-filled cheeks looked like apples in the cast, and no tricks with paint could reduce them.

We were far more successful with the mask of Shelby Grove, whose modestly attractive appearance was much enhanced by being transferred to colored plaster, and the face was so realistic that by putting it on the pillow of a padded bed and pulling covers over the neck we deluded people into thinking it was a real person.

Of the two finest masks we made, one was of Eunice Merrill, an Occidental student whose facial contours had attracted me as being ideal for the purpose. Her face was thin with good cheek bones, her nose straight and narrow, her chin firm, and her lips sensitive and not too full. In applying the Negocol we took care to have her lips parted, and for the first time succeeded in getting a natural cast of the teeth without a mouth distortion or a gaping space between the teeth and lips. Blaine did an unusually good job of delicate coloring and the result was lovely—a beauty that eclipsed the charm of the girl herself and enraptured everyone who saw it.

The mask of Carlos Escudero, a student at USC, was our greatest achievement. Carlos was a native of Mexico, and his claim that he was of pure Spanish descent was bolstered by his face—lean, imperious, sensitive, with a hawk-like nose that might have graced a conquistador or a young Roman emperor. Not only was his facial beauty heightened by the cast, but we succeeded for the first time in making separate molds of the face and the back of the head and putting them together, although the joining of the two parts required very delicate work. The finished head, bronze-gilded and mounted on a pedestal was so handsome that it was breath-taking.

That triumph should have marked the beginning of success for the Faster Master Plaster Casters, but apart from a few later experiments it was the last real achievement. Archie, as our business manager, suddenly revealed that his expense account had eaten up what remained of our microscopic fluid capital, and that in addition we owed $30 or more for Negocol and other supplies, without settlement of which our supplier, the only one in the Los Angeles area, refused to let us have any more. We quarreled with Archie and he withdrew. Blaine and Ritchie had both grown increasingly temperamental and unwilling to take suggestions. John was tired of the whole thing, for it increasingly was degenerating into artistic puttering, bickering, and dissention without getting any nearer to being a money-making proposition. Besides, it was an activity in which he took no real part other than the furnishing of ideas which were rarely carried out, and he was restless to devote more time to his writing, with which the mess and turmoil of production seriously interfered. I too was getting disgusted, for it had cost me more money than I could afford and showed no signs of getting anywhere than to a more complete disruption of my house and living arrangements.

And so, with the departure of Archie, the whole project collapsed. Today I do not know for sure where a single one of the masks and objects d'art we produced is, or if any of them survive.

Fortunately for the nerves of everyone concerned, the congested state of our menage did not remain at its original peak throughout the few months of our experiment. The stresses of group living, fact, grew unpleasant after a relatively brief time, particularly with the constant depletion of my beer supply, of which all the trouble and expense of brewing, tending, and bottling devolved on me.

The Russians were the first to go. (Ritch, of course, was not a Russian, but we tended to consider him as part of the actively Slavic group.) Something less than a month after their arrival, they found a little house a block down the street and moved into it. Thereafter, though work on the project continued at our house and we visited each other frequently, the enforced intimacy was eased and our quarters seemed delightfully spacious and uncluttered—

and blessedly quiet—even with John and Carol still there, for both of them were neat and cooperative in helping with household tasks. (Within a few days after Ritch, Tal, and Nadja moved, their house became messy and chaotic and remained so until they departed.)

John liked to see a semblance of order; and frequently, after scowling over the condition of the floor, would get a broom and sweep vehemently. The fact that he usually raised a cloud of dust in the process and often left the sweepings in a pile at the center of the room did not detract from his good intentions or his achievement. He and Carol often took over the cooking, at times producing ingenious results with high economy.

It was in this period that Carol fell in love with my accordion. The instrument had two-and-a-half octaves of button keys (no lower A) with only four basses, so that even in skilled hands its limitations were notable. Carol's hands were not skilled but they were busy, and she worked very hard learning to play a number of simple tunes. In fact, she worked so hard and so constantly that John fled to a spot where he could write in quiet, and my nerves and musical sense both began to suffer. Eventually I offered to sell it to her for one cent if she would agree not to play it within five hundred feet of the house when I was there—a condition to which she gaily agreed. Suspicious, I drew up what seemed to be an unbreachable contract covering every possible contingency, and we solemnly signed it before witnesses.

I am not certain that Carol had already made her discovery, but within a couple of days my teeth were again being set on edge by the discordant strains of the instrument, haltingly repeating the same old tunes. Indignantly I went looking for Carol, who, from the loudness and clearness of the sound obviously must be either in the house or just outside it. She wasn't. She was sitting on a huge rock at least a quarter of a mile up the hill—a place from which by some atmospheric or acoustic peculiarity every sound, even a low-voiced conversation, was carried undiminished and undistorted throughout our house. Thereafter, she made the rock her conservatory and favored us and the neighborhood with regular recitals. Her excuse was that I had humiliated her with a contract which impugned her sense of honor, and I deserved to be punished for not trusting her.

After they had been with us for two or three months, John and Carol decided to get married, though I believe it had been their intention when they started south together. What really spurred them into it was the discovery of a house of their own, for, as Carol decreed, it wasn't proper to move into one's own home without being married.

The house they had found didn't look much like one—it really resembled a small barn that had been abandoned as hopeless after having been hit by a cyclone. It had walls, floors, and a roof of sorts, but there were great gaps in all of them. Windows were broken, plumbing was almost non-existent, and the place was ankle-deep in dirt and filth, not to mention the vintage spider webs which hung like curtains. John, after making a critical study of the shack, believed it could be made livable and had no difficulty in persuading the owners to rent it to him for $15 a month, letting him supply all materials and labor for the renovation.

Fortunately it was only two or three hundred yards from our house—up the hill and around the corner on El Roble Drive, a quiet little street with few other structures—so that he could work on it whenever he wanted to, and we could at times help. The first job was cleaning the place of its stratified contents, and after he had removed the old lumber, broken furniture, and miscellaneous junk, he and Carol went after the rest of the debris with shovels. Next came the major jobs of replacing broken floor boards, patching the gaping walls, and replacing broken panes. At Carol's inspiration, they cut out much of the front of the house and installed a huge, multi-paned window at least six-by-six feet square that they acquired from a wrecking company. That alone did a great deal toward making the hovel a home. Virtually unversed in the arts of plumbing, John asked questions, borrowed tools, and made mistakes, but eventually had gas and water pipes hooked up to his satisfaction. As a particular triumph, he bought a second-hand water heater for $10 and after a fiasco or two got it working properly.

While John installed or replaced various pieces of hardware, patched the roof, and coped with things like chimneys and doors, Carol devoted herself to floors and walls. At her direction, a partition was removed, making one large, well-lit room of what had been two small, dark ones. Excavation and scrubbing with lye revealed a floor that was for the most part sound, closely laid pine. Properly braced and supplied with a few new boards, it became a level, solid surface. Eventually we all helped in smoothing it, rubbing it with bricks, skating around in old shoes on loose sand, and dragging weighted boxes. The result was astonishingly good.

Carol tore down the remnants of patchy, faded paper and composition board with which the walls had ben spottily covered, baring the unfinished boards and open studs. Then John started the job of painting the place inside and out. With an eye to economy he bought several gallons of what he called box-car paint—dark red and very cheap. Despite the color, which softened as it sank into the ancient woods, two coats made an extraordinary improvement in the exterior of the house; and inside it gave richness and charm to the rough walls. Then, with the approval of Carol but to our horror, he darkened the paint and applied it to the now well-rubbed floor, which, after being waxed until it gleamed, was a genuine triumph of wine-dark luxuriousness.

In the meantime, too, Carol had been planting geraniums and other quick-growing flowers in a plot she dug in front of their picture window. She also cut down accumulations of weeds, cleaned the yard, and made ready to plant a little lawn in front, while the neighbors looked on incredulously.

From the north they had brought down one piece of furniture—a small, leather-covered sofa, seating two and known with affection as "the liver-colored couch," for the leather was indeed a deep brownish maroon and seasoned with use. Its rear covering half torn away in no way impaired their love for this sofa. Our cats nearly caused a bitter feud between us when, in our absence one evening, they sharpened their claws all over the seats and back, tearing tiny triangles that Carol later spent hours gluing back in place with colorless cement.

The couch became the initial unit of their furnishings, matching the floor and walls almost perfectly. Next they procured a second-hand set of box springs and mattress, which, placed under the picture window and draped with a colorful Mexican rug, served admirably as an ample divan by day and a bed by night. John patched up some of the old furniture that had been in the house, built some from boxes and old lumber, borrowed some spare pieces from us, and picked up a few things from places like the Goodwill Industries, while Carol assembled bright curtains, rugs, and hangings. Completed at last, the place was amazingly attractive and inspired envy and admiration in everyone who saw it.

But as they were adding the finishing touches, they were troubled by the thought of the marriage ceremony. They loved each other tremendously, but something about licenses and rituals frightened them. The house was almost ready for occupancy and Carol had vowed that she wouldn't move into it without being married, but we couldn't persuade her to make the necessary trip with John to the license bureau in Los Angeles. Finally Maryon provided the solution. She accompanied John to the court house, and solemnly avowing herself to be Carol Henning, spinster, signed the application for license, which could be picked up after a three-day wait. Three days later we all drove down while John went inside and collected it.

Then we had two neurotics on our hands. When they refused to make any preparations for the marriage or even to talk about it other than to vow that they wouldn't enter any God-damned church, Maryon again took the initiative and by telephone made tentative arrangements with a justice of the peace in down-town Glendale. Now as we headed for his office, both of them were jittering badly and urging us to go home instead so that they would have time to prepare themselves mentally for the ordeal, although they had carefully dressed in their best street clothes before we started.

Obdurate to their entreaties, we parked in front of the big building on Colorado Boulevard near Brand and made them get out of the car, but we had to half-wrestle them through the door and into the elevator. Fortunately there was no delay in the judge's office—he was expecting us and ready to go immediately to work. So the four of us stood before him while he read the brief civil ceremony—John completely rigid with one eyebrow raised nearly to his hairline and Carol twisting her face to suppress hysterical giggles. Later, John said she had been tickling his palm through the whole rite. But with extreme dignity he paid the justice his fee, accepted congratulations, and then, as if on the verge of suffocation, broke for the outer air.

For a wedding breakfast we took them to a nearby White Spot, where we treated them to hamburgers—not just the ordinary ten-cent ones (which were pretty good) but to the super deluxe fifteen-cent ones with a generous layer of cheese—and two apiece. But by the time we got back to our house, the newlywed swore snapping profanely at each other and would probably have worked into a violent fight if Maryon and I hadn't separated them by force and lectured them on the responsibilities of marriage. It worked and we ushered them to their new house. John didn't carry her over the threshhold because they'd both already crossed it so many times in the preceding weeks. Once inside they were soothed and very happy to have their own home at last.

In August, 1930, John and I deserted our wives and went mountaineering after a fashion, but not because either of us had an Everest or Annapurna complex. The idea started with our friend George Macon, a technical director for one of the motion-picture companies. His enthusiasm sold us on the idea of a two-week trip into the High Sierras, carrying with us all the essentials for the maintenance of life. Exercising a mathematical bent that we hadn't suspected, George made all the plans for supplies and equipment, as well as for routes and destination. He calculated the basic requirements per person of food, adjusted those with an eye for minimum bulk and the capacities of pack animals and potential spoilage, and then took over the job of purchasing all supplies.

We drove to Bishop, about 250 miles away, spent the first night sleeping in a pasture outside the town (discovering in the morning that there were tarantula holes around and under our sleeping bags), and continued after breakfast to South Lake, where George had made arrangements with a packer for rental of animals. Those were not quite what he had expected, but we had to take what was available—a horse, a mule, and a burro, which the packer managed to load with the food and paraphernalia that George had deemed not too excessive for three horses. And we set out on foot for Bishop Pass, several steep miles ahead.

John was the only one of the five of us—George had recruited two other young men to make up the party—who had had any appreciable experience with horses, and he knew almost nothing about pack animals. Thus, when we came to a spot where a snow slide had deeply covered the trail, it was he who persuaded the reluctant beasts to climb high above the slide while he perilously braced them from below to prevent their sliding down the nearly vertical slope. The horse, however, had to have its pack unloaded halfway through the exercise, and John denied any knowledge of the intricate hitches necessary for repositioning of the load. That job fell to George, and his improvizations gave us trouble for the remainder of the trip.

In mid-afternoon we got within a thousand feet of the 13,000-foot pass only to find that the sun had so softened a snow bridge on the trail that it was impassable, nor was there a suitable spot for an overnight bivouac. Since we couldn't go forward and had no intention of going back, we camped on a small, semi-level area with a surface of boulders and pointed rocks around which we tried to arrange our sleeping bags during a miserable night with the temperature far below freezing and a strong, chill wind blowing steadily. By arising at five we crossed the snow bridge, refrozen during the night, and guided the animals up a kind of giant's causeway of huge blocks of stone to the summit of the pass. From there the trail was easy but arduous, leading through mud flats and a couple of waterfalls down 3000 feet to the middle fork of the Kings River and the

Muir Trail. We set up our camp in Little Pete Meadow, a beautiful spot by the river with a floor of soft greenery.

I found myself elected cook, working with a highly restricted larder, as designed by George's concept of the balanced portable diet. The two friends he had enlisted for the trip were accustomed to the business-man's lunch type of nourishment, preferably with toasted sandwiches, roasts, and carrots and peas, none of which were available to us. They viewed with suspicion and apprehension my discovery that along the stream was a plentiful supply of wild onions, providing us with the only fresh vegetables we were to have. They ate them, but complained. They also complained when it was their turn to wash our limited dishes, and were consistently unhappy at the lack of variation that I was able to contrive from the block of dried beef and the cans of corned beef that George had chosen.

A few golden trout were visible in the nearby stream but they showed little initial interest in the flies and other equipment that George and his two friends had brought along. So the three men rose at dawn, loaded themselves with poles and creels and set out downstream in search of better fishing. John and I remained lazily in camp, drinking coffee after a leisurely breakfast. With the sun well up and the temperature beginning to get comfortable, we strolled up the stream. About a hundred yards away we discovered a deep pool at the side of a huge, overhanging rock, with sizeable fish visible in the water. By the sheerest luck, John spied a piece of what looked like string, and pulling on it, salvaged a length of line with a good hook at the end, the bequest of some prior fisherman. Neither of us had brought angling equipment, or for that matter, a fishing license. Nor were we fishing enthusiasts, but this opportunity couldn't be ignored. We returned to camp to look for bait and came back with a bit of bacon and some red berries that John thought looked a little like salmon eggs. We also brought some peanuts in the shell and a volume of Elizabethan plays by Ben Jonson that I had included in my pack. For the next couple of hours we sat on the big rock taking turns holding the line with the variously baited hook close to the noses of inquisitive fish while the unoccupied person read aloud from the plays, and each of us ate peanuts. John played on a harmonica that he had brought along. The trout loved the whole thing—bacon, berries, a piece of yarn from a red sweater, even the peanut shells in the water.

By noon we had read *Bartholemew Fair* and caught about a dozen fine golden trout, but the rock was getting hard to sit on. For lunch we had trout rolled in corn meal and fried in bacon grease. At 4:30 when the sun had retreated far up the side of the mountain, our sportsmen returned, scratched, insect-bitten, and tired, bearing three small fish between them, the longest six inches. They were humiliated by our artless success and denounced our baited-hook technique as reprehensible, but they willingly shared the remainder of our catch when I prepared it for dinner.

During our stay there, two Forest Service men came through on a trail-clearing assignment and stayed with us for a meal, telling stories of the people, animals, and difficulties that they encountered in their work. John questioned them closely, and echoes of that conversation are discernible in several of his works. He asked the name of an unusually sharp peak near the camp and was delighted to have *one* of the woodsmen tell him that he'd never heard it called anything but Dog Prick Peak—but then, as he said, "It *looks* like a dog prick."

That was what John meant in *Sea of Cortez*, when he notes: "in the same way Dog —— Point (and I am delicate. . . .) had finally to be called in print 'The Dog.' It does not look like a dog, but it does look like that part of a dog which first suggested its name."[12]

Our animals broke away one night, and with the help of some other campers—the only ones we saw—we reclaimed them downstream at Grouse Meadows, to which we shifted our equipment. Later, as our scheduled time was running low, we moved them farther down to Deer Meadows, where the soggy ground and the mosquitoes made us glad to pull up stakes for the homeward trip.

As we started back, John was fascinated by the way paradise Creek came roaring down the side of the canyon, striking a solid spur of granite and sending up a high spray as it made a right-angle turn after creating a circular, wildly whirling vortex of a pool, and plunged down over a foaming bed of sharp-toothed rocks to the stream below. I climbed up with him to examine it, and on the instant he decided to have a shower bath. He stripped and walked to the edge of the swirling pool where the spray was falling—and that came close to eliminating a budding novelist from the world. He ignored the coating of wet moss at the brim, his feet slipped on it, and he plunged into the giant eddy, which swept him helplessly around, nearer and nearer the exit channel to the fanged bed of the almost vertical cascade. He had been whirled around several times and was getting dangerously close to the outlet before I managed to find a stick that would reach him as he came within range. Even so, the rescue was difficult as I stood on the slippery moss and pulled against the force of the violently circling water, but eventually he crawled out, cut, bruised, and exhausted. Had he been swept into the main channel with its razor-edged rocks, he would have been lucky to survive intact. There had been no heroics on my part. I was afraid of slipping too and only by the merest chance did I find a branch that was sufficiently long and strong enough to stand his weight and the power of the water.

He did not emerge unscathed. He was a mass of cuts and bruises and had taken an almost disabling blow on one kneecap, which, I believe, had been damaged earlier while he was playing polo at Stanford. The injury was so severe that he could hardly put his weight on the leg, and before we could proceed, we had to devise a crude crutch. By that time, the rest of the party, which had gone on ahead, returned. Seeing that John was nearly incapacitated, they urged him to ride the horse, whose load, diminished by exhaustion of most of our food supplies, could be distributed between the other animals. John would have none of it, even though a 3000-foot climb up a steep and rocky trail lay ahead. He seemed to feel that to ride would be to confess weakness before men whose outdoorsmanship and horse knowledge he did not regard highly. It was a tough decision for him and for me too. Every step hurt him and the make-shift crutch was clumsy and painful to his armpit. I stayed with him in his slow progress up the side of the mountain, while the others took turns on the horse and waited for us at well-spaced resting points. He made it, though, hobbling slowly and silently up the rough and sometimes vertiginous trail, reluctant even to stop for rest lest he hold up the group even more.

Eventually we arrived at the packer's camp, settled our accounts, and headed for home, stopping half-way to gorge ourselves with a meal that contained red meat, fresh vegetables, and other delicacies that we had gone without for two weeks. When we finally got back to Eagle Rock we found a party in progress, either to welcome us back or, if we didn't come, to assuage the sorrow of our absence. The girls didn't say which. And before the night was over, John had gone with Maryon, Carol, and a couple of the guests into Hollywood, still limping but in good spirits, returning much later with two young self-proclaimed lesbians whom they had acquired at a spot called Jimmy's Back Yard. Those hung around till the next day, and after they had gone, we discovered that they had stolen my new watch and cleaned out our jewelry box containing such items as grandfather's gold watch chain, my Sigma Delta Chi pin, and one that I had designed as an eighth-grade graduation pin for my grammar-school class and that had cost fifty cents each on a wholesale order.

Soon John was hard at work on a new book about which he had been thinking for some time. In wrestling with the characters of his various books and stories, he had become fascinated with the idea that personalities are not factual, objective qualities but interpretations formulated in the minds and eyes of observers, almost like two chemicals interacting on each other, changing the original character of each. He was thinking about the many factors that enter into the pictures people have of other people: prejudices, associations, social and economic relationships, mental states, and the like.

He knew, of course, that the idea was far from novel—that in one form or another it is inherent in almost all literature and implicit in the most elementary psychology, but he found endless ramifications and applications for it, and realized that it might be the key to the understanding and depicting of character.

The central figure of the book, he decided, was to be a man

with the general characteristics of his father—a kind man, honest, reserved, strong-minded, imaginative, and gently humorous. But instead of being a protagonist in the literal sense, he was never to appear in his own person, save, perhaps, through excerpts from a diary, though such inclusions were only tentative. The book as planned would start with a simple statement of the man's death, perhaps through an obituary notice appearing in a typical small-town newspaper. From there on, at least six people who had known him well during his life would tell of the man as they had known him, with their interpretations not only of his deeds, character, and motives, but also of his relationship with close associates. Among such apologists were to be his wife, his son and/or daughter, his business partner, his best friend, a business rival, one of his parents, and such other possibilities as a servant, a lodge brother, and a secretly maintained mistress. Thus each one would present varying portraits of the central figure, of himself, and of some of the other characters, providing unique aspects in each case. The intertwining structural pattern delighted John, as did the intrinsic irony, the kalaidescopic shifts in points of view, and the composite character he hoped to produce while attacking the concept of an absolute and immutable truth.

For a time he worked assiduously on it and completed rough drafts of two or more sections, probably more. He read me only segments of what he had done. His tentative title was *Dissonant Symphony*, which fitted his working plan very well, at least in structural pattern. Soon, however, he became dissatisfied with the story or the way he was handling it and laid it aside, saying that it wasn't going well. He threatened to destroy the manuscript but it is reported to have survived and to be a part of a university collection.[13] I believe that the limitations imposed by such a form were largely responsible for his abandonment of the project, though he was also not happy with the character he was creating or the way he was doing it. Possibly his deep-seated love and admiration for his father, who was still alive and had neither mistress nor servants, also produced a guilty feeling of semi-betrayal in the creation of a story about an individual inspired by and similar to him.

Then they had automobile trouble. Something went wrong in the differential of the Marmon that had "belonged to Barney Oldfield," and by painfully disassembling the back axle, John discovered that he needed a new ring gear. Parts for ten-year-old Marmon specials were not easy to find (the cost of a new one was prohibitive), and we toured wrecking establishments for twenty miles in all directions before we found a second-hand replacement in good condition. John was never a mechanic, but he borrowed tools, studied automobile manuals, and asked questions while applying trial-and-error methods. The job took him days of hard work, during which he barked knuckles and saturated himself with black grease. Eventually the gear was in place and everything fastened where it should be. We all cheered as he lowered the heavy machine from the blocks on which it had been resting, and we took turns riding with him on test runs around the block. The car ran beautifully and he was very much pleased with himself.

A couple of nights later, John and Carol started out to visit some friends on the other side of the city. They had gone only a few miles when they heard a loud crunch and the Marmon stopped. They had it towed to a garage, where an examination the next day revealed that in installing the gear he had over-tightened some part of the assembly, with the result that the gear had broken. In disgust, he negotiated with the proprietor of the garage and came away with a battered, topless Chevrolet touring car, built in 1923 or earlier. Its contours were such that they automatically named it "The Bathtub."

Its appearance was disreputable, but for the most part it ran pretty well, though the radiator leaked badly and had to be constantly refilled. Then someone told John that a little corn meal would often stop such radiator leaks. Knowing that the leak was a large one, he poured in a liberal amount one Sunday morning before starting on a twenty-two mile trip to the beach at Santa Monica. The motor soon got hot and the front of the car began to send up jets of steam as they moved along the heavily traveled roads. On Wilshire Boulevard as they kept up with a steady stream of sea-bound cars, the radiator cap flew skyward with a bang, followed by a mighty geyser of yellow mush. It coated the hood and the windshield; it plastered John and Carol and the inside of the car and even spread generous portions on nearby automobiles. Almost blinded and in some pain, John managed to pull off to the side of the road and stop without an accident. No serious damage was done, but an extensive job of cleaning themselves and the car was necessary before they could continue. A few days later they bought a second-hand replacement for the radiator and the car gave them several more years of service.

Our Eagle Rock house was on a hillside, and behind it was a long, unpopulated rising slope with no close neighbors on either side, making it an ideal location for a sun-bathing area. We leveled off a suitable spot, put down two old mattresses, and screened off two sides with burlap and canvas, so that even if neighbors craned their necks their sensibilities would not be offended by the sight of unclothed flesh. It was a fine place to sit and bake and drink home-brewed beer in good weather, and not only the Steinbecks but many of our other friends made extensive use of it. Some of them started undressing in their cars when they got within a mile of the house and arrived wearing only the last vestiges of their clothes. Often as many as six or eight nature lovers were basking, sweating, and passing the pitcher of cold beer—or grumbling when, having emptied it, they had to comply with the house rules and put on a robe to go into the house and fill it again.

One afternoon while only the four of us were sunning, Maryon and Carol started experimenting with the bleaching properties of strong peroxide and ammonia, using their pubic hair as test material. It proved resistant, and Maryon suggested that they try the stuff on John's hair, which was normally dark, coarse, and wavy. Surprisingly, he agreed, and girls gave it successive packs with both fluids. The results were amazing. With each application his hair grew pinker. After the final one it was a flaming pink with strong overtones of salmon—a color that none of us had ever seen in hair before and that I doubt I shall ever see again—or want to.

Instead of being outraged or even indignant as the rest of us expected, John seemed pleased and even fascinated. He insisted that he wanted to wear it that way, though Carol was already protesting. A few days later on a Sunday, the four of us, with him driving, went to Santa Monica to meet his sister Mary (by then the wife of William Dekker) on the beach. The shocking pink hair blowing in the breeze above the topless Chevrolet proved to be a traffic hazard. Driver after driver would suddenly focus his eyes with incredulous horror on the radiant hair and follow us with turning head and open mouth and would ignore the course of his own car. People froze on the sidewalks and stared as we passed . Children shrieked and pointed. When we reached the rendezvous, Mary and her offspring took one look and refused to recognize us. We had to settle our blankets several yards from hers, and she continued to ignore us for the rest of the afternoon.

For a week or two John was stubborn about his hair and insisted that he liked it that way, but at length he yielded to Carol's entreaties and dyed it jet black, a color which in its own way was just as startling as the former auroraborealic pink.

They were very happy in their little home, which, with constant improvements and gardening, was admired by everyone who saw it. By careful management, culinary imagination, and selective shopping, the $25 a month from his father and occasional small contributions from other members of the family sufficed for their $15 rent, their food, and their other expenses, since in 1930 living costs were very low. They ate a great deal of stew, tamale pie, beans, hamburger, and the like, but it was tastefully prepared and varied with interesting spices. Life was very pleasant.

Not, however, for long. After they had lived there for only two or three months, the owners of the property, who lived in another city, came to see what had been done to the uninhabitable shack that they had given John permission to improve, so long as they didn't have to pay for any of the improvements or be bothered by them. They were astonished with what they found. The former eyesore was now a trim, attractive cottage with a large new front window fronted with diminutive lawn and well-kept flower beds. And the inside embodied dignified simplicity—rich, dark walls and ceilings, contrasting decorations, and furniture in good taste. Even the plumbing worked, as did the hot water and the fireplace.

That settled it. The place was just perfect for their son and the girl he was about to marry. John and Carol were given a month in which to get out and they weren't even compensated for the paint and fixtures, let alone the labor they had put in. They considered possible reprisals, but in the end left quietly, laying a few fearsome curses upon the property and scattering hex marks.

For the next month or two they inhabited a gloomy little house down Rock Glen from us and just inside the west borders of Glendale. Then they found a more suitable house in Montrose on the edge of the Coast Range foothills and remained very quietly there for a few subsequent months.

John was working very hard on a series of short stories and destroying them almost as soon as they were completed. He did not make any sales, I believe, though some of the stories may have been among those which he later collected into *The Long Valley*. We still saw each other several times a week, for only a few miles separated us.

John and Carol's lack of money was acute, and I think both of them were beginning to get discouraged at John's failure to make any commercial progress with his writing. They amused themselves by inventing a poltergeist to live with them, and they reported a number of peculiar and inexplicable phenomena that they laid to him—locked doors that suddenly opened in the middle of the night, articles hurled to the floor, drawers that mysteriously opened or slammed shut, unmistakable footsteps in unoccupied parts of the house. During one of our visits a heavy book was dislodged from its secure position well back on a shelf near the ceiling and narrowly missed me where I sat below. Carol even claimed to have seen the creature a few times, moving in obscure corners or showing a grinning face from behind the furniture. As nearly as she could explain it, he seemed to be something like one of Palmer Cox's brownies with a malicious leer. Both of them seemed genuinely convinced that they were host to a real poltergeist and were quite proud of him—as John had been of the one he professed to have experienced in the Salinas house.

Eventually the cumulative effect of poverty, of literary frustration, and of a Southern California in which neither of them felt really at home got the best of them. Particularly Southern California. There is a vast difference in atmosphere, scenery, and ways of life between the northern and southern parts of the state, and they had spent most of their lives in the crisper atmosphere of the north. They became, in fact, homesick, even though Carol, I believe, was not completely at ease about the prospect of close association with John's parents, whom she had probably met several times before coming to Los Angeles. The serious—and terminal—illness of his mother might have been factor in their departure.

In the autumn of 1931 they loaded the Chevrolet with all the possessions it could carry, shipped some others, threw the rest away, and headed north. They moved into their favorite of the two family cottages at Pacific Grove, the one at 147 Eleventh Street, which remained their home for almost the next ten years until they built their first house on Greenwood Lane in Los Gatos.

Both of them worked diligently in improving the cottage with paint, wallpaper, drapes, and the like. Within the limitations of its size, flimsy construction, and tiny log, they made it livable. One of John's contributions was the construction of an against-the-wall fireplace with a tall, half-cone of bright copper reaching almost to the ceiling and radiating heat with great efficiency. They also constructed a small but deep rock pool in the garden, stocking it with fish and bullfrogs and planting its edges with moss and rock plants. They cultivated every available inch of ground, growing not only many kinds of flowers but several rows of carefully calculated vegetables to augment their frugal fare. This could now include fish and crabs from the Pacific, either caught personally or bought very cheaply from commercial fishermen. Sardines and other canned fish were also very inexpensive, but after having worked one summer at a Monterey packing house on Cannery Row, Carol would touch no fish that came from a can.

Maryon and I visited them there during the next summer. We were expected, but when we arrived no one welcomed us at the door although Omar Kiyi II announced us. But our knock went unanswered. Peering into the brightly lighted room we could see John and Carol sitting stiffly in front of their radio, so we entered, only to be *sss*hed by John's finger across his mouth. So obediently we sat until the day's episode of *Frank Watanabe and the Honorable Archie* had ended. Then we were greeted enthusiastically and the wine jug was brought out. The program had been a favorite of all of us, and listening to it was almost ritual. Vic and Sade was another radio series to which we were all addicted. As at Angelus time, all conversation was to cease when the theme music sounded.

Part 5:

Writing "Like Sparks Out of a Bonfire"

It was about this time, I believe, that John met Ed Ricketts—according to him, when they were both in a dentist's office, awaiting treatment. The letters we burned contained many details of the consequences of that meeting, which certainly influenced permanently the directions of his thought, but my memory of dates, sequences, and details is sadly deficient. He was writing steadily and purposefully, for part of the period making a final revision of *God Unknown*, started as *The Green Lady*, reworked into the rejected To An *Unknown God*, and then into its ultimate form.

Early in 1933, they spent a month or two in Laguna Beach, though I have no memory of their reasons or the length of their stay. The *God Unknown* was, I believe, just published, and word of a resident novelist penetrated to the staff of *Laguna Beach Life*, the weekly paper on which I had once served briefly and embarrassingly. According to Carol's subsequent report, a young-woman reporter appeared one morning as she and John sat drinking coffee under a tree. John was stripped to the waist and perhaps concentrating on something he was writing or preparing to write, and was not pleased by the interruption. Nor were the girl's opening questions well chosen—things like "How do you get your ideas?" and "What have you written so far?"

Carol went in the house to get her a cup of coffee while John started doing a magnificent con job. "Blood sacrifice," he told her, "that's what the world needs to purify and rededicate itself." While the girl listened and scribbled on her pad, he embroidered the subject with mystical and pseudo-religious overtones, doubtless tinctured with some of the concepts in the newly published book. The world is full of sin, he said, and expiation can be gained only by purging it with a flow of redeeming blood. He quoted from what he said was the Bible and from *The Golden Bough*. Carol reported that it was a superior performance.

I regret that I never got to see the story when it appeared in the paper. But again, according to Carol, it pulled out all the stops and was impressive. An earthquake kept me from reading it. My wife and I had started on March 10 for Laguna to visit the Steinbecks, but as we stopped briefly at my mother's apartment in Long Beach, the severe quake struck, wrecking buildings, killing numbers of people, and blocking roads, so we returned to Eagle Rock to see if our house was still standing. It was undamaged.

In the ledger which contains the holographic text of *God Unknown* and *The Pastures of Heaven* there are many notes squeezed into the margins, for the most part directed to me.[14] They at least reveal some of the things he was thinking as he wrote, as well as one entertaining bit of jubilant humor that deserves to be salvaged. Just when he gave me the ledger I do not remember. It was probably in 1933 or 1934, but the notes reveal that he had been planning the gift for some time. When Maryon and I separated in June, 1933, I may already have received it, for at some time after that, I took it for safe-keeping to my mother's apartment in Long Beach, where it stayed, almost forgotten, until Mother's death in 1945, when my sister found it and returned it to me.

The book consists of 300 numbered pages with 38 lines per page; and the writing, ranging from small to minute, averages from ten to more than twenty words per line. Written on the fly page is a rough index of the contents, listing the eleven narratives of *The Pastures* in the order in which they were written: *Helen Van Deventer and Daughter, The Maltby, The Lopez Sisters, The Deserted Farm, Miss Morgan, Discovery, Tularecito, Shark Wicks, Raymond Banks, John Whiteside and House*, and *Pat Humbert.* [15]

At the foot of the fly leaf is a faint, penciled line: "With footnotes to Dook," which was probably the last thing written in the volume, since the idea of giving it to me and of including progressive notes as the work proceeded apparently came just before John made the beginning of the *God Unknown.*

Immediately after the Pat Humbert story on page 114 is a long penciled note occupying most of page 115:

To Dook

When I bought this book and began to fill it with words it occurred to me that you might like to have it when it was full. You have that instinct so highly developed in magpies, pack rats, and collectors. If this were a blank book, you would probably like it better. I can imagine you keeping a book blank because of your hatred of change. In spite of all this, I should like you to have this book and my reasons are all sentimental, and therefore, of course unmentionable. I love you very much. I have never been able to give you a present that cost any money. It occurs to me that you might accept a present that cost me a hell of a lot of work. For I do not write easily. Three hours of writing requires twenty hours of preparation. Luckily I have learned to dream about the work, which saves me some working time.

What I wanted to say was this. Up to this page the stories are the best I can do at the present time. Now the series is through and I am going to take two months vacation. In that time I shall try six or seven short stories, light, amusing, restful. I may even try to sell some of them, and if I do, it will be under a mom [sic] de plume. So I'm asking you to keep quiet and mouselike about the stories which follow this. I'll make a note when the ban is off.

The only story which follows this note is the "unnamed Narrative" starting on page 119 and abandoned after three pages. The "fragment" consists of about 1,600 words starting the story about a little boy named Mizpah living in Pacific Grove during the days when that village was still basically the gathering place for annual Methodist camp meetings and evangelical gatherings. The Steinbeck family acquired its property at the Grove during the latter part of this period, and John saw much of the surviving religious strictness and fanaticism during his regular visits to the family cottage.

On the next page is a long note, almost an invocation, with elevated language and high emotion. It was written after the story was well under way. Fifteen pages following have been cut out of the book, indicating that the first start at the new novel was destroyed, and a fresh beginning made on page 137. The note on page 122 reads:

Again

Now the new work starts—a good plan, a good story; strong, sturdy, standing with fine legs set wide, and contemplating the wreckage of the earth-body. His chin is down and his bewildered eyes look at the ground. And then his active love arises, a force as mighty as the thrust in the thighs of a bull when he drives the invincible phallus into the quivering yoni. And the love grows like a black rain until he rains the good blood from his throat upon the dying earth.

Now as always—humility and terror. Fear that the working of my pen cannot capture the grinding of my brain. It is so easy to understand why the ancients prayed for the help of a muse. And the muse came and stood beside them. And we, heaven help us, do not believe in Muses. We have nothing to fall back upon but our own craftsmanship, and it, as modern literature attests, is inadequate.

We might be wrong. Somewhere in a cave dug by the young and insolent brains of our times a spirit who delights in literature might languish. Some immortal intelligence there may be which understands the hunger man has for beauty. If such there is, may he or she help me, for I am afraid.

> May my words be burned with the flame of my desire to produce some beautiful thing before I die and am sucked into the hungry earth.
>
> My story is better than I am. It seems to be contrived by a better brain than I possess. If I hoped enough and prayed enough, might not the spirit which helped me to design my plan, help me to bring it into the land.
>
> May I be honest; may I be decent; may I be unaffected by the technique of hucksters. If invocation is required, let this be my invocation—may I be strong and yet gentle, tender and yet wise, wise and yet tolerant. May I for a little while, only for a little while, see with the inflamed eyes of a god.

The progress footnotes are written in the inch of space at the top of the page, obviously so that none of the precious lines, into each of which can be crowded so many tiny words, will be wasted. The first appears on page 157 in the middle of Chapter 6. It is written minutely in pencil:

> Well, how do you like it so far. It seems strange how the thing grows, how the people become more essentially real than the people I know. This is a week's work from the beginning. I am going very fast—too fast, I'm afraid. But my story is impatient. Besides, I have said that I will submit it by July and this is the end of [next page]

But there is no continuation on page 158. Instead, on page 159, is another note:

> These heads make good places for notes. I wonder how you'll like this book, whether Joseph will be to you the person he is to me. Of course that is impossible. It seems very strange that this book will be finished before I see you again. Maybe: And I'll know whether or not I've failed again. I think this is a better, tighter story than any I've done yet.

On page 167, halfway through Chapter 8, the green ink stops and the rest of the volume is written in blue-black which has now turned almost black. Such details are unimportant except that they provide the background for one of his most charming notes, starting on page 168:

> An examination of this mss., should anyone be interested, should be of interest to the camp followers of literature. The change of ink colors, for example, might to those students of influence in the life of an artist, be of the rarest significance. This volume begins in purple ink—my mood was rich with the blood of youth, rich with the intricacy of style. I was beginning to feel the purple of the Caesar. [ink changes to green] Old Nature, bless her. The trees and all the green earth, stems straining to lay their leaves in heaven. Youth again, but green youth, not the earth purple, the soil purple, the purple of seeds—but the green of growth toward what comes now—the blue—blue of heaven—the mysterious end—the finish—blue of philosophy, of quiet maturity. Indeed, there is room for thought in all this. And lest some god dam fool should devote time to this subject which might better be employed—say in a concordance on Zane Grey, I shall explain. A year ago Holman's department store had an ink sale—ink that had been so long in stock that it was as ripe and rich as Napoleon brandy, cobwebs on the bottle. Two bottles for five cents. I bought two and used them. On page 167 the green was exhausted and I went back, but the sale was over and I bought one bottle of blue for ten cents. Purple of soil, green of growth, blue ten cents. Media are ridiculous. And Duke—should you ever look over this book which I am intending you should have, if I have as good a story as I think I have, you may have a little chuckle to yourself. For you know that only the end counts.
>
> This story has grown since I started it. From a novel about people it has become a novel about the world. And you must never tell it. Let it be found out. The new eye is being opened here in the west—the new seeing. It is probably that no one will know it for two hundred years. It will be confused, analyzed, analogized, criticized, and none of our fine critics will know what is happening. I could name four who know, one with his brain and three with their bodies. This must be cryptic.
>
> Duke, this novel is just under way. I don't know how it will be when it is finished. That's funny, isn't it? If you ever see this, the birthing pains will be over. And here am I sitting and wondering how I can bring off

the thing. All the scenes aren't born yet. It would be much less fun if it were sure. There are things in my mind as strong as pure as good as anything in the structure of literature. If I do not put them down, it will be because I have not the technique. The story is too big, Duke. I am so afraid of it sometimes—so fearful of its implications that I am tempted to burn it as an over-evil thing. And it is not evil. It is good and timeless. Joseph is a giant shouldering his way among the ages, pushing the stars aside to make a passage to god. And this god—that is the thing. When god is reached—will anyone believe it. It really doesn't matter. I believe it and Joseph believes it. The story is a parable, Duke. The story of a race, growth, and death. Each figure is a population, and the stones, the trees, the muscled mountains are the world—but not the world apart from man—the world and man—the one inseparable unit, man plus his environment. Why they should ever have been misunderstood as being separate I do not know. Man is said to come out of his environment. He doesn't know when. Now this note is over.

The next note is written in ink:

Note: I wonder how you are liking it now. There seems to be no end to my excitement on this theme. The pass is my pit next to the circle in the pines. But the circle in the pines, as you have no doubt surmised, is the citadel of the story. Curious: I am adding these notes as if you might be reading this from mss. And it is probably that you will never look through this book. But it does me good to talk thus to you now and then it does the mss. no harm. There are beautiful things to come. I wonder if you know why I address this manuscript to you. You are the only person in the world who believes I can do what I set out to do. Not even I believe that all the time. And so, in a kind of gratitude I address all my writing to you, whether or not you know it.

[No further comments until the story's completion—a final entry is on page 260.]

Note: Now this book is finished, Dook. You will have to work on it; to help straighten out the roughness, to say where it falls short. It will be much better when your work on it is done. In giving you this manuscript, I do not give you anything I value very highly. I wish I valued it more so that it would be a better gift. The book had plans beyond my abilities I'm afraid. It isn't nearly all I hoped it would be. But it is finished anyway and done with. You haven't read it yet. I hope you will like it some. I remember when I finished the earlier book of the same title. I took it to you and you said, "It is very good." And I knew you knew it was terrible and you knew I knew you knew it. And if this one is as bad I hope you will tell me. I know it isn't as a matter of fact. I know enough of technique to be sure it is much better constructed. But I've worked too hard on it. I can't tell much about it.

Anyway this is your book now. I hope you'll like to have it.

love John

Part 6:

A "New Start" with "Big Writing": *Grapes of Wrath*

In a letter written to me from Pacific Grove on June 21, 1933, is the tentative statement of Steinbeck's "Phalanx Theory," or his version of the well-known Gestalt thesis that the behavior of groups differs from that of individuals acting individually, and that such groups tend to become separate entities with their own laws of being and conduct. This principle, about which we had many subsequent conversations and discussions, became the formative idea of *In Dubious Battle*, and indeed, some of the arguments and concepts which are loosely phrased in the letter are carried virtually intact into the book.

The book, however, is a synthesis of two largely unrelated ideas: the phalanx concept and a project to write the life story of a young man with whom he had become acquainted. As I remember it, the individual, who had served as a Communist organizer for a time, was the son of a Polish butcher who attributed his own strength to drinking blood daily in the Middle Western stockyards where he worked.

Whether the theory or the life of the young man came first I don't know, but I believe that John had formulated the theory and laid it temporarily aside after searching for a story to which it could be applied. Originally he planned to write the organizer's story in the first person and publish it anonymously. But when he had completed twenty-five or thirty thousand words of it, he showed it to Robert Ballou, then his publisher, and Ballou persuaded him to change it to the third person and the true novel form, making a longer book than he had intended. In doing this, Steinbeck found that he had an ideal vehicle for developing the phalanx thesis, and at the same time that he could still utilize a roughly accurate version of the young man's story, giving it new force and meaning while endowing the theory with life and dramatic significance.

Since the letter, bubbling with excitement and enthusiasm, fits so significantly into *Dubious Battle* and provides seed for later developments in other novels and in influencing the course of some of his subsequent thinking, I shall quote significant parts of it.[16]

> This is not a letter to read unless you have so much time that you just don't care. I just want to talk and there is no one to talk to. Out of the all encircling good came a theme finally. I knew it would. Until you can put your theme in one sentence, you haven't it in hand well enough to write a novel. The process is this (I am writing this at the risk of being boring. One can refuse to read a letter and the writer of it will never know.) The process is this—one puts down endless observations, questions and remarks. The number grows and grows. Eventually they all seem headed in one direction and then they whirl like sparks out of a bonfire. And then one day they seem to mean something.
>
> When they do it is the most exciting time in the world. I have three years of them and only just now have they taken a direction. Suddenly they are all of one piece. Then the problem begins of trying to find a fictional symbolism which will act as a vehicle. And for such a theme, that is going to be difficult. The Greeks generalized without considering with any accuracy the units which made up their generalization. And after that method had been mauled and worried through many centuries the modern school abandoned the generality for the unit, and in the end lost

all sight of the generality. Dr. Fletcher, a good mind and a good observer, has never for fifteen years moved his mind from one small species of nematodes.[17] . . . I believe that there is a change going on.

For a number of years I have been very much interested in certain reactions and phenomena which seemed to indicate a racial physiology. I have a good many hundreds of notes. Certain groups of human units, their boundaries usually topographical, react to stimuli much as if they were a unit much more close knit than is generally thought.

Let me quote a few of the notes. The coral insect working with hundreds of billions of others, eventually creates a strange and beautiful plant-like formation. In the course of time numberless plants create the atoll. Architecturally the atoll is very beautiful and good. Certain groups in Europe at one time created the Gothic spire. They seem to have worked under a stimulus as mysterious, as powerful and as general as that which causes the coral insects to build, and their product, while not of their own bodies, is built of a fluid more fine, but none the less material. The human biologic unit, has the ability to join with other units into a new unit so compact as to be thought of as a unit, a pathological unit.

Note—in nineteen-seventeen this unit was in a physical and psychic condition which made it susceptible to the inroads of the influenza germ. This germ at other times was not deadly, and, when encountered now, causes discomfort but not ordinarily death. It has been shown that at the time mentioned the germ had not changed but the receptivity of the race had. Note—A few years ago nearly half a million people bought and read a book called [*The Bridge of San Luis Rey*]. Not one in a hundred knew what that book was about but some mysterious stimulus made them read it.

Note—In Mendocino county a whole community turned against one man and destroyed him although they had taken no harm from him. This will sound meaningless to you unless you could see the hundreds of notes that make them meaningful to me. The larger unit, and it may contain any number of the biological units, has a nature entirely different from its parts—as different in fact as a man is from the single cells of which he is composed. As an example—The biologic unit has a mechanism which allows him to profit by experience. If he follows a course and is hurt, he changes his process. The larger unit has not this mechanism. The group unit never learns by experience, in fact has not such a faculty. The group unit is so strong that it can change the nature of its biologic units. It is quite easy for the group unit, acting under stimuli to viciousness, to eliminate the kindly natures of its units. When acting as a group unit, men do not partake of their ordinary natures at all. These things seem very obvious. If it is so, why is it that the group unit has never been observed and studied as a unit instead of as a mass of individuals. Such it certainly is not. The group unit can change its nature and can even change the biologic structure of it units if the stimulus be strong enough. It can alter the birth rate, diminish the number of its units, control states of mind, alter appearance, physically and spiritually. All of the notations I have made begin to point to an end—That the group unit is an individual as boundaried, as diagnosable, as dependent on its units and as independent of its units' individual natures, as the human unit, or man, is dependent on his cells and yet as independent of them.

Does this begin to make sense to you? The greatest group unit, that is the whole race, has qualities which the individual lacks entirely. It remembers a time when the moon was close, when the tides were terrific. It remembers a time when the weight of the individual doubled itself every twenty eight days. It remembers that the moon was the most terrible thing that it had to contend with, and strangely enough, it remembers every step of its climb from the single cell to the human. The human unit has none of these memories.

The nature of the group units, I said, were [sic] changeable. Usually they are formed by topographical peculiarities. Sometimes a terrible natural stimulus will create a group unit over night. They are of all sizes, from the camp meeting where the units pool their souls to make one yearning cry, to the whole world which fought the war. In dealing with this one cannot stop with the human race. The process of evolution might be one of splitting up the group units. A great many of the lower life forms are able to act in no way except as a group unit. The higher forms seem able temporarily to tear themselves loose from the group unit. You are better able to understand the indication of all this than anyone I know. But I am writing it to you more to clear up for myself. I forecast that before many years are gone, the group units in all their number and in their changing moods and reactions will be considered as units. Russia is giving us a nice example of human units who are trying with a curious nostalgia to get away from their individuality and reestablish the group unit the race remembers and wishes. I am not drawing conclusions. Merely trying to see where the stream of all my notes is going.

One could easily say that man, during his hunting period had to give up the group unit since all hunters must; and now that food is not to be taken by stealth and precision, is going back to the group which takes its food by concerted action. That if one lives by the food of the lion he must hunt singly, if by the food of other ruminants he may live in herds and protect himself by his numbers. There is too much of this. I'll have to arrange and arrange.

It can be placed some what like this for the moment—as individual humans we are far superior in our functions to anything the world has born,—in our group units we are not only not superior but in fact are remarkably like those most perfect groups, the ants and bees. I haven't begun to tell you this thing. I am not ready to.

Half of the cell units of my mother's body have rebelled. Neither has died, but the revolution has changed her functions. That is cruel to say. The first line on this thing came from it though. She, as a human unit, is deterred from functioning as she ordinarily did by a schism of a number of her cells.

The human unit is capable of the same diseases as the group unit. I told you you didn't have to read this. My thesis is, then, the group unit is an individual as calculable and studyable as the human unit. It may not be in our time. Perhaps it will never be.

And, when the parts of this thesis have found their places, I'll start trying to put them into the symbolism of fiction.

The fascinating thing to me is the way men, completely without conscious volition, arrange themselves into these units, and that the units are entirely different from the natures of their component parts. The group unit has a soul, a drive, an intent, an end, a method, a reaction and a set of tropisms which in no way resemble the same things possessed by the men who make up the group unit. These group units have always been considered as individuals multiplied. And they are not so. They are beings in themselves, entities, to put it harshly, the group units are creatures in themselves. Just as a bar of iron has some of the properties of the revolving, circling, active atoms which make it up, so these huge creatures, the group units do not resemble the human atoms which compose them. By studying the group units one may come to a conclusion about their nature which could never be arrived at by studying the humans who compose them. The nature of a bar of iron could never be understood by studying the atoms which compose it.

This is muddled, Dook. I wouldn't send it to anyone else in this form. But you and I have talked so much together that we can fill in the gaps we leave. I'd like you to think this over rather carefully. I know it is full of holes. So is the theory of relativity, but if one could, by beginning with the axiom of the group creature, discover that it reacts in given ways, and we know that in thousands of cases it does, we would have a base to start an investigation into a new and profitable field. You will remember that I often spoke to you about a field for investigation, that of race psychopathology? This is the base from which to start that investigation. The thesis can be attacked from a great many angles and very successfully. Perhaps when it is more carefully worked out, it will not be so easy to refute it. Give it your thought and your reaction anyway. . . .

. . . And you might put your mind on the problem I have stated. If you could help me put it into form, and to help me formulate it, I probably would have less trouble finding my symbols for reproducing it. And by the way, it is a gorgeous field for research by a young savant. There's a reputation to be made by it. You will find the first beginning conception of it among the anthropologists, but none of them has dared to think about it yet. The subject is too huge and too terrifying. Since it splashed on me, I have been able to think of nothing else. It is an explanation of so many mysterious things, the reason for migrations, the desertion of localities, the sudden diseases which wiped races out, the sudden running amok of groups. It would explain how Genkis [sic] Khan and Atila [sic] and the Goths suddenly stopped being individual herdsmen and hunters and became, almost without transition, a destroying creature obeying a single impulse. It would explain the sudden tipping over of

Prohibition, and that ten years ago the constitution of the US was a thing of God and now it is abrogated with impunity. Oh! It is a gorgeous thing. Don't you think so?

I am ignorant enough to promulgate it. If I had more knowledge I wouldn't have the courage to think it out. It isn't thought out yet but I have a start. Think of the lemmings, little gophers who live in holes and who suddenly in their millions become a unit with a single impulse to suicide. Think of the impulse which has suddenly made Germany overlook the natures of its individuals and become what it has. Hitler didn't do it. He merely speaks about it. The thing is automatic. Suppose there were no final units of life, but suppose life were like the Martians in that book.[18] Creatures of varying sizes and impulses, a series of arrangements and rearrangements of units, each arrangement being a creature with a nature of its own and impulses and ends of its own, yes and individual appetites and satisfactions. The individual being not the final unit, but merely a step.

I'll stop before I drive you as crazy as I have become since all my wonderings have taken a stream like force. All the things I've wondered about and pondered about are seeming to make sense at last. Why the individual is incapable of understanding the nature of the group unit. That is why publishing is unsure, why elections are the crazy things they are. Why a lecturer cannot tell in advance which [idea] will get over. The group unit has its own sense of humor, its own methods of enjoyment which are foreign to its component parts. We only feel the emotions of the group beast in times of religious exaltations, in being moved by some piece of art which intoxicates us while we do not know what it is that does it. Are you as nuts as I am now? [marginal note:] We are prone to think of individuals as entities separated by space. The atomic theory gives us no such justification. [Dated: Pacific Grove (June 21, 1983)]

I replied to the letter with some probably inept suggestions, and received another dated June 30, 1933, which continued the subject and said in part:

I had your letter in answer to my hectic one, and I was sorry that you went off into consideration of the technique of the novel which will result. I can see how it will be done, all right, but I am more interested just now to get the foundation straight and the physical integrity of it completed. The investigations have so far been gratifying. I find that in anthropology, Doctor Ellsworth Huntington, in History and cultural aspects, Spengler and Ouspenski, in folklore and in unconscious psychology, Jung, in economic phases of anthropology Briffault, in biology, Allee, and in physics Schondringer, Planck, Bohr, Einstein, Heisenberg have all started heading in the same direction. None has gone far, and none apparently is aware of the work of the others, but each one is headed in the same direction and the direction is toward my thesis. This in itself would indicate the beginning of a new phalanx or group unit. One finds that the Soviets have destroyed the boundaries of the sciences in teaching their children, and the logical conclusion of my thesis is exactly that destruction of boundaries. It knocks the three Biology, zoology [sic] into one piece instantly. The corroboration of innumerable investigators is available, conclusions reached individually and without reference to the others. Jung goes so far as to postulate what he calls, a third person, which is exactly what I have called the keying mechanism of the individual with which he plugs into the phalanx. It is curious to notice what happens to the individual when that mechanism is allowed to atrophie [sic]. I noticed it in the mountains. When the possibility of joining and becoming part of a phalanx is taken away, the mind becomes dull and those individual qualities which have raised the human race become lacking. It would seem from this slight example that even those qualities which we call individual gain strength and force from participation in the phalanx. You understand of course that all this investigation and correlation is simply to establish a basic integrity. In the projected novel they will be covered, and I assure you it will not be a tract describing an investigator who discovers such things. I'd rather write a treatise . . .

Both these letters were written in Salinas while John was undergoing the long ordeal of waiting for the slow death of his mother. He spent much of his time in Salinas, helping to care for her, while Carol remained in the Grove. He was working on short stories and had completed two or three with which he was reasonably satisfied, though he did not identify them and said that writing them was good training in self-control if nothing else, adding that, "Now I have my new theme to think about there will be few loopholes in my days. I can think about it while helping with a bed pan. I can make notes at any time of the day or night, and I think I shall delay the writing of it until I have the ability for sustained concentration. However, if the time is too long I can't even wait for that. I'll have to go to work on it. The pieces of it are fast massing and getting ready to drop into their places."

~

I was again at Stanford by this time and whatever correspondence there was is lost, but I visited in Salinas and Pacific Grove over the next three years, and John and Carol made visits to me, usually on their way to or from San Francisco, so we kept in touch.

It was during one of my trips to the Grove that I first met Ed Ricketts and visited his laboratory, viewing with interest the jars of specimens which lined the walls and the glass-topped compartment where he kept his lethargic rattlesnakes, later dealt with in a Steinbeck story. On the day I saw them Ed put a white mouse in with them for my benefit and the snakes would have nothing to do with it. It was perhaps on the same visit that Ed produced a Ouiji board which spelled out impressive answers to our questions while John, Ed, and I all kept fingers on the table. We also experimented with "spirit writing," using an oversized pencil which we all clutched lightly. I have no explanation for some of the "messages" that we got—they were coherent and "signed" by two or three controls, each of which had a distinctly individual handwriting. Whether or not Ed and John believed in the apparent phenomenon I do not know, but they seemed convinced—and convincing—at the time. John, Carol, and I experimented with the board and pencil a number of times afterward, and we all enjoyed our attempts to have faith, though when we tried to follow leads provided by the messages, the results were totally disappointing, as when a control named Jackie told us to look in certain volumes for bonds which my late aunt had hidden. We searched but found nothing, and other suggestions proved equally valueless. All of us *wanted* to believe.

Around Christmas, 1935, John and Carol drove in with a present of a Benjamin pump rifle for me, with an ample supply of BB shot and we spent hours shooting from the living room of my Menlo Park cottage at a target that we rigged up on the kitchen wall. John proved to be the superior marksman by a considerable margin. Carol was no slouch either. As for me, my parents had never permitted me as a boy to have even an air rifle. I was a terrible shot.

I am unable to provide much in the way of exact chronology, dates, or episodes from 1933 on. In 1933, *To a God Unknown* was published, three different publishers having a successive hand in it. John later boasted ruefully to me that his books had been responsible for the demise of almost every firm which had undertaken them, up to a point. I know that he had given me the manuscript for criticism and editing, as he had with at least parts of *The Green Lady* and *To an Unknown God*, its earlier versions. And he was mildly annoyed and argumentative about some of my comments, as well as with my rather pedantic rigidity in matters of punctuation. His rhetoric was rarely at fault and he always had a sense of the precise word.

And in 1935, *Tortilla Flat* finally found a home, to the delight of all his friends, to whom he had now and then been reading parts of it as we gathered in the Pacific Grove cottage. John stood as he read, his one eyebrow characteristically lifted and his voice tending to move toward the upper registers as he came to parts that he particularly liked or found moving. The episodes, he said, were all essentially true, and many of them had been told to him originally by Susan Gregory, teacher at the "Tortilla Flat" school, who had heard them from her pupils and even seen some of them happen. The Modern Library edition of the book bore a dedication to her. According to John, the manuscript had gone the rounds of most of the major publishers without success—he said nine of them had turned it down, but he sometimes changed the number—and was gathering dust in the drawer of his agent (presumably McIntosh and Otis) when Ben Abramson, the Chicago bookseller, who had previously bought up some hundreds of unbound copies of *Cup of Gold* as an investment, persuaded Pat Covici to look it up. He did, and the house of Covici-Friede presided over John's first real literary success, establishing Covici as his friend and life-long editor, as well as an important influence on every remaining volume. They were affectionately close, as is clearly evidenced by the "warm-up letters" that John wrote to him while working on *East of Eden*, prefacing each day's production with an often lengthy discussion of the problems, intentions, and dissatisfactions he was encountering, as well as often unrelated comments on personal affairs and abstractions.[19] John invited me to meet Pat, as he called Covici, in 1940, and I spent the night there after dinner and a long evening together in the house west of Los Gatos.

Until the success of *Tortilla Flat*, John and Carol had some lean times as detailed poignantly but entertainingly in a 1960 issue of *Esquire*.[20] Both he and Carol did work for the W.P.A. and perhaps other government-sponsored projects, one of his jobs being "taking a census of the dogs on the Monterey Peninsula,, their breeds, weights, and characters." Carol was writing ironic little verses, some of which appeared in the *Monterey Beacon* over the pseudonym of Amnesia Glasscock.[21] Earlier, Carol had made a typed edition of some of those verses titled "A Slim Volume to End Slim Volumes," a copy of which was promised me but never delivered. Also in 1934 she had written a long and sardonic marching song to the tune of "The Daring Young Man on the Flying Trapeze," titling it "The Man in the Shiny Silk Hat" and signed, "Carol, the Sweet Singer of Moscow." It had five verses with a chorus that went: "He rides through the streets in the shiniest cars,/ A man who should obviously be behind bars./ He starves little babies, seduces their mars,/ And no one does nothing to him."

They claimed that on Black Thursday, July 5, 1934, when San Francisco was tied up by a general strike and longshoremen paraded on Market Street in a compact body that police fired on with fatalities; the strikers had sung Carol's song as they marched, but it is doubtful that dock workers could have coped with the vocabulary or the often complex sentiments it contained, or could have remembered its more than fifty lines. Someone, of course, could have sung it from a written text and the men could have cheered its ribald lines.

Carol also was painting in water colors and creating a series that she called "American Sportswomen." It started during one of my visits at the Grove on a morning when she asked what I would like to do. For no particular reason, I replied, "Paint pictures," and she produced a box of water-colors with which I struggled to create lamentable art of which she was scornful. "I can do better than that," she said, and proved it by turning out the first of the ridiculous naked fat women whom she later perfected. Within a year or two, she had a one-woman show of them, running, jumping, throwing things, and participating in almost every field that America considers as sport. They were satiric and delightful.

Holman's department store in Pacific Grove is mentioned in several of John's books, and it served as a treasure house for the community, being the only large general store in the area, where agricultural implements, clothing, hardware, and devices for every taste and occupation—within the limits of the town's moral standards—were available. It was a part of the sight-seeing trips the Steinbecks offered their visitors, and sometimes they went through it just to browse.

The public library was another place where they spent much time, although it steadfastly refused for many years to have any of John's books on its shelves. Monterey, too, failed to recognize the tourist value of *Tortilla Flat*, and Steinbeck was denounced and even threatened for publicizing that area of the town, which it considered an embarrassing slum inhabited by undesirables. There were reports of visitors who asked about its location only to be told that there was no such place, that the book was a libelous attack on the fair name of the community. Even in Salinas, where the social and economic status of the family was of the highest, the name of John Steinbeck was anathema in many circles and his books were—and still are, to some extent—considered both dirty and traitorous to the city and its residents, though indignation and denunciations did not reach their peek until "The Harvest Gypsies" series began appearing in the *San Francisco News* in October, 1936, to be followed in 1939 by *The Grapes of Wrath.*

Not until almost ten years after John's death in 1968 did Salinas begin revising its opinion of its only major writer. It started with the establishment of the John Steinbeck Library, containing books, taped reminiscences by people who had known him, and a slowly accumulating assortment of memorabilia about him. Then the John Steinbeck Foundation was formed and on February 27, 1978, celebrated what would have been his 76th birthday with a First Annual Steinbeck Country scavenger hunt for further articles associated with him.[22] Joining in the sponsorship was the Salinas rock station, KDON. With encouragement from the Chamber of Commerce, the John Steinbeck Commemorative Stamp Committee was formed, with a resulting thousand-plus letters pouring into sources at Washington, with the resulting announcement by the Postal Service of a stamp bearing his picture on his 1979 birthday, with accompanying festivities. In addition, a medallion honoring him and Helen Hayes, as part of a government-sponsored series featuring notables in the Arts, was announced for 1984. But even with such acclaim, students in one of the Salinas schools working on a Steinbeck assignment were reported to have encountered a surprising amount of animosity as they interviewed citizens about the writer. In June, 1981, however, Salinas played host at a thirteen-day Steinbeck Festival, funded by the national Endowment for the Humanities and featuring tours, speakers, panel discussions, and dramatizations, with a wide attendance from various parts of the country.

John had written several sketches and satires for Stanford publications as early as 1924, and his first national publication was a short story, "The Gifts of Iban" in the short-lived *Smoker's Companion* of March, 1927. But it was the old-established *North American Review* that provided him with a wide audience for his short stories, many of which had been circulating fruitlessly over the editorial desks of major magazines. First to appear there was "The Red Pony" in November, 1933, to be followed the next month by "The Great Mountains," by "The Murder" in April, 1934, and "The Raid" in

October of the same year. Those stories with several others were later collected in *The Long Valley*. (I read the original manuscript of "The Red Pony" while sitting in the upstairs hall of the Salinas house, and repelled by the grisly details of the operation on the neck of the horse, I told him emphatically, "You can't publish that." I have had ample reason to change my mind. "The Red Pony" remains one of the most frequently anthologized stories in American school anthologies.)

His articles and sketches were also appearing in the *Monterey Beacon* in 1935, which printed at least nine of his contributions, including "The Snake" during 1935.

Although his stories and articles were beginning to find places in various periodicals and to draw reservedly favorable comment, he detested publicity and refused to permit photographs to be taken for publication, reluctantly approving a sketch when his publishers demanded a picture to go with his books. His first official picture was taken in 1935.

His deep-seated need for privacy continued throughout most of his life, and while he learned to make compromises that the promotion of his books required, he refused to face the camera whenever possible, avoided all possible interviews, and steadfastly turned down invitations for speeches, honorary degrees, and appearances on radio and television. He did, I believe, act as commentator on a film prepared for television that I have never seen, and cut at least one record in which he read material that he had written. The single appearance he could not avoid was before the Swedish Academy, and the prospect of facing the members and making a speech gave him a bad case of nerves. In apologizing for not writing to me he said, "Maybe when this literary bull-running is over, I can complete some kind of communication castrated of self-consciousness. . . . Meanwhile pray for me some. I've always been afraid of such things." In another letter dated September 28, 1962 but not sent until later, he wrote:

> I'm going to Stockholm and I'm going to make a speech—the first and last of my life. I have it cut to 500 words now and it can be trimmed. I'll

> do everything expected of me for five days . . . I think I can pull it off. If I can't I'll probably shoot myself because I am the least likely public character who ever came down the pike. If they wanted a front they picked the wrong guy. I'll let you know if I can pull it off. I think I can.

~

With the success of *Tortilla Flat*, John and Carol had real money for the first time together, and they invested some of it in a house, built in an undeveloped area on Greenwood Lane in northeast Los Gatos. Specifications were their own and the plan was simple: a huge living room with rafters and an inverted-V roof, an ample kitchen, two bedrooms, a small study for John to work in, and a long porch across the front of the house looking down over a wooded slope that fell away below. A speaker system was set into the upper wall of the big room to carry music from a specially designed record player for their growing collection of good music. The house was set in the center of the lot, which comprised an acre or more, so that they could keep a maximum distance from potential neighbors. They called the place "Arroyo del Ajo," which they translated as "Garlic Gulch."

The privacy they sought did not last long. Almost before their house was completed, a woman started building on an adjoining lot and within a few feet of the property line. "She spent all her time watching us," the Steinbecks reported, and on occasions, John urinated off the end of the porch, facing her in reprisal.

The news quickly got around that a controversial young novelist had moved into Los Gatos, and that brought further harassment. People came looking for him and boldly walked into the house, even trying to look over his shoulder as he was working and growing abusive when they were asked to leave. To stop such invasions, John put up a tight six-foot grape-stake fence around the property, and when the visitors without hesitation began coming through the gate, he equipped it with a special lock that could not be opened from the outside. After that, the sight seers parked and peered through the fence, some of them even bringing picnic lunches and quite audibly discussing what they could see: "I bet that's his wife. You'd think she'd wear more clothes than that. Pretty unsociable of them to lock out folks that just come to see them." As an active deterrent, John's sleek Doberman, Bruga, was permitted to patrol the yard. Bruga was a temperamental dog, and at one time during a fit of recalcitrance bit John's hand so badly that it was incapacitated for weeks.

By the time *In Dubious Battle* appeared in 1936, mail was pouring in at a rate of twenty or thirty letters a day, a few praising, some denouncing or calling John a Communist, and many asking for something: copies of books, speeches, reading of manuscripts (which often arrived without return postage), contributions to causes, or just money. One that he showed me contained a picture of an attractive woman with an earnest request that he father a child by her.

They lived there less than two years. In a later letter when they had moved to a more inaccessible place, John wrote:

> . . . We moved back into the hills because the house was flooded with strangers all the time. And because in the year we lived there six houses went up all about us and it was like living in an apartment house. Besides, the land was too expensive. It grew to be three thousand dollars an acre and you couldn't raise a radish in it. . . . We hadn't known [it] was a fashionable district when we went there. But it was.

I visited the Greenwood Lane house only a few times, finding them happy in the first house that was really their own but already beginning to be annoyed by the penalties of even a moderate fame. Carol was planting flowers and shrubs, and they seeded the sloping area below the big front porch. Grass was just starting to grow when a girl who had come with me walked on it in high heels, bringing howls of rage from both Steinbecks. On one of my visits I met Larry (Lawrence Clark) Powell, now librarian emeritus of UCLA, whom I hadn't seen since he was a student at Occidental. Carol was making a collection of outstanding jazz and boogie-woogie records, and they alternated those with classical selections on the fine phonograph. It was a pleasant establishment.

Part 7:

The Estrangement and After

I had been continuing with my graduate work at Stanford, teaching bonehead composition courses, which paid $50 a quarter, but by 1936, with only the oral examination and the formal writing of my thesis ahead of me, not enough teaching jobs to keep me solvent were available. After a period of editing a weekly throw-around paper in Redwood City, I took a job in Marysville on the *Appeal-Democrat*, where I remained for four years, working up from an initial salary of $20 a week to a princely $22.50.

Marysville did not have a book store when *Of Mice and Men* was published, so I had to send away for the book. A few people in town had heard of Steinbeck and some had even read one or more of his books, but praise for them was rare. That part of the Sacramento Valley was a focal point for migrants and fruit tramps during the growing and harvest seasons; sometimes more of them were camping in the river bottoms, open spaces, and newly-opened migrant camps than there were people in the town itself, and the residents regarded them with suspicion and even enmity. That was the sort of people John was writing about, just as if they were human, and it made him suspect too. Why would anybody want to write about ignorant, dirty people, they asked, especially about a half-wit like Lenny? Generally, I avoided any mention of John Steinbeck, the expounder of dangerous ideas very close to socialism, for as a newcomer I was suspect myself. The community did not take readily to strangers.

Thus, when John came visiting me there in 1937, I did not introduce him around very widely, though he accompanied me around my beat and to some of the more interesting spots—the police station, the Chinese Joss House, a couple of the Chinese lotteries, which ran wide open, and some of the more colorful bars. Primarily, he had come to visit the local migrant camp, operated by the federal government, having already visited the ones at Weedpatch, Winters, and a few others.

At the time I got the strong impression that he had indeed been traveling across the country from Chicago with the Dust Bowl migrants along Route 66 in an old car he had purchased for the purpose, but people close to him have since insisted that he did not, in spite of many published descriptions of the journey. It is true, I believe, that he refused permission to stay in one of the camps, even though he had gone out on a fruit-picking job with the regular crews. And Tom Collins, manager of the Weedpatch camp near Bakersfield, provided him with much of his basic information about migrants and their problems. John eventually dedicated *Grapes of Wrath* to him.

I was delighted to see John, but the effects of the visit were unfortunate and led to a virtual estrangement for a while. In his mind was the intention to do something for me—specifically to enable me to finish my graduate work, aborted by lack of funds. He was excited about his plan as he told me about it. Friends had told him, quite correctly, that I was not very happy in the Marysville atmosphere, and he had devised a splendid way to get me out of it. I could choose a university anywhere in the world—he suggested the University of London—and he would pay all my expenses for as long as I wanted to attend. I had scholarly capabilities that he lacked, he said, and this would be a wonderful way to indulge them to the hilt.

The proposal did have enticing aspects but I turned it down. And explaining why was not easy. He had been counting on taking me away from a place and job that I did not like, giving opportunity for new dimensions to my intellectual potential, and in addition providing a chance for foreign travel and experience, something that he had always yearned for and was later to indulge extensively. I tried to tell him that leaving a reasonably comfortable college background for a job in an unfamiliar city where I had no friends had been difficult and a little bit frightening, but that having made the change, I felt that I must prove myself by fitting into the new milieu and by making a success of my duties. For a number of years I had been more or less drifting along on a benign current without surpassing problems. Now I was living in a disinterested community, not suffering exactly, but completely on my own. The temptation was great to accept his offer—go back to the life of books, ideas, and pleasant friendships, but such a choice would leave me with the feeling that I had failed to face a test of character. If I took the easy way this time, I might go on doing it for the rest of my life, with a progressive loss of respect for myself. This was something that I had to see out, although reluctantly.

John was disappointed and he didn't understand, misinterpreting when I described some of the more-tolerable features of the job and the town. Those attempts merely proved that I "adored Marysville," as he put it in a later letter, and that I wasn't really unhappy after all, taking pleasure in "being liked and admired at the police station, and . . . having fun at the wrestling matches," which I had to cover for the paper. We parted sadly and without warmth. For the next year or so, all I knew about him was what I read in the papers.[23]

When *The Grapes of Wrath* was published in 1939, its reception in Marysville was hostile, especially among the Associated Farmers, who are not kindly treated in the book, and in the newspaper for which I worked. Earl Brownlee, the city editor, knew the influence that the organization had in the largely agricultural community and in addition welcomed the opportunity to get in occasional semi-humorous but often malicious jabs at me as an outlander and friend of the author. The death of Zane Grey gave him an early editorial opening:

HE DID NOT SPEAK THEIR LANGUAGE

That element in a self-appointed intelligensia, with representatives in every scene, whose chief occupation is tearing down illusions and ideals, to say nothing of idols, for the rest of us, will not be impressed with news of the death of Zane Grey.

Grey did not speak their language in the tales he wrote. He was no John Steinbeck, glorifying his rugged yarns with all the filth he dared dish out to certain receptive minds. He was no pinko, putrifying a parlor with his presence or desecrating bookshelves by his presence. The worst a Zane Grey shelf ever gets is a supercilious sneer from those whose superior intelligence is beyond his reach.

The prodigious production of Grey's hand and mind may not survive the ordeal of time, but this generation will not forget that he brought entertainment to millions and offered nothing to offend the decency of any household or institution. More than 17,000,000 copies of his books have flooded the reading world. If the intelligencia [sic] can produce his counterpart, it can then flaunt its superiority.

A splendid tribute to Zane Grey, but the objective of the barb is quite apparent and almost overwhelms the tribute. Brownlee must have felt that he should do more in scourging the smut-peddlers from the shrines and temples of decent American literature, for a little later he made a more-direct attack in an editorial—with a side glance at me:

CENSORSHIP THAT IS JUSTIFIED

Generally we are dead against censorship, but it must be admitted there is some justification for the action of the Kansas City board of education in removing "The Grapes of Wrath" from public libraries. There must be a limit of indecency to which authors may descend and still have their works accepted for general reading. John Steinbeck reached that limit in his story of California's transient labor. The obscenity of "Grapes of Wrath" would not be tolerated in a newspaper; it would not be tolerated in the movies, and it would not be tolerated on the stage, which has gone pretty far itself in the name of realism. Dirt for dirt's

> sake, appears to be the rule in this book. Steinbeck never chooses a term of accepted usage when he can select a synonym from what used to be known as the language of the barroom before the feminine influence modified it to a degree.[24]

Interestingly, the central theme of the book—the problems and economics of the westward migrant movement—was totally ignored in a community where agricultural migrants surpassed the population in number seasonally, where government camps for them were being set up, and where strikes fostered by the newly formed CIO were affecting the harvest of fruits and other produce.

In 1939, having exchanged a few cards with John, I accepted his invitation and visited his new ranch in the hills west of Los Gatos. It was known as the Biddle ranch and was located off Hebard Road that joined the Santa Cruz highway. He had described it as: ". . . the most beautiful place in the world on rich land with plenty of water and forest and view and big vegetable gardens and a little lake." Carol's father had told them of the property and they fell in love with it—especially with the privacy and space it offered with its forty-seven acres, the difficulty of access (sometimes the road washed out in winter), and the quiet. In writing about it, he said:

> If we were going to sell it, the description would certainly sound like an estate. At the Greenwood road place we were finally surrounded with little houses and right under my work room window a house was built by a lady who was studying singing—the mi-mi-mi kind so we finally went nuts. Carol's father found this little ranch far up the mountain. It is forty-seven acres and has a big spring. It has forest and orchard and pasture and big tress. It is very old—was first taken up in 1847. The old ranch house was built in 1858 I think. So we came up, built a four-room house for ourselves, much like the Greenwood road house. There had been an oil well on the place and we used the big timbers and boards

> for our house. Then we refinished the inside of the old ranch house for two guest rooms and a big winter playroom where one can have parties. So far in our ad we have 'two houses—four bedrooms.' Then since Carol loves to swim I asked about swimming pools and I discovered a curious thing. The cost of swimming pools isn't the pool but the machinery for filtering the water over and over since water is expensive. But we had a four-inch head of spring water. Now we built a long, narrow swimming pool and turned our spring into it.
>
> . . . Then we have a Japanese boy who cooks, gardens, and looks after the place when we are away. And in the summer I have an Okie boy by the day to work around mainly because he needs the money so dreadfully. So there's a staff of servants. You see, it really is an estate.

His description did not do justice to the place. The forest that he mentioned was a designer's dream. In fact, Charlie Chaplin on his first visit described it as a "forest by Adrian," who was one of the leading Hollywood set designers. And at a time when Chaplin was having domestic troubles, John quoted him as saying, "When I get this picture opened and all the formal things done, can I please go up to your ranch and kick all the servants out and just talk a little bit quietly about how lonely and sad I am?"

In the midst of the fairy wilderness of lacy trees and vines was the tiny lake, itself looking like something from a movie set with masses of green algae around the edge, trailing branches, and dancing shadows. The effect was unreal and delightful.

The swimming pool was not large but it was clear as crystal with the fresh, cool water running through it, and was painted an azure blue. As he had said, the house was similar to the one they had built earlier, but better organized and equipped. The living room had a fine big fireplace and many large windows. The effect was spacious and warm. Not far from the house was a pleasant little hill, the summit of which produced a copious crop of meadow mushrooms in season, and near the foot of it was the shed and ample yard of their one-eyed pig, Connolly, named after the famed gatecrasher. I can't recall about horses, though I'm sure they had one or two. There was also a milk cow. And of course, a second Bruga dog. The first one was disposed of after it had mangled John's hand.

Carol, as usual, was busy planting things, and John later gave her a small greenhouse to protect her bulbs, slips, and seedlings. He always spoke of it as Carol's ranch.

I spent a night or two in the renovated old ranch house, part of which was devoted to the game room, with ping-pong table and a variety of other amusement devices. Together with a kitchenette and refrigerator. It was a pleasant place.

On one of my visits I found two members there of the crew that had sailed with them on the *Western Flier* into the Gulf of Lower California to gather material later shaped into *The Sea of Cortez*, and assorted friends from other areas kept dropping in. John was serving an excellent red wine that he had discovered at a nearby winery and laid in a couple of barrels of it. He was also demonstrating his marksmanship with a high-powered, English air pistol that could send a bullet through an inch of pine board. There was always something new and diverting, and conversation never flagged, though often, after much wine-drinking, the rough, twisting, exit road proved a bit hazardous.

In 1940, between writing-projects, often tied in with motion-picture activities, John also took flying lessons and seemed enraptured by the freedom and excitement of the sky. He wrote in August of that year: "There's something so god-damned remote and beautiful and detached about being way to hell and gone up on a little yellow leaf . . . a sense of being alone in the best sense of the word, not loneliness at all but just an escape into something delightful. . . ." For a while at least he drove every morning early from Los Gatos to Palo Alto for his flying lesson, but there were constant interruptions—trips to Hollywood, Mexico, and New York. Whether or not he ever got his license I do not know, nor did he mention flying in his letters after that year, except, of course, as a passenger.

In October, 1940, I quit my newspaper job in Marysville and moved to a house in Menlo Park near the Stanford Campus, enabling me to see John and Carol more frequently, both by visiting at their ranch and having them stop to look in on me. Early in 1941 they came in happily and Carol exhibited a fine star-sapphire ring that John had given her for her birthday. That, however, was shortly before they separated on April 27, according to the papers, which were my only source of information about their estrangement. She was granted her final decree in March, 1943, on charges of extreme cruelty involving "other women—particularly a Hollywood blonde."

I never learned who the blonde was. In subsequent visits he mentioned a well-known motion-picture actress with whom he said he had spent a week in Texas and hinted at an active social life in the film capitol with very little more explicitness. Nor did he mention his separation from Carol.

On one occasion he arrived in mid-afternoon and had clearly been drinking—for him to let it show was unusual—scorned my offer of assorted wines and liquors, and produced a bottle of a special brandy from his car, saying that it was the only thing he could drink. That too was a departure from the old days when anything in a bottle was welcome, from cheap red wine to bootleg whisky or gin. By dinner time he was even a little maudlin, weeping sentimentally about a girl he had known in the South. After dinner, he drove me to see a girl he had gone with in college, now married and living in Palo Alto, and again, he insisted on bringing in his own brandy instead of accepting what the host was serving. And going back to my place he frightened me by driving both fast and badly at a time when local police were conducting a campaign against speeders, as I warned him. Nor would he agree to spend the night but set out for Los Gatos with the bottle on the seat beside him.

That was one of the few times that I saw him badly affected by liquor, and he had often spoken approvingly of his parents' method of letting him get acquainted with alcohol in the home, resulting in his knowing how to deal with it. He compared it to my rearing, during which alcohol in any form was considered as an absolute Evil. That invested it with an irresistible fascination for me, often bringing deplorable consequences while I tried to learn to cope with it. In one of his letters he wrote a devastatingly painful indictment of what liquor sometimes did to me. As frequently was the case, he got into the spirit of what he was writing and overdid a bit, but the effect on me was doubtless salutary.

I knew little of his Hollywood activities. He told of trips there and other places, mentioning that he was working on a picture or learning techniques but almost never giving details. He spoke of dining with Chaplin and Paulette Goddard but gave few other names. Another woman, the wife of a producer—we had both known her before her marriage—told me of what sounded like an improbable episode at one of the restaurants frequented by the cinema celebrities. She and her husband, she said, had been dining there when she saw John come in. She invited him to their table for a drink. He accepted, proceeded to order a squab under glass, and, when it arrived, sent it back as underdone. He even carped at the waiter about other things. Such behavior may be common in Hollywood, but I never saw John act boorishly. His politeness was inherent. Perhaps his dislike of the movie colony could produce a defensive rudeness. The producer's wife herself was capable of arousing hostility at times, and she may have triggered his response. Her account, too, could well have been distorted.

In one of his letters there was an echo of the trip to Mexico we planned to take together but never did. He made many trips there, chiefly in connection with various motion pictures—*Viva Zapatsa!*, *The Forgotten Village*, and *The Pearl* in particular.[25] He wrote: "It is so strange—remember how we used to think of Mexico as the golden something and we never really thought we would get there for all our talk? Certainly I never thought I would be going again and again and not particularly wanting to. It's like all the beautiful ladies. . . . And now they bore me so completely because they aren't really beautiful after all."

Early in 1940 he spoke of working with Ed Ricketts on a "collectors' handbook on the invertebrates of an area near San Francisco bay but using this as a microcosm." Stanford University Press was to publish it, he said, and he was "studying harder than [he] ever did in school and doing some independent research also . . . I've grown more and more dissatisfied with my work and this will help it I hope. Besides, it will drop me out of this damnable popularity."

As far as I know, the handbook was never published, though he indicated that advanced preparations for it had been made at the Stanford University Press, which had published *Between Pacific Tides* by Ricketts and Jack Calvin.

The various aspects of "popularity" had been annoying him for some time. In March 1939, he wrote: "I have been desperately worried by the pressures which have been put upon me. Success is the most stultifying thing in the world and I have been dodging that sort of thing." Three months later he was more explicit about the "pressures" resulting from *The Grapes of Wrath* and "The Harvest Gypsies":

> . . . the Associated Farmers have tried to make me retract things by very sly methods. Unfortunately for them the things are thoroughly documented and the materials turned over to the La Follette Committee, and when it was killed by pressure groups all evidence went to the Attorney General. . . . They can't shoot me now because it would be too obvious and because I have placed certain informations in the hands of J. Edgar Hoover in case I take a nose dive. So I think I am personally safe enough except for automobile accidents, etc., and rape and stuff like that so I am a little careful not to go anywhere alone nor to do anything without witnesses. . . . So they have gone to the whispering campaign . . . but unfortunately that method only sells more books. I'm due to topple within the next two years but I have that little time left to me. And in many ways I'll be glad when the turn of the thing comes. As it must inevitably.

On two or three occasions he wrote of trips he was taking to escape unwelcome attentions, binding me to secrecy as to his objectives. He was unhappy when items about him appeared in Herb Caen's *San Francisco Chronicle* column and said he finally traced them to a musician who had a summer place next door. John named no names, but one of his nearest neighbors was Yehudi Menuhin. The constant publicity and "pressures" were arousing his fighting spirit. By November, 1939, he announced:

> I'm finishing off a complete revolution. It's amazing how every one piled in to regiment me, to make a symbol of me, to regulate my life and work. I've just tossed the whole thing overboard. I never let anyone interfere before and I can't see why I should now. Now as far as I know I'm absolutely free—in reason. This ultimate freedom receded. I'm keeping more of it than I need or even want, like a reservoir. The two most important [things] I suppose—at least they seem so to me—are freedom from respectability and most important—freedom from the necessity of being consistent. Lack of those two can really tie you down . . . Of course all this will die down in a very short time. In a year no one will ever have heard of me and my projected work is not likely to create any hysteria.

He was speaking of the tide-pool handbook and the realization that he lacked many of the essentials for such a study, even though he was by then a partner in Rickett's laboratory, having "bought half the stock . . . which gives me equipment, a teacher, a library to work in," but:

> . . . I find that I have no education. I have to go back to school in a way. I'm completely without mathematics and I have to learn something about abstract mathematics. I have some biology but must have much more, and the twins, bio-physics and bio-chemistry are closed to me. So I have to go back and start over. . . The world is sick now. There are things in the tide pools easier to understand than Stalinist, Hitlerite, Democrat, capitalist, confusion, and voodoo. So I'm going to those things which are relatively more lasting to find a new basic picture. . . Communist, Fascist, Democrat may find that the real origin of the future lay on the microscope plates of obscure young men who, puzzled with order and disorder in quantum and neutron, build gradually a picture which will seep down until it is the fibre of the future. . . I am quite sure that changing the rules as Stalin, Hitler, and Mussolini are doing is not effective. Systems of thought and action are as unarbitrarily mutant as any other physical change. . . The point of all this is that I must make a new

> start. I've worked the novel—I know it as far as I can take it. I never did think much of it—a clumsy vehicle at best. And I don't know the form of the new but I know there is a new which will be adequate and shaped by the new thinking.

Shortly before Pearl Harbor John visited me in my Menlo Park home, filled with apprehension about the war that he was sure we were soon to be involved in. He had been predicting it for at least two years. And he said that if by any remote chance I should get drawn into it by the draft (I was 40 years old) to let him know promptly and he would pull strings to get me into the communications section of the Signal Corps, where he expected to be. It didn't work out that way exactly. I received my draft notice in June of the next year and passed the physical examination with the help of a harried medical officer who was anxious to get away for lunch and consequently marked my heart-beat rate down from the 120 which it had consistently registered to a more reasonable 100—and I was a soldier. On receiving the "Greeting" I had written to John but got no reply, doubtless because he was off on one of his trips. Nor did I hear from him for more than two years, though I occasionally saw his name in the paper.

Not until later did I get even partial details of what he had been doing. Sent by the *New York Herald-Tribune* Syndicate in 1943 to cover the war in Europe, he mailed back a series of dispatches subsequently published as *Once There Was a War* and consisting of vignettes, episodes, and commentaries, often with repulsion and usually with intense humanity, tempered by ironic humor.[26] He traveled for a time in British torpedo boats as they raided shipping off the coast of Italy "at Garta and Genoa and over between Corsica and Sardinia." It was there that his ears were damaged, not from the big guns but from the six-inchers. He was under fire on one of the runs.

~

In 1944, after I had served in the Army, gaining a discharge when the military decided it would be happier with men thirty-seven years of age and under, Bob Cathcart, then in the Navy, gave him my address and he reestablished contact, writing somewhat apologetically from New York:

> . . . About two years ago Maryon wrote me your army address which I promptly lost and lost track of Maryon too. It has been a very long time of not writing and not hearing. During my fuss in California [his divorce from Carol] I rather purposely cut myself off because I didn't see any reason for putting a very unhappy thing on other people, and then the war came along and I got mixed up in it. You will laugh to think that for a year and a half I tried to get into the army but was blackballed for this largest club in the world. [His activities in behalf of the Spanish Loyalists may have had something to do with that.] I am very glad of it now but at the time I was very sad about it. Had I succeeded I would either have been guarding a bridge in Santa Fe or writing squibs for the Santa Ana Air Force Monitor. As it is I've had a look at the war, too much of a look I guess.

He went on to describe how a doctor had found that "both ear drums had been burst and that there are probably little vissicles [sic] burst all over my body" as a result of "a very bad pasting in Italy but oddly enough was not hit at all." His hearing was returning as the drums healed, but "the nervousness, dreams, sleeplessness, etc., have to take their own time."

By that time he had married Gwyn Conger, a radio singer to whom he had been introduced in Hollywood by Max Wagner, brother of Rob Wagner, then editor of *Hollywood Script*. They were living in a New York apartment and Gwyn was looking forward to the birth of their first child in July. After that he planned to make a picture in Mexico (probably *The Pearl*) and then move to California. He said that he had "just tossed away" the book he had been working on for several months because it "wouldn't jell," but gave no hint of the subject.

By September they were tearing up the apartment in preparation for a return to Monterey, where he had "rented two small houses down the coast—one to live in and one to work in. I've had a wonderful sense of going home but just lately I'm a little scared. There must have been a change in me and in everyone else, I'd like to settle there if I can. . . I am so looking forward to sitting on the rocks and fishing. I like that. And the little houses I've rented are right near the ocean." He was also eager to do some more work in Ed Ricketts' lab. The start of his work on the script for the Mexican picture had been postponed till October or November, and he planned to watch it being filmed in January.

He mentioned that he had completed *Cannery Row*, which was written "on four levels and people can take what they can receive out of it. One thing—it never mentions the war—not once. . . The crap I wrote overseas had a profoundly nauseating effect on me. Among other unpleasant things, modern war is the most dishonest thing imaginable." He also said, "Within a year or so I want to get to work on a very large book I've been thinking about for at least two years and a half." Obviously he meant *East of Eden*, but I had no further word of it until it appeared.

He sent me a bound set of *Cannery Row* galley proofs and I was enthusiastic about it as a highly entertaining story, but I was surprised and somewhat disappointed in its descent (as I saw it then) from the serious and idealistic level of *The Grapes*. The verdict I wrote too hastily to him was unfortunate:

> It is almost the book that I hoped you would have written when I heard the title. In its own right it is a swell book, and it is one which I enjoyed thoroughly. The thing that chiefly bothered me is the loopholes that it affords the carping coterie of critics, since it will, of course, be judged not for itself but as it fits in the Steinbeck bibliography. I'm afraid the literary Petronii will be something like this: 'The vagaries and minor felonies of brown-skinned indigents, naive, amoral, and lazy, can be entertaining, but the same formula applied to American Bums gets a little out of focus. Angels, saints, etc. forsooth—a bum is a bum and we got a war on.' Some of them will wickedly point out that you conscientiously got a couple of bad words in to assure its being banned in Boston, and sadly remark that the world marches on but Steinbeck wallows in the

same old trough. . . The wolf pack will say with extreme cleverness that Steinbeck, California white hope, has at last started to repeat himself.

Well, a good many of those predictions came true, though I failed to find anyone saying that *Cannery Row* was *Tortilla Flat* in white face, as I rather expected. And my comments apparently did not sit very well.[27] I had no reply and didn't hear from him until 1952.

During that interval I knew of him only from news stories, articles he had written for various magazines and other publications, and once in a while, reports from mutual friends. I learned of his divorce from Gwyn, which left him very bitter, as he later told me; his projects, some of which were total fabrications from the Aladdin's lamps of columnists, Hollywood and elsewhere; and his travels. It was probably a short article in the *Saturday Review* which inspired me to write him a card, care of Viking Press, and shortly afterward I got a letter dated February 25, 1952, soon after his marriage to Elaine Scott.

Surprisingly, it was hand printed in fairly large letters, which he explained by saying that he had given up typing for good, and his handwriting had become execrable to the point that everyone complained. (Of course he returned to typing and cursive script, usually with the soft lead pencils that he bought by the gross and sharpened by the dozen in preparation for his daily stint.) My card had come, he said just as he was packing to leave on a six-month European trip sponsored by *Colliers*, for whom he had contracted to write a number of articles. He was rather apologetically resigned to his departure:

. . . I have never lost the basic restlessness. Thought I would with the years but it was probably glandular all along. I still have to turn over boards. I have a beautiful little house in New York with a pretty little garden and bulbs coming up, so I run to Europe. I guess it's always going to be that way. I got my brains beaten out with a play last year [*Burning Bright*], so I'll have to do another play next year. I don't understand this. I just do it. And it is far from a bad life.

By September he and Elaine had returned from the "grand tour . . . Spain, Africa, Italy, France, Scotland, Ireland, England," and he was glad to be back. He was fifty years old now and he philosophized a little about it:

> Fifty is a good age, the hair recedes, the paunch grows a little, the face—rarely inspected—looks the same to us but not to others. The little inabilities grow so gradually that we don't even know it. My hangovers are less bad, maybe because I drink better liquor.

He also spoke of his writing:

> I do pretty much work and as always—90 per cent of it is thrown out. I cut more deeply than I used to, which means that I overwrite more than I used to. I cut 90,000 words out of my most recent book [*East of Eden*], but I think I must have put them in to be cut. I think it's a pretty good book. It was a hard one. But they're all hard. And if I want to know I'm fifty, all I have to do is look at my titles—so god-damned many of them.

In the same letter he mentioned something about which I have never since seen or heard anything further. He says he wrote a picture script "based on an early play of Ibsen's called *The Vikings at Helgeland*—not very well known—a roaring mellow [sic] drama, cluttered and verbose but with the great dramatic construction and character relationships he later cleaned up. Anyway, I shook out the clutter and I think it will make a good picture."[28]

He noted that he had three more articles to write for *Colliers* magazine to complete his agreement with them, and said:

> Then I want to learn something about plays. I've had three plays produced. Two of them were successful and I don't know a single thing about plays. . . . I've always tried to make a composite or compromise between play and short novel and only now do I know why this cannot work. I have gone about it backwards . . . I've learned that a play has to go through production. Lines have to be changed to match the incredible

> unconscious criticism of the audience. When the play is on—then you could go back and make a novelette of it. But by then you are through with your story anyway. So I've abandoned the form—for the present anyway. But I want to learn about straight plays, so I'm gong to try to plunge into that form this winter. You may look for some collosal [sic] flops. But I do maintain that gigantic stupidity that will let me try it.

He had been bitter about the irreplaceable reference library that Gwyn took ("not to read") when they were divorced. Now, he said, he was gradually accumulating

> a library of words—all dictionaries—12 vol *Oxford*, all of Menken [sic], folklore, Americanisms, dic. of slang—many—and then all books and monographs on words. I find I love words very much. And gradually I am getting a series of dictionaries of modern languages. The crazy thing about all this is that I don't use a great variety of words in my work at all. I just love them for themselves. The long and specialized words are not very interesting because they have no history and no family. But a word like claw or land or host or foist goes back and back and has relatives in all directions.

He sent me a copy of *East of Eden*, which he was sure was the best thing he ever wrote, that everything else he'd ever written was a preparation for, and that if it wasn't any good, nothing he'd ever written was any good, and asked for my honest opinion without reservations. That made comment difficult, the more so when I remembered the year or two of silence which followed my slightly tempered praise of *Cannery Row*. I praised its many virtues but remarked mildly that I had trouble believing in Cathy until the final sequences. He dealt with that problem in his reply:

> You don't believe her, many people don't. I don't know whether I believe her either but I know she exists. I don't believe in Napoleon, Joan of Arc, Jack the Ripper, and man who stands on one finger in the circus. I don't believe in Jesus Christ, Alexander the Great, Leonardo. I don't

> believe them but they exist. I don't believe them because they aren't like me. You say you only believe her at the end. Ah! But that's when, through fear she became like us. This was very carefully planned. All of the book was very carefully planned. And I'm forgetting it so soon . . .
>
> The Book—it's been capitalized in my mind for so long that it was a kind of person. And when the last line was finished that person was dead. Rewriting and cutting was like dressing a corpse for a nice funeral. Remembering the book now is like remembering Ed Ricketts. I remember nice things about both but a finished book and a dead man can never surprise you nor delight you any more. They aren't going any place.

Then he spoke of a project that never developed, or rather, that developed into something else. "Frank Loesser and I are going to make a musical comedy of *Cannery Row*." Instead, Loesser dropped out for reasons I never learned, and Rodgers and Hammerstein collaborated with John on the production in 1955 of *Pipe Dream*, with Helen Traubel as the ebullient madam of the brothel and most of the original *Cannery Row* characters in extended roles and situations.[29] In a letter of December 3, 1952, answering my comments involved, he wrote of the difficulty of transferring *Cannery Row* to the stage:

> You are right about the difficulty of transferring C.R. to the stage. I'm not going to do exactly that, I have a whole new story. It will simply be set against the old background. You know Dook—it never gets any easier. Starting a thing still brings the same helpless desolation it always did. I do believe that just the practice has made me less likely to make the old errors in form and so forth. But I have learned new errors to make. The process of writing a book is the process of outgrowing it. That is the dreadful fact. Each one is completely new. Now—criticism dwells on your mistakes—in other words critics can tell you what *not* to do. If they could they would be doing it rather than criticizing. I am just as scared now as I was 25 years ago.

Whether *Sweet Thursday* was written primarily as a book in itself or as a kind of back-formation from his plans for the play I do not know. The book appeared in 1954, more than a year before the play opened in December 1955. But in the same letter he was definitely thinking about the play and repeating some of the ideas he had expressed to me earlier about the problems of writing for the stage:

> Now I want to talk about the play. It is going to be called *The Bear Flag Café*. I am going to do it the best I can. One of my wrongnesses lay in my belief that I could write a short novel that could play from the lines. I arrived at this (naturally) without any knowledge of the theatre. I did *Mice and Men* and later *The Moon Is Down*. And I never went near production. Then I did *Burning Bright* [an experimental play panned by the critics]. This time I worked with the production, went on the road with it and I learned a very simple thing. What I had tried couldn't be done. A play is only a play after it has been through production and faced an audience. I'll bet Shakespeare worked his through production—changing to meet audience reaction. There are things you can't foresee. I had gone at it backwards. After a play has been produced—then it can be put in novel form but it can't be the other way around. . . .

Clearly, he was writing on the play with the probable intention of turning it into a novel afterward. In none of our correspondence did he mention what happened to the intended collaboration with Frank Loesser. I next heard in April 1953, that he was just back from "a number of trips" and trying to work but that "it is coming very hard." He had had his typewriter equipped with extra-large primer type because "My eyes aren't what they used to be up close," a fact that he had mentioned earlier. In November he wrote that he had a new book finished in first draft, but did not identify it. Almost certainly it was *Sweet Thursday*: ". . . I'm going to put it away for a few months. See whether it makes any difference in the rewrite. It should. I always want to rewrite them after it is too late." He expressed the desire to do some more short stories, lamenting the badness of some of his earlier ones that he had reread, and wondered whether he had learned anything. "I'm going back to Spain in the Spring. I feel an affinity there. Mexico is a kind of fake Spain. I feel related to Spanish people much more than to Anglo-Saxons. Unusual with my blood line—whatever it is. But they have kept something we seem to have lost. I don't know quite what it is."

Issuance by Viking of *The Short Novels of John Steinbeck* in 1953 gave him "a shock at the passage of time" as he looked at the list of his titles.

> . . . Lord, there are so many of them and they took so long. Recently I had an amusing lunch with six critics. They were the men who knocked each book as it came out. Reading the books over again, they said they couldn't recall why they had got so mad. Harry Hanson said the books were so different one from another it used to make him mad because he thought it was a trick. Only now he said was he conscious of the design. Well there wasn't any conscious design. I suppose what it boils down to is this—a man has only a little to say and he says it over and over so it looks like a design. And the terrible thing is that I still don't know what it is I have to say, but I do know it isn't very complicated and surely it isn't new.

The next letter came in September, 1955, and told for the first time of his out-of-town hideaway on the tip of Long Island at Sag Harbor:

> . . . We have a little shack . . . It's a whaling town or was and we have a small boat and lots of oak trees and the phone never rings. We run there whenever we need a rest—no neighbors and fish and clams and crabs and mussels right at the door step. I just got it this spring and I love it.

By the time *The Bear Flag Café* had metamorphosed under the aegis of Rodgers and Hammerstein into *Pipe Dream*, and John was actively involved in the production, although he was simultaneously working on a new book, *Pippin IV*:

> . . . it is fun. They are all painful fun while I'm doing them. I have a show in rehearsal too so I work on the book until 3 and then go to the

> theatre. It is a musical and I love to see them put it together. It's a mystery to me how they do it. The dancers and the singers and the actors. I am very much the spectator in this one. Such pretty people—such pretty girls. Remember how we used to sit in your car in Long Beach and look at girls? Well I still like that. We have some show girls who are perfectly exquisite. I'm not afraid of pretty girls any more as I once was and these kids are real warm and pleasant. And if you think they aren't smart, you're wrong. You've got to be smart to be a good show girl . . . the era of the dumb blonde is definitely over. It's going to be a very good show.

He revealed plans to cover both Presidential conventions in the following year—never having seen a national convention—while reporting primarily for the *Louisville Courier Journal* but also doing some pieces for the *Reporter.* His contract with *Colliers* was finished, but I had noticed that he was still being listed in their promotion material as a contributor and mentioned it to him, which brought him an apology from the "deeply embarrassed" top management and a promise that the use of his name, to which they had had no right for two years, would be stopped immediately. He also told me that he had been having fun doing some little pieces for *Punch*—"real crazy ones but the English seem to like them."

In October he wrote about dogs, including Charlie, his most famous one:

> Do you still have a dog? We have two—an ancient cocker bitch—a spinster, mean and crotchety and old—very like my grandmother, and a gay young big poodle who thinks of himself as one hell of a guy. I bought him for Elaine in Paris. He has been trained in French. The feeding plan that came with him was wonderful—everything had to be *bien sucre*, but the drinking habits were the best—weak tea or wine and water. I named him the worst pun in the world—Charles le Chien, le Policier de Paris. He is known as Charley. Dogs are spoken to in the second person and my second person is notably weak. We moved him over to English by combining words, *Couche-toi* became *Couche it down. Assez-toi-Assit. Fais le beau—hands.* It worked but he was eleven months

old when we got him and if you want quick obedience you have to do it in French. I guess he is still translating and my French is lousy as always. A beautiful accent but no vocabulary.

In my reply, I answered his questions about my dog Ichabod, and that inspired him to give further details about his canine menage.

. . . I particularly liked your dog and your attitude toward him. We have now a big poodle and an ancient spayed cocker, as ugly-tempered an old virgin as I have ever met in human skin. Selfish and self-centered, with all her impulses which might normally have gone to pupping, all turned into an appetite for food. A swine in every direction. I would very gladly take her out and shoot her, but it seems we owe this monster a debt of gratitude because once she was company to Elaine's daughter many years ago. The dog feels no loyalty of any kind except to the person who has anything in the world she can eat, and she can eat anything. And the daughter has long ago lost interest. But we've got to keep this mean and evil sausage around until she succumbs to fatty degeneration of the heart muscles. The poodle is a gay and humorous person and I love him very much. . . .

He went on to tell of his plans to go to England in the following February, where he hoped, among other things, to acquire a white "triangular-eyed English bull terrier," a kind of dog he had never owned but always wanted. He planned to "find a good bitch and have her bred to a fine dog and bring her back." He even offered me one of the hypothetical offspring. I demurred, chiefly on the grounds that a dog of such aristocratic ancestry would produce an inferiority complex in my aging Australian shepherd (plus some undetermined genes) and in me. He did return with such a dog, but a handsome male whom he named Angel Biddle Duke and was very proud of.

In November he wrote of the progress of *Pipe Dream*, still with excitement but with some disappointment:

We opened the show a week and a half ago in New Haven and it was lousy. But the audiences don't know it is lousy. Anyway we are gradually

> cutting, changing, and adding and I think now it is a little better. We moved to Boston last Sunday and will be here three and a half more weeks. I am going to stay until all the changes have been made and then go home to New York. It still is pretty bad but do you know we are sold out solid here and tickets are being scalped for a hundred dollars apiece. And we are going into New York with over a million dollar advance. This is absolutely crazy. The show isn't anywhere near that good. I only hope it is much better than it is now by the time we go in. It is my first experience with a musical and it is really nuts. All those pretty girls and the pairing off and the scandals and the fights. It is a complete and self-sufficient world. On the road morals disappear completely and it is all very gay and shrill. I love the company. I really adore them and it is all unreal as hell and I am never going to do it again. But I must say I am glad to see it once.

In July, 1956, he was looking toward his contract coverage of both conventions in about a month but was currently involved in the wedding of Elaine's daughter, which he described as "only slightly less lavish than the Aquacade." Meanwhile he was "trying to make an August deadline with a new little book," *Pippin IV.* His political column was to be called "On Both Your Houses" and he said he would be filing for thirty papers. He mentioned that he had had "a bare-knuckle affair with ospreys" at his Sag Harbor retreat and was writing the story, which "in essence is true, but I got so fascinated with the character of the man supposedly writing the story and his attitudes and the planting of evidences of his background and erudition and lack of it, that the whole thing will only be true in essence." The story eventually appeared March, 1957, in *Holiday.*

I don't know what happened during his covering of the San Francisco convention, but he did not manage to get down the Peninsula to visit me as he had promised. Not only did he have to cope with Republicans and newsmen, but there were innumerable Bay Area friends and relatives.

There was another major gap in correspondence—John and Elaine were traveling extensively and he was constantly beset with mountains of mail to a point that attempts to answer it were hopeless, especially when he was trying to work on his own material over handicaps of health, which included failing eyesight and back trouble among other ailments. There was also something in 1959 which he describes in a later letter as "the light tap on the shoulder." It was, I learned later, a slight premonitory heart attack.

A coincidence started the correspondence again. My sister, Marion Adams, wrote a note to him praising one of his articles that she had just read, and he replied to her with a long and retrospective letter, chiefly about me and his analysis of the things that had caused us to drift apart:

> I think I know the beginning of the break between Dook and me, the point from which no return was possible. It was due to a stupidity of mine, but I have been guilty of many. I'll tell you about it. I don't think I've ever told anyone else because of a flood of shame at my own lack of sensitiveness.
>
> There were the years of the rejected work and the published books that were financial flops and they went on so long that they became the normal life. Then without warning my books began to sell and money began to come in. It scared the hell out of me because there was not and is not any payment that relates to the work in a book. So I gave the money away in all directions. And then I got my ill-conceived plan, and I worked it out in detail by myself. Dook was to go on with his formal education—Oxford or Cambridge for a Masters and the University of London for his doctorate. It seemed so simply. I had the money. It didn't seem to be my money. Dook was broke. He was academic material and I wasn't. Well, I took the finished plan to him stupidly thinking he would be glad. His rage was cold and fierce. I see it now and I see why now. But I swear to you I had no feeling of charity, only of sharing. And a coldness set in that has never been overcome. Oh! I see how he felt. From my misguided impulse both of us got hurt feelings and suspicions. He felt insulted and I felt slapped down. And there were no words for either of us for the truth. And by the time we were ready for truth, the drift had taken place and you can't do anything about drift. Since then I've learned what a dreadful weapon or tool money is, but then I'd had

> no experience with it. It was bright stuff and I wanted to spread it around, overlooking the brighter stuff of human feelings. Isn't it remarkable how suspect good intentions must be? If I had to do it again, I think I would still find the plan good and valid but perhaps I will have learned the technique of giving without wounding. Of course Dook had the much harder row—that of receiving and he wasn't any more prepared for receiving than I was for giving. It seems to me a little sad that we are only prepared to live at about the time of leaving life. Now I don't think I ever told that to a soul before because I was ashamed and when one is ashamed, he builds a wall of defenses and justifications. And on such small ineptnesses and accidents lives are changed and destinies directed.

It was three years—October 24, 1959—before I heard from him again, and then only after a letter from me had chased him around and finally caught him in New York after his return from an idyllic six months "near a little town named Bruton in Somerset," where he and Elaine had rented a tiny stone cottage that in the *Domesday Book*: "I have never known such a time of peace. There was time to think and to read and to wander. I went up to the hill forts and dug about, talked to people, slept enormously. . . . "

So it is that I would greatly prefer to die in the middle of a sentence in the middle of a book and so leave it as all life must be—unfinished. That's the law, the great law.

—John Steinbeck, 12 June 1961

Epilogue:

Atque Vale

Late in 1959 John, Elaine, and the two boys left aboard the SS *Rotterdam* along with an Irish tutor so that the boys' school work could go on while they all took a leisurely trip around the world, visiting historic sites.[30] He wrote that "Geography doesn't mean much until you've moved over it and one bicycle trip along Hadrian's wall makes you know the Roman Empire as you never could otherwise. . . . I don't think anyone can be a snob after Israel and India, and anyone who doesn't respond to Greece and Crete and Egypt is crippled emotionally. And we'll hear the music of the world, and about music both boys are passionate. . . One thing I insist on is that we don't move constantly. Here and there we will sit down for a week or a month. . . At the end of a year I think I will have carved very deeply in them the one thing I truly believe—that all that is is holy, with its subhead—a penny has two sides.

The real coincidence was that my sister, too, was planning a trip to Europe, and she too had reservations on the Rotterdam for the same sailing date. So they became shipmates, and she saw John for the first time in many years and met Elaine and the boys, with all of whom she had further contacts after they had disembarked. But John's careful plans were disrupted before they really got under way. He became ill while they were still in Europe, perhaps from the same ailment that had brought the "tap on the shoulder," and they returned to New York. In the letter to Marion before they started, John had written:

> . . . I've had a good, full, painful life. I've thoroughly enjoyed my work. I believe that is one of the critical charges leveled against me. I've tried to write the truth as I saw it and I have not held on to a truth when it became false. When the tap came, I was ready—too ready—even anxious. But on inspection this seemed wrong to me and I closed that door and I can't ever open it again. And it hasn't seemed long, but sometimes it seems endless. And then the radishes came up and there are baby rabbits on the lawn and a small delighted conceit becomes the sound of a book and the whole world is fresh and new and wonderful again. So if there is any overtone of regret in this letter, ignore it. I regret my stupidities but only as I might regret my big ears and shapeless nose. They are all a part of me and I could no more cut off my stupidities than my nose to spite my face.

~

In September, 1962, he was notified that he would be awarded the Nobel Prize for Literature, and I sent him a card which started: "I suppose it was really almost forty years ago that a guy moved in with me and told me, 'I want to be the best writer in the world. . ." He replied,

> I've learned a few things since. I would say now that I want to *try* to be the best writer in the world. That's a very different thing. In our base-

ment room in Encina I didn't know the tendency of horizons to jump back as you move toward them. And I didn't know that the tired farther you go, the farther there is to go. But these are the realities. This prize business is only different from the Lettuce Queen of Salinas in degree. Basically it's the same thing. There's no sadness in this. It's a kind of a joke. The sad thing would be to believe it.

In a subsequent letter, started September 28 but not mailed in a sectionally augmented form till December 1, he meditated on the meaning of the award and what it had already done to him.

. . . I have been answering about a hundred and fifty letters a day—all written by well-meaning and flattering people and all requiring an answer. I have achieved a soapy style all sweetness and gratitude. Of course a great many people want something, school girls want me to do their term papers or think to flatter me by asking "interesting" questions. The whole thing is incredible. Of course it is tapering off now and will soon disappear. . . The award in some way has gathered to itself a mystique and I don't know how. What it is is a money prize awarded geographically and sometimes politically. The Swedish Academy of 17 members lays the finger on and presto—everything is changed. . . I've always been afraid of it because of what it does to people. For one thing I don't remember anyone doing any work after getting it save maybe Shaw. This last book of Faulkner's was written long ago. Hemingway went into a kind of hysterical haze. Red Lewis just collapsed into alcoholism and angers. It has in effect amounted to an epitaph. Maybe I'm being optimistic but I wouldn't have accepted it if I hadn't thought I could beat the rap. I have more work to do and I intend to do it. I discover to my horror that everyone expects me to stop working and make a career of the prize—lectures, dinners, honorary degrees. I even had a letter from the President of Stanford. It is just generally considered that I am finished and have become an ornament. I am offered honors all over the place. Now you know damned well, Dook, that an honor is wonderful the first time, pleasant the second, but along about the fifth honor, it gets to be a goddamned nuisance.

With the letter he sent me a tentative version of the speech he would make in Stockholm—"the first and last of my life," asking me to let no one see it until he delivered it December 10.[31] Always before, winners of the Nobel and other major literary honors were given extensive treatment or reasonable attention at the very least. But although the award was announced fully in the press and on radio and television, with special articles in almost every magazine of literary, cultural, or news presentation, not a word of the award appeared in *Saturday Review*, nor did his name appear in any context other than in the masthead for many months.

John later told me that he had stopped contributing after an argument (with whom he did not say) over some drastic editing on one of his pieces, but I never learned the real explanation.

And when John died, the magazine made no mention of his demise until almost two months later, which was just three months before his death. These things are puzzling.[32] In January he was still suffering from the side effects of the award but wrote with some excitement about getting ready to start work on the Arthurian myth, which had been of lifelong interest to him and on which he had already labored, apparently without feeling that he was making the proper approach. I believe, indeed, that at the time when T. H. White's *The Once and Future King* appeared and became a bestseller, to be followed by the stage success of *Camelot*, partly founded on it, John had a treatment of the legend that was almost ready for publication. If so, it was withdrawn and laid aside, though periodically he mentioned it as a continuing project. Now he spoke of accumulating a "library second to very few on the middle ages," with Caxton Malory, the Winchester Malory, Dugdale, both the antiquities and the other. And the Kings' rolls of the period all on microfilm" He said he had "read so much middle English that I can write it as well as modern." And he enclosed a dedication of the book-to-be to his sister Mary, all in Middle English vernacular and spelling, which he had had "emblazoned by the best man living in England . . . beautiful with the names in red."

His sister, Mary Dekker, died January 23, 1965, and in April of that year he wrote:

> Well finally I am ready for the Arthur. It was to have been Sir Mary's [she was described that way in the dedication] book and she had to die to get me to start it. I have to before she fades. And by that I mean before I fade. Sir Mary is permanent now. But I'm not and so I must get it to her . . . Do you know, I couldn't find an approach to get into it until she died. And it's so very simple. I wonder why it escaped me for so long . . . And now I'm aching to get to it.

I can remember only one later reference to the book, and that was an oblique one which happened with reference to a dinner given by Adlai Stevenson for the visiting Algerian leader, Ahmed Ben Bella, who spoke only French. John said that Stevenson called him over and asked him to "explain the Arthurian Cycle to our honored guest." John tried, in his "barbarous French," while Ben Bella's eyes grew more and more puzzled and suspicious, and Stevenson leaned back and thoroughly enjoyed himself, every once in a while feeding John a French word he couldn't place."

The last time I saw John was in November, 1964. He wrote that he would attend a family gathering at the home of his sister Esther (Mrs. C. J. Rodgers) in Watsonville at Thanksgiving. Twenty-three relatives would be there, and he assured me I would be welcome if I wanted to come. I replied that to be an outsider in a family convocation of that size would be uncomfortable for me and probably for the others as well. Instead, after he had arrived he borrowed a car and with Elaine, whom I had never met, drove the hundred-odd miles to my Los Altos Hills home, where we spent a pleasant afternoon reminiscing, exchanging information, and getting acquainted again. It was all too brief for the many things we had to say. I was charmed with Elaine, with whom I felt no strangeness. And I had no inkling as they departed that I would never see John again.

We continued to correspond, though his various illnesses and trips abroad made our communication irregular. In July of 1963 he had needed surgery for a detached retina, after which he was kept in darkness for a while and his secretary and wife answered letters until his eyes were well enough to let him leave with Elaine on an Iron Curtain journey for the State Department. His knee, injured in college, I believe, gave him periodic trouble, and there had been that prodromal "tap on the shoulder." He produced *America and Americans* and a number of magazine articles but no more novels. He worked on the Arthurian book, saying prophetically of it, "Sometimes I think this might be that Life Work that never gets done. I have worked for years on the preparation for it and I can't see that I have got much of anywhere." He boasted of a new typewriter with eight instantly interchangeable type faces, all of which he gleefully illustrated in one letter with commentary on the essential character and overtones of each. He wrote of some of the cars he'd had—a Continental of such sturdy materials that it was undamaged in a collision which almost bisected the car he hit; two Cadillacs, and a Jaguar XK120, which got the sports pitch out of his system; a Mustang; a Land Rover for use on the beach at Sag Harbor in the summer, given him by the manufacturer in return for copy he'd written for the firm; and a Rover 3 litre.

There were deaths: Pat Covici, "Gov." Adlai Stevenson, Tal Lovejoy, who died from a fall, and her husband "Ritch," who preceded her. Of Covici he said that he now hated to go to the Viking office, "not because he wouldn't be there but because he would." And when Stevenson died, "leaving us with that sort of hollow grey feeling in the pit of the stomach," they went with President Johnson to the funeral in Bloomington after having been invited to Camp David, where Billy Graham and Justice Goldberg were among the other guests.

He wrote of the swimming pool he gave Elaine for a birthday present ("It couldn't be a secret"); of making things like his first completely satisfactory typing table, constructed from an old screw-type piano stool; his work cottage that he built at Sag Harbor, octagonal in shape with windows on every side and purposely too small to be used as a guest house; of Angel Biddle Duke, the handsome English bullterrier of aristocratic lineage, who never barked and shunned fights with other dogs, subduing them with one warning glance. He was delighted with a Polaroid camera someone gave him and sent me a number of photographs taken with it, thereby proving his assertion of being "the world's worst photographer." He marveled at seeing snowflakes borne upward by air currents as he looked out over the city from the window of his high apartment; and he related how he had to shoot snapping turtles in his garden at the upper tip of Long Island because they killed his baby ducks.

There were episodes, amusing encounters such as the one where a drunk insisted that John was Nick Kenney, popular newspaper versifier, becoming angry at his denials and then denouncing him for posing as Kenney! There was the handyman who he was sure would bore him with interminable questions or folksy confidences, but who instead spoke hardly a word until John blurted out the answers to all the questions he expected to be asked. He would apologize for breaks in letters, explaining that a "person from Porlock" had caused them mentioned that on one of his trips to England he had made a special visit to Porlock merely to see the village itself.

I had no word from him during his visit to Viet Nam and saw only a few of the dispatches which stirred up rancor in some people, including individuals who had been among his enthusiasts, nor do I know what his actual feelings were about our tragic involvement there. I refused to believe some of the views ascribed to him.

Then, late in October, 1967, Elaine wrote the details of the long and intensely painful operation to perform a spinal fusion almost simultaneously with his son John's argument with the law over loud parties and charges of marijuana possession. She said, "It's a good thing he's tough or Johnny's mess with its superbly cruel timing would have been too much." He did survive, and a few weeks later he was learning to walk again and starting swimming-pool therapy. By the next March he was hoping his back would improve enough to enable a trip to Tanganyika [Tanzania] "to see the animals—not to shoot them or even photograph them but just to look at them." He never made it.

John Steinbeck died December 20, 1968, after a succession of heart attacks, but he did it in his own apartment with Elaine as the only nurse during the final few days. She said, "He didn't want to die [but] he died splendidly." There was a simple funeral at St. James Church near where they had lived, with "old and dear friends around and many a friend reader." Henry Fonda read poetry that she had chosen. She and his son Thom, on home-leave from Viet Nam, took his ashes to Pacific Grove on Christmas Eve, and his sisters arranged a little service, just the family, on Point Lobos overlooking Whalers' Bay—a spot John and Mary especially loved. "It was heart-breakingly touching, an otter playing in the bay and the gulls flying over. And now he is buried with his ancestors in the Salinas Cemetery under an old oak—with the lettuce fields all around and Fremont's Peak looking down."

Now it is a friendship in memory. It is one that has been a major influence on my life—for the good, both in providing me with confidence and a companion whom I could love and respect.

C. A. S.
Woodside, CA

ENDNOTES

Introduction

1 Carlton A. Sheffield, *Steinbeck, the Good Companion*, ed. Richard Blum (Portola Valley, CA: American Lives Endowment, 1983), to which all references here pertain. Sheffield also wrote an introduction to the Steinbeck–Elizabeth Otis letters in 1978 (see Shafsky and Riggs in Works Cited). Two Elizabeths matter to Steinbeck's life: Elizabeth Otis of McIntosh & Otis was an early believer in Steinbeck's great talent as a writer and worked for him as a friend as much as his literary representative for forty years. Elizabeth Anderson, who wrote under pseudonyms of John Breck or John Barton (or E. C. A. Smith and Elizabeth Smith), was a brilliant, liberated woman from the Midwest who ran a household of bohemians, including Steinbeck's bug-infested, shed-like attachment the "Sphincter." Anderson's daughter, Polly Smith, was as independent as her mother; she had been arrested for smoking in public in downtown Palo Alto and flying solo over Stanford football games in an unsafe plane without flying lessons. In one of the strangest acts of John Steinbeck's life, in a drunken, lust-fueled rage, he dangled the teenaged Lolita out of a two-storey window after she refused his advances (See Note 6).

2 Jackson Benson's outstanding biography was preceded by Thomas Kiernan's The Intricate Music (Boston: Little, 1979) and Sheffield had much to say about this in the Blum edition. Kiernan's antipathy to Steinbeck the man is openly avowed repugnance: Steinbeck, he claims, is "pompous," "literarily hostile," full of "vindictiveness and petty intolerance" (ix). Kiernan's eagerness to pick Steinbeck's brain in the later interview is clearly suggestive of his own desire to psychoanalyze the writer's motives, to which he will later impute an obsessive loneliness that Steinbeck's life belied; Sheffield, commenting on Kiernan in the Blum edition, was indignant: "[His biography presents] a mass of misinterpretation and distortion. The very plethora of incident, quotation, and localized description, along with the lack of attribution . . . may cause incredulity and dismay in some of those who knew Steinbeck well" (qtd. in Sheffield 12). There is Steinbeck's view of himself, writing in a letter to filmmaker John Huston in one of the letters collected by Elaine Steinbeck and Robert Wallsten on March 2, 1965 (hereafter Steinbeck: Letters): "I'm a guy with lots of friends, good friends" (812).

3 Giambattista Vico (1668—1744), a religious humanist and professor of rhetoric at the University of Naples, who reacted against the Cartesian analytic movement. There is, he wrote, a field of knowledge beyond what we make for ourselves and know from within. "Human history did not consist merely of things . . . ; it was the story of human activities, what men did and thought and suffered, of what they strove for, aimed at, accepted, rejected, conceived, imagined, of what their feelings were directed at" (Isaiah Berlin, *Against the Current*, ed. Henry Hardy, introd. Roger Hausheer (New York: Viking, 1980) 95).

4 Blum is not alone in lamenting the loss of these letters from this "inadequately documented period" of Steinbeck's life. However, his opinion is worth hearing (syntactical filler provided in italics): "My guess, worth nothing but as speculator, is not so much that JS [John Steinbeck] had spoken of great exploits in the whorehouses (which Dook did speak *and* brag of), nor in the bars (*Dook* also *did* this) but of self-criticism. Dook, who was himself quite self-demeaning, . . . would likely in a true and great friend provoke a reassuring 'me too' self-confession of a similar sort that, *when* offered in a compassionate and reassuring way, would also set forth one's worst and most hated self." One further comment regarding the Steinbeck's boon companion of his reckless youth: Sheffield had become chaste in later life owing to his impotence and could no longer tolerate alcohol. Blum adds a wry comment on this aspect of Dook's self-effacement: "Sheff had always been the kind of man to wear three rubbers to the whorehouse. Even then Sheff would be the one standing around outside drinking bootleg beer!"

Preface to the Reader

1 Harry Thornton Moore, *The Novels of John Steinbeck*, 2nd ed. (Port Washington, NY: Kennikat, 1968). The English title of the first edition is *John Steinbeck and His Novels: An Appreciation* (London: Heinemann, 1939). In the foreword to the second edition of this volume, Moore claims to be embarrassed by his "verbal clumsiness" of parts belonging to 1939, but not apparently his analytical judgments of Steinbeck's work before *Grapes of Wrath*. Moore adds an egregious "Contemporary Epilogue" to his early and superficial "appreciation," lowering further still his estimation of Steinbeck in the novels after *Grapes*: "We can perform a service to our culture . . . by not overrating the work of this man of goodwill who is sometimes a competent novelist, though never 'great'" (106). Moore's own service to culture is of course the academic's harmless battening upon a greater host—in his case, D. H. Lawrence and J. D. Salinger providing most of the sustenance. In any event, he need not have feared for his other subject's reputation. (See Appendix A for a list of Steinbeck's fiction with reprint dates.)

2 Elaine Steinbeck, and Robert Wallsten, eds. *Steinbeck: A Life in Letters* (New York: Viking, 1975). All letters or portions of letters published here are found in other works, principally in the collected letters edited by Steinbeck and Wallsten and the Steinbeck-Covici letters edited by Thomas Fensch. The University of Texas' Humanities Research Center in Austin, TX, purchased the latter, whereas the Steinbeck archive of Stanford Libraries holds originals of the letters to Sheffield.

3 Peter Lisca, *The Wide World of John Steinbeck* (New Brunswick, NJ: Rutgers UP, 1958). Lisca authored three more books of biography and criticism on Steinbeck.

4 E. W. Tedlock, Jr., and C. V. Wicker, *Steinbeck and His Critics* (Albuquerque: U of New Mexico P, 1957).

5 Joseph E. Fontenrose, *John Steinbeck* (New York: Barnes, 1963).

6 Jackson J. Benson, *The True Adventures of John Steinbeck* (New York: Viking, 1984). Benson's biography contains many letters that are not found in the "edited" collection of Steinbeck and Wallsten. He records the Polly Smith incident in Note 1 on pp. 136–37.

7 Nelson Valjean, *John Steinbeck* (San Francisco: Chronicle, 1975). Valjean in 1971 uncovered Stanford records indicating that a poor scholastic standing, rather than a shattered love affair, caused Steinbeck's sudden departure "for China" (p. 6). He found a dean's warning that Steinbeck's registration was to be suspended or canceled. Steinbeck never gave Sheffield, or anyone else, an explanation.

8 Sheffield's *Note* from the American Lives publication in 1983 modestly acknowledges assistance to scholars and biographers seeking information on Steinbeck besides Steinbeck and Wallsten. The Steinbeck-Sheffield letters were made available and later donated or sold to Stanford and are, as he modestly avers, an integral part of his own memoir. Furthermore, some portions of that ms. were taped by Spyglass Productions, Inc. of Monterey, CA as part of the "Friends of John Steinbeck" series (Sheffield 19). (See Hossick and Le Bris bibliographic entries for two recent videorecordings of Steinbeck with both black & white and color sequences, but a caveat on the co-production by Gedeon/France 3 and its "new" interpretation of Steinbeck's work: this is the same country responsible for Jacques Derrida and Michel Foucault.)

Letter to Jawn from Dook

1 A portion of the letter referred to is reprinted from Fensch's *Steinbeck and Covici* and dates from December 6, 1948:

> . . . Duke Sheffield was down last weekend. He has not changed. His is a very little mind. I had forgotten how small. He is still picking at pronunciations and grammatical excellences. In many ways he has the qualities of a mediaeval schoolman. And he does not change [sic] only it seems to me that his horizons have narrowed. I find that I don't like him. Perhaps I never did. . . . (93)

It must, indeed, have been a stunning blow to come upon this seeming betrayal so abruptly, but a sidenote on the psychodynamics of this friendship is offered by Blum. What matters is this, as *Steinbeck: Letters* notes:

"Carlton A. Sheffield, variously called 'Duke,' 'Dook,' 'Juk,' or even 'Jook' . . . is Steinbeck's closest male friend . . . and is his only correspondent who appears throughout this book . . . (9–10). On the nickname, Blum writes: "Note again Sheff hated being called 'Dook' by JS, that JS continually so called him [or] was at least indifferent [about it, which fact of their relationship implies] a commentary on power and disdain of 'who the hell are you to say what I call you' . . ."

2 Steinbeck's early anti-Semitism has not proved fodder for the archly sensitive revisionists who have taken Faulkner and Hemingway to task for similar utterances; there is, of course, a case for Steinbeck's having the reflexive prejudice of his generation. He first referred to playwright George S. Kaufman, anxious to purchase stage rights to *Of Mice and Men* as "wiseacre New York Jew" (qtd. in Kiernan 222). When the Reverend L. M. Birkhead, mouthpiece for a patriotic organization called Friends of Democracy, wrote Steinbeck to query the author's ethnic origin in the wake of sharp attacks against *Grapes of Wrath* as Anti-American or, worse, Jewish propaganda, Steinbeck wrote back "with a good deal of sadness": "It does not seem important to me whether I am Jewish or not" (*Steinbeck: Letters* 203–04; Parini 236; Benson 420). An exchange of letters between Birkhead and Steinbeck was published in 1940 and in September of 1940, rpt. and retitled *A Letter Written in Reply.* As a writer of war dispatches during the invasion of Italy, whose eardrums had burst while witnessing the shelling of the Salerno beachhead in 1943, he expressed profound compassion for the suffering incurred by Nazi Germany's victims, and during the time of America's strife with civil rights, while composing his travel memoirs, he witnessed and wrote with disgust of the vileness of racial animosity toward blacks—for example, in "Atque Vale" about whites' hypocritical and unrealistic expectations of "Negroes."

Memoir

1 Ella Winter, "Sketching the Author of 'Tortilla Flat,'" *San Francisco Chronicle* 2 June 1935, sec. D: 4.

2 *The Wrath of John Steinbeck* (Los Angeles: Albertson, 1939). The 1975 rpt. includes Lawrence C. Powell's foreword.

3 Steinbeck at least once parodied in a letter his friend's effort at free verse, ignoring his own poor efforts. Minor poet Herbert Carruth's English 35 course elicited a number of bad poems from both students. Sheffield, however, kept up his poetry writing throughout his life, and Blum's edition includes a sampling which shows a later preference for the epigram over free verse:

> All men have hangups, it is said;
> I can tell mine in a minute:
> I hate to see an unmade bed
> or an unmade woman in it.
>
> I love sweet, sexy, stupid Trish;
> Her body language is commanding;
> her talk, alas, is gibberish—
> She's the peace that passeth understanding.
>
> If you think that the Lord is ignoring your lot,
> That He pays you no notice at all,
> One course you can try to gain favor on high—
> Just make like a sparrow, and fall.
>
> But that was written long ago;
> By Time I've been betrayed;
> And now it's comforting to know
> At least my bed gets made.
>
> The hand of God is vast and stern
> Escape it if you can;
> But pity all who chance to fall
> Into the hand of man.

"How do men act in a cat house?"
Asked a girl of her working friend, Flo.
And Flo, with a grin just suggestive of sin,
Said, "Baby, they come—and go."

Sheffield also notes that the final assignment for Professor Carruth's class was a sonnet and includes the "tortured" Steinbeckian product that resulted:

To Death—and Life

A little era of discordant days,
And then an endless line of thoughtless peace.
Come, Lily Death, and break my bonds; release
Me from this shallow hole; oh! Let me raise
My head above the rim. What piercing maze
Of stars are there? Where do the heavens cease?
I see five specks and such a little piece
Of everything. Anticipation flays
Me with desire, yet Nature shelters me.
Above may be a stealthy, gripping cold,
That hideously sinks into the breast
Of such a worm as I. No if I be
A worm, I'll burrow deep within the mold.
Go, loathsome Death. 'Tis here I find my rest. (qtd. in Sheffield 35)

Steinbeck once presented a copy of a sonnet to Sheffield's mother, and she copied an untitled bit of blank verse that he showed her on June 7, 1923:

I am not any less nor more a fool
Than sturdy Atlas, bearer of the skies;
Nor would I any less than he forego
The heavy heavens for the precious fruit
Of Greek Hesperides or mortal earth.
As life is short, so are the planets high

But life is real, concrete and tangible,
While blazing planets which we see tonight
May not have graced our solar universe
For thirty thousand times a thousand years.
So give me life with all its petty thoughts
Of Spring, and benches and a glowing moon.
Aye, rather give me one short hour of joy
In worldly things, than pious, carking days
Of contemplation of an after-life.
And when the moment comes when I must die
I shall then be afraid like other men,
But fear shall not have dogged my other days,
Been fell companion of my every thought—
I shall have really lived, not hoped to live.

4 Joseph H. Jackson, ed. and introd., *The Short Novels of John Steinbeck* (New York: Viking, 1953). Jackson refers to Chapter 20 as one of the great examples of the "yarn-spinning" of Western-American literature, but does not allude to Steinbeck's letter to him in August 1944, in which Steinbeck claimed "several layers of understanding are possible" for *Cannery Row*. Steinbeck later told Sheffield there were exactly four (qtd. in Simmonds 224).

5 Jeffery Farnol (1878–1952). The author's wild popularity with romances and buccaneer tales like *The Broad Highway* (London: Marston, 1910) lasted into the twenties (*Black Bartlemy*, Boston: Little, 1920).

6 James Branch Cabell (1879–1958) *Jurgen: A Comedy of Justice* (New York: McBride, 1919); Donn Byrne (1889–1928) *Blind Raftery and His Wife Hilaria* (New York: Century, 1924) and *Messer Marco Polo* (New York: Century, 1921). Sheffield admired Branch Cabell's rococo allure, but worse, Donn Byrne's "wistful Celticism" and "subtly Gaelic twisting of phrase and overtones of brogue."

7 Steinbeck's reticence toward Hemingway is genuine, for Steinbeck rarely spoke of serious rivals in his letters. Although he had spoken freely of his admiration for the early Hemingway, Steinbeck later retracted those feelings and replaced them with spite. Benson describes a memorable meeting at Costello's in New York that gave Steinbeck a firsthand glimpse of Papa's boorish behavior when Hemingway shattered a blackthorn walking stick over his own head, a gift from Steinbeck to John O'Hara (547–49).

8 Mary Ardath is noted by both Parini and Benson as a *Greenwich Village Follies* chorine, not an aspiring concert pianist. According to Benson, she deserted her banker husband and showed up at a campground off the Pacific Coast highway where Steinbeck and his first wife Carol were staying; the Sheffields were living in Palo Alto, hosting the Steinbecks on weekends, and Sheffield was working on his master's degree at Stanford. Benson writes that she showed up with her little girl, apparently hoping to rekindle the romance with Steinbeck (157). *Steinbeck: Letters* refers to Ardath as a "statuesque beauty," confirms the Benson version, but claims "children in tow" (93).

9 Sheffield is kind to the memory of Ruth, his former wife, who had spent time in mental institutions before her suicide. The letter's passionate excess makes it an extraordinary letter, even though JS frequently struck a romantic pose. Brian St. Pierre dismisses it as a "snotty and vindictive . . . parody of male bonding" (34). Jay Parini, however, claims that Ruth [Carpenter Sheffield] believed Steinbeck "had tried to discourage Dook from getting married" (59). The complete letter is found on pp. 126–27 of the Blum edition and 12–14 of *Steinbeck: Letters*. It is dated from Gramercy Park, New York City, and dated between June and July 1926.

10 George Borrow (1803–81), *Wild Wales: Its People, Language, and Scenery* (London: Murray's; New York: Putnam's, 1906). Borrow was a self-taught, brilliant hack writer and novelist, a major figure of the naturalistic school.

11 Sea *of Cortez*, John Steinbeck and Edward F. Ricketts, 1941; rpt. Mamaroneck, NY: Appel, 1971) 54.

12 *Midsummernight* (New York: Farrar, 1930). Sheffield notes that the book had "almost no sale" (Sheffield 36).

13 Neither Benson nor Parini can confirm Sheffield's speculation about the lost mss. of this period. Without speculating, Parini notes that Steinbeck was one of those literary "burners" (Steinbeck had told George Albee that he burned between 60 and seventy stories and quotes a portion of a letter from Steinbeck to Kate Beswick from this period): "It's exhilarating to get rid of old work. I am writing so well now [*The Pastures of Heaven* would come out in November of 1932] that I don't want the old stories around. They are terrible reminders of where I've come from . . ." (qtd. in Parini 125). Benson suggests that the ms. of "Dissonant Symphonies" and an unnamed novel did indeed go up in smoke (200). Assuming Sheffield is correct that portions of the ms. exist, Stanford Archives or the University of Texas at Austin's Harry Ransom Center for Humanities Research are the leading repositories of Steinbeck papers and letters. John Hooper, Director of the National Steinbeck Center in Salinas, maintains Steinbeck papers acquired from the Salinas Public Library and affirms the possibility of its existence and the likelihood of portions of the mss. from this period being blent into the tales of *Pastures of Heaven* (Telephone interview, 16 Nov. 1999). According to Tara Wenger, Research Librarian at Texas, "We have nothing in our collection entitled "Dissonant Symphonies."

14 Sheffield's clinical synopsis of the ledger's contents belies the enormous importance of his gift from Steinbeck. Although *To a God Unknown* is 1933, the date of Dook's *Ledger* is less critical than the fact that Steinbeck had one person in mind during the creative process; this was, as biographers have noted, a real "crossroads" for Steinbeck the artist. From now on, says Benson, he wrote with a single person in mind. "Steinbeck's work could have gone in any one of several directions" (200). Not only did Sheffield open his house and larder to the struggling writer but he lent his persona to Steinbeck for what is retrospectively considered Steinbeck's most important creative breakthrough. In contrast to the letter to Sheffield's wife Ruth, professing a chest-thumping friendship of soulmates, the dedication is a seasoned statement of a mature artist.

15 Sheffield adds that, though "Discovery" is indexed and presumably refers to the opening episode in which the valley is discovered, it is not present in the volume and might have been written on pages 99–102, which have been cut out of the book. No text or mention of the brief concluding episode of the published book, in which a busload of tourists passes the valley and comments on it. Presumably this was added to round off the story, perhaps at the suggestion of the editors. The index contains only two other items: "Unnamed Narrative . . ." p. 119 and "new Novel. . . p. 123." The former runs for a scant three pages and peters out in the middle of a sentence; and the "new novel," *To a God Unknown*, fills the book to page 160."

16 The so-called "Phalanx Theory" letter appears in *Steinbeck: Letters* (74–76) with some deletions. I have followed Steinbeck and Wallsten's paragraph divisions.

17 Richard Astro is acknowledged to be the most informed critic on Steinbeck's "teleological" thinking, but it is the influence of Ed Rickets, more than Steinbeck's reading of Fletcher on nematoda, where the influences are found. Fletcher is not mentioned in Libbie H. Hyman, *The Invertebrates*, vol. 3 (New York: McGraw, 1951) 572 ff. (See Benson 241 ff. for a discussion of the "superorganism" theory Steinbeck borrowed from William Emerson Ritter.)

18 Olaf Stapledon, *Last and First Men* (London: Methuen, 1930). Sci-fi with an undertone of H. G. Wells. The prose ranges from pedestrian through purple to godawful: "It was for this that we stayed our time, and must watch ourselves decline from spiritual estate into that brutishness from which man has so seldom escaped" (352).

19 The *East of Eden* notes were published posthumously as *Journal of a Novel* (New York: Viking, 1969). Pascal Covici (1888–1964) looked up Steinbeck's agents in 1934 when he visited Abramson's bookstore in New York and was encouraged to read *Cup of Gold* and *Pastures of Heaven* by the owner. Steinbeck paid tender tribute to his friend of many years at Covici's funeral: "If the book of Pat Covici is really closed, then all of us have marked many pages for rereading and remembering."

20 "A Primer on the 30's," *Esquire* June 1960: 85–93.

21 Amnesia Glasscock, pseud. [Carol Steinbeck], *The Collected Poems of Amnesia Glasscock* were published in the *Monterey Beacon* during Jan.–Feb. 1935. They have since been published (South San Francisco: Manroot, 1976) but erroneously attributed to John Steinbeck. "Glasscock was a humorous use of the name of California's 'poet laureate' Carl Burgess Glasscock" (Benson 314).

22 Brownlee and the *Appeal-Democrat* were of course not alone in the attacks on the book. The *San Francisco Examiner* for Sunday, June 4, 1939, devoted almost an entire double-page spread to an attack by Arthur D. Spearman, S. J., director of the library of Loyola University, Los Angeles, who says in part:

> . . . [Steinbeck] has used his book to discredit religion, to honor and encourage lechery, and to inculcate contempt for the law enforcement officers of America, whom he depicts one and all as the dishonest and cruel bravos of a universally Frankinsteinish [sic] group of large owners, bankers, and capitalists. As St. Paul might say of the 'Grapes of Wrath' as pictured by Mr. Steinbeck, 'there is little of profit in them.'
>
> [The novel] may be summed up as a brief written in terms of human misery, for the adoption of the philosophy of life called Communism. The arguments are selected from the customary communistic sources and strategy; a highlighted appeal for the behavioristic philosophy of sex-indulgence; an animated cartoon of the useless, discouraging influence of religion upon human welfare, a tincture saturating the whole book and made personal in the warping sin-remorse of Uncle John, brooding upon his past; a portrayal of law enforcement officers as the tools of the rich with no care or interest in protecting the legal rights or life and limbs of the poor worker. . .
>
> . . . [The book] is a plea for a fundamental change. It does not see any possibility of American life on a basis of the Ten Commandments, liberty under law, guidance from true religion, or a relationship of mutual duty and right of employee and employer.

23 The John Steinbeck Foundation has been renamed, and relocated, as the National Steinbeck Center, in Salinas, and in 1998 acquired the Steinbeck collection from the Salinas Public Library, according to current director John Hooper.

24 Sheffield's account of the estrangement over the misguided generosity of his friend to pay his way through the doctoral program is typically self-effacing. Steinbeck anguished over the separation and in a 1961 letter to Sheffield's sister Marion, wrote an account of the event:

> . . . I think I know the beginning of the break between Dook and me—the point from which no return was possible. It was due to a stupidity of mine but I have been guilty of many. . . . without warning my books began to sell and money began to come in. It scared the hell out of me because there was not and is not any payment which relates to the work of a book . . . And then I got my ill-conceived plan, and I worked it out in detail by myself. Dook was to go on with his formal education . . . It seemed so simple. I had the money. It didn't seem to be my money. Dook was broke. He was academic material and I wasn't. Well, I took the finished plan to him stupidly thinking he would be glad. His rage was cold and fierce. I see it now, and I see why now. *(Steinbeck: Letters* 709–11)

25 See Appendix A for a complete list of Steinbeck screenplays.

26 *Once There Was a War* (New York: Viking, 1958).

27 Steinbeck and his publisher wrote letters discussing Sheffield's comment that Steinbeck was beginning to repeat himself. Covici's letter of 15 Nov. 1944 is typical in its flattery in defending an author who was more friend than client. Steinbeck's is a curious response: trivia and then a sudden swing at ex-wife Carol, "drunk and formidable," whose man-hating skills were transferred from her husband to the wounded in France during the war in one of his most wicked *bon mots*: "I am told that when she washed them, they bled" (qtd. in Fensch 93). For Sheffield, the gaffe, if that is what it was, resulted in a second strike—but not with the rapier used on Carol; this was a bludgeoning of hammer blows. (See Note 1, *Letter to Jawn.*)

28 Ibsen's *The Vikings at Helgeland* (1858) is one of the playwright's last verse dramas, full of night and murk, before the strong-personality plays commencing with *Brand* (1866).

29 Richard Rodgers (1902–1979) and lyricist Oscar Hammerstein II (1895–1960), famed for pap productions like *Oklahoma!* (1943) and *The Sound of Music* (1959). Steinbeck was displeased with the Rodgers and Hammerstein version of *Cannery Row* as *Pipe Dream* because, among other genteel touches, they changed his prostitute to a nurse. In a complaining letter to Elia Kazan, he wrote: "What really is the trouble is that R. and H. seem to be attracted to my kind of writing and they are temperamentally incapable of doing it" (qtd. in Benson 781). Parini records Steinbeck's reaction to the producers via Ethan Mordden's *Rodgers and Hammerstein* (New York: Abrams, 1992, 174): "You've turned my prostitute into a visiting nurse!" (385).

30 The person Steinbeck hired for his two sons, fresh from Actors Studio, was playwright Terrence McNally (*Terrence McNally: 15 Short Plays* (Lyme, NH: Smith, 1994)). His reminiscences of his days as tutor within the strained Steinbeck family circle at this time are summed up in the Parini biography (455–57; 436–37. See also Benson 900–10). A recent play is *Corpus Christie* (New York: Grove, 1998).

31 *Speech Accepting the Nobel prize for Literature, Stockholm, December 10, 1962* (New York: Viking, 1962). Sheffield mentions a singularity in the failure of *Saturday Review* to follow up on the newest laureate as had been their tradition, blaming it on the lack of enthusiasm Granville Hicks, longtime editor and literary reviewer, had for Steinbeck's fiction. Steinbeck's name had been carried in the masthead of *SR* for some time, although he had not been a "Contributing Editor" for several months. In Sheffield's words: "As a subscriber I watched each issue minutely and incredulously and I am sure that I overlooked no mention. A card I sent asking about the omission was acknowledged but not printed and my sister had a similar experience" (Sheffield 254).

32 Daniel Aaron, "The Radical Humanism of John Steinbeck," *Saturday Review* 28 Sep. 1968: 26–27. Aaron, an English professor at Smith College and author of *Writers on the Left*, condescends to the writer and his thirties' politics as being as bland as a "classroom assignment" (26). Apropos Sheffield's comment about Granville Hicks' (possible) enmity to Steinbeck or to his novels, this issue also contains a review article by Hicks that pronounces the new fiction of William Gass, John Barth, and Anthony Burgess worthy of respect but that "at this moment all the arts seem to be threatened by the frantic demand for novelty" (26). No mention of Steinbeck.

Works Cited

Aaron, Daniel. "The Radical Humanism of John Steinbeck: *The Grapes of Wrath* Thirty Years Later." *Saturday Review* 28 Sep. 1968: 26–27.

Bennett, Robert. *The Wrath of John Steinbeck: Or, St. John Goes to Church.* Fwd. Lawrence Clark Powell. New York: Haskell, 1975.

Benson, Jackson J. *The True Adventures of John Steinbeck, Writer.* New York: Viking, 1984.

Blum, Richard H. A. Telephone interview. 8 Sep. 1999.

———Letter to Terry White. 6 Oct. 1999.

———Letter to Terry White. 2 Jan. 2000.

Fensch, Thomas. *Steinbeck and Covici: The Story of a Friendship.* Middlebury, VT: Eriksson, 1979.

Fontenrose, Joseph E. *John Steinbeck: An Introduction and Interpretation.* New York: Barnes, 1963.

Hicks, Granville. "The Up-to-Date Looking Glass." *Saturday Review* 28 Sep. 1968: 31–32.

Hooper, John. Telephone interview. 16 November 1999.

Hossick, Malcolm, writ., dir., and prod. *John Steinbeck: An American Novelist, 1902–1968.* Skan Productions. Falls Church, VA: Landmark Media, 1994.

Jackson, Joseph Henry, Introd. *The Short Novels of John Steinbeck.* New York: Viking, 1953.

Kiernan, Thomas. *The Intricate Music: A Biography of John Steinbeck.* Boston: Little, 1979.

Le Bris, Michel, writ. *John Steinbeck.* Dir. Alain Gallet. Prod. Anne-Françoise de Buzareingues. Narr. Nick Calderbank. Princeton, NJ: Films for the Humanities, 1996.

Lisca, Peter. *The Wide World of John Steinbeck*. Rev. ed. New York: Gordian, 1981.

———*John Steinbeck: Nature and Myth*. New York: Crowell, 1978.

———*Steinbeck: The Man and His Work*. Corvallis: Oregon State UP, 1971.

———*The Grapes of Wrath: Text and Criticism*. 2nd ed. New York: Penguin, 1996.

Moore, Harry Thornton. *The Novels of John Steinbeck: A First Critical Study*. 2nd ed. Port Washington, NY: Kennikat, 1968.

Parini, Jay. *John Steinbeck*. New York: Holt, 1995.

St. Pierre, Brian. *John Steinbeck: The California Years*. San Francisco: Chronicle, 1983.

Sheffield, Carlton A. Introduction. *Letters to Elizabeth: A Selection of Letters from John Steinbeck to Elizabeth Otis*. Eds. Florian J. Shafsky and Susan F. Riggs. San Francisco: Book Club of California, 1978.

———*Steinbeck: The Good* Companion. Ed. and Introd. Richard Blum. Portola Valley, CA: American Lives Endowment, 1983.

Simmonds, Roy. *John Steinbeck: The War Years*. Lewisburg, PA: Bucknell UP, 1996.

Stapledon, Olaf W. *Last and First Men: A Story of the Near and Far Future*. London: Methuen, 1930.

[Steinbeck, Carol.] *The Collected Poems of Amnesia Glasscock: By John Steinbeck*. Afterword Robert Peters. South San Francisco: Manroot, 1976.

Steinbeck, Elaine, and Robert Wallsten, eds. *Steinbeck: A Life in Letters*. New York: Viking, 1975.

Steinbeck, John. "Atque Vale." *Saturday Review* July 1960: 13.

———*Cannery Row*. New York: Viking, 1975.

———*Journal of a Novel: The* East of Eden *Letters*. New York: Viking, 1969.

———*The Log from the Sea of Cortez: The Narrative Portion of the Book, Sea of Cortez, by John Steinbeck and E. F. Ricketts, 1941, Here Reissued with a Profile, "About Ed Ricketts," by John Steinbeck.* New York: Viking, 1951.

———*Once There Was a War.* New York: Viking, 1958. Rpt. New York: Penguin, 1977.

———and Edward F. Ricketts. *Sea of Cortez: A Leisurely Journal of Travel and Research.* 1941. New York: Appel, 1971.

Taylor, Horace Platt. "The Biological Naturalism of John Steinbeck." Diss. Louisiana State U, 1961. Ann Arbor: UMI, 1962. 6200064.

Tedlock, E. W., Jr., and C. V. Wicker. *Steinbeck and His Critics: A Record of Twenty-Five Years.* Introd. and notes E. W. Tedlock and C. V. Wicker. Albuquerque: U of New Mexico P. 1957.

Valjean, Nelson. *John Steinbeck, The Knight Errant: An Intimate Biography of His California Years.* San Francisco: Chronicle, 1975.

Wenger, Tara. Letter to Terry White. 22 Nov. 1999.

Wilhelmson, Carl. *Midsummernight.* New York: Farrar, 1930.

Appendix A: Works by John Steinbeck

Novels

American publishers are noted here, but a majority of Steinbeck works were simultaneously published in London, Toronto, and less frequently Melbourne, by Heinemann's of London.

- *Cup of Gold: A Life of Henry Morgan, Buccaneer.* New York: McBride, 1929. Rpt. Penguin, 1976.

- *The Pastures of Heaven.* New York: Viking, 1932. New ed. 1963. Rpt. New York: Penguin, 1982.

- *To a God Unknown.* New York: Viking, 1933. Rpt. New York: Penguin, 1976.

- *Tortilla Flat.* New York: Viking, 1935. Illust. ed. 1947. Rpt. New York: Penguin, 1977.

- *In Dubious Battle.* New York: Viking, 1936. New ed. 1971.

- *Of Mice and Men.* New York: Viking, 1937. Rpt. New York: Bantam, 1970.

- *The Red Pony.* New York: Covici, 1937. Rpt. New York: Penguin, 1989.

- *The Grapes of Wrath.* New York: Viking, 1939. Introd. Carl Van Doren. Cleveland: World, 1947. Rev. ed. Ed. Peter Lisca. 1972. Rpt. New York: Penguin, 1989. 2nd ed. Ed. Kevin Hearle. New York: Penguin, 1996. Ed. Peter Lisca. New York: Penguin, 1997.

- *The Forgotten Village. New York:* Viking, 1941.

- *The Moon Is Down. New York:* Viking, 1942. Rpt. New York: Penguin, 1982.

Cannery Row. New York: Viking, 1945. New ed. 1963. Rpt. 1975.

The Wayward Bus. New York: Viking, 1947. Rpt. New York: Penguin, 1979.

The Pearl. New York: Viking, 1947. Rpt. New York: Bantam, 1986.

Burning Bright: A Play in Story Form. New York: Viking, 1950. Rpt. New York: Penguin, 1979.

East of Eden. New York: Viking, 1952. Rpt. New York: Penguin, 1979.

Sweet Thursday. New York: Viking, 1954. Rpt. New York: Penguin, 1979.

The Short Reign of Pippin IV: A Fabrication. New York: Viking, 1957. Rpt. New York: Penguin, 1977.

The Winter of Our Discontent. New York: Viking, 1961. Rpt. New York: Penguin, 1982.

Saint Katy the Virgin. Mount Vernon, NY: Jacobs; New York: Covici-Friede, 1936.

Nothing So Monstrous [rpt. episode from *The Pastures of Heaven*]. New York: Pynson, 1936. Rpt. Folcroft, PA: Folcroft Library, 1977. Rpt. Norwood, PA: Norwood, 1978. Rpt. Philadelphia: West, 1984.

The Long Valley [fourteen short stories, including "The Red Pony," "Saint Katy the Virgin," "Johnny Bear," and "The Harness"]. New York: Viking, 1938. Rpt. New York: Penguin, 1986. Pub. as *Thirteen Great Short Stories from the Long Valley*. New York: Avon, 1943. Pub. as *Fourteen Great Short Stories from the Long Valley*. New York: Avon, 1947.

How Edith McGillicuddy Met R. L. S. Cleveland: Rowfant Club, 1943 [152 copies printed for members of the Rowfant Club at the Grabhorn Press, San Francisco, 1943].

The Crapshooter. New York: Mercury, 1957.

Plays

- *Of Mice and Men: A Play in Three Acts.* With George S. Kaufman. Prod. on Broadway at The Music Box Theatre. 23 Nov. 1937. New York: Viking, 1937. Rpt. New York:
- Dramatists Play, 1964. Pub. in *Famous American Plays of the Nineteen Thirties*. Ed. Harold Clurman. New York: Dell, 1980.
- *The Moon Is Down: Play in Two Parts*. Prod. on Broadway at Martin Beck Theatre. 7 April 1942. New York: Dramatists Play Service, 1942.
- *Burning Bright: Play in Three Acts*. Prod. on Broadway at Broadhurst Theatre. 8 Oct. 18, 1950. New York: Dramatists Play, 1951. Rpt. New York: Penguin, 1979.

Screenplays

- *The Forgotten Village.* Dir. and Prod. Herbert Kline. Narr. Burgess Meredith. Pan American/Mexico, 1940. Videocassette. Sunnyvale, CA: Video-Sig, 1980.
- *Lifeboat*. Dir. Alfred Hitchcock.. Perf. Tallulah Bankhead and Walter Slezak. Twentieth-Century-Fox, 1944.
- *A Medal for Benny.* Dir. Irving Pichel. Perf. Dorothy Lamour, Arturo de Cordova, J. Carrol Naish. Paramount, 1945. Pub. in *Best Film Plays—1945*. Ed. John Gassner and Dudley Nichols. New York: Crown, 1946.
- *The Pearl*. Dir. Emilio Fernandez. Perf. Alfonzo Bedoya and Pedro Armendariz. RKO, 1948.
- *The Red Pony*. Dir. Lewis Milestone. Perf. Myrna Loy, Robert Mitchum, and Peter Miles. Republic, 1949.
- *Viva Zapata!*. Dir. Elia Kazan. Perf. Marlon Brando, Jean Peters, and Anthony Quinn. Twentieth Century Fox, 1952. Ed. Robert E. Morsberger. New York: Viking, 1975. Rome: Edizione Film Critica, 1952. New ed. Ed. Robert Morseberger. New York: Viking, 1975.

Film , TV, & Other Adaptations of Steinbeck

- *Flight.* Adap. *"Flight."* Dir. Louis Bispo. Writ. and prod. Barnaby Conrad. Narr. Burgess Meredith. Perf. Efrain Ramirez, Amelia Cortez, and Andrew Cortez. Videocassette. Minneapolis, MN: Festival Films, 1980.
- *The Forgotten Village* [book with 136 photographs from the film] New York: Viking, 1941.
- *The Grapes of Wrath.* Dir. John Ford. Writ. Nunnally Johnson. Perf. Henry Fonda, Jane Carwell, and John Carradine. Twentieth Century Fox, 1940.
- *Of Mice and Men.* Dir. Lewis Milestone. Writ. Eugene Solow. Perf. Burgess Meredith and Lon Cheney. United Artists, 1939. Opera adapt. Carlisle Floyd. Seattle Opera House. 1970.
- *Tortilla Flat.* Dir. Victor Fleming. Writ. John Lee Mahin. Perf. Spencer Tracy, Hedy Lamarr, and John Garfield. Metro-Goldwyn-Mayer, 1942.
- *The Moon Is Down.* Dir. Irving Pichel. Writ. Nunnally Johnson. Perf. Cedric Hardwicke and Lee J. Cobb. Twentieth Century Fox, 1942.
- *East of Eden.* Perf. James Dean and Jo Van Fleet. Warner Brothers, 1954. TV miniseries. Musical adapt. *Here's Where I Belong.* Billy Rose Theatre. 1968.
- *Pipe Dream.* [*Sweet Thursday*]. Musical adapt. Oscar Hammerstein II. Music Richard Rodgers. 1955 . New York: Viking, 1956.
- *The Wayward Bus.* Dir. Victor Vicas. Writ. Ivan Moffat. Perf. Dan Dailey, Jayne Mansfield, and Joan Collins. Twentieth Century Fox, 1957.

Television:

America and Americans. NBC, 1967.

East of Eden. ABC, 1981.

Travels with Charley. NBC, 1967.

Omnibus Volumes

Steinbeck. Ed. Pascal Covici. New York: Viking, 1943. Enlarged ed. *The Portable Steinbeck*. 1946. Rev. ed. 1971. Rpt. New York: Crown, 1986. *Steinbeck Omnibus*. New York: Oxford UP, 1946.

Short Novels: Tortilla Flat, The Red Pony, Of Mice and Men, The Moon Is Down, Cannery Row, The Pearl. New York: Viking, 1953. New ed. 1963.

East of Eden [and] *The Wayward Bus*. New York: Viking, 1962.

The Red Pony, Part I: The Gift [and] *The Pearl*. Toronto: Macmillan , 1963.

The Pearl [and] *The Red Pony*. New York: Viking, 1967.

Cannery Row [and] *Sweet Thursday*. London: Heron, 1971.

To a God Unknown [and] *The Pearl*. London: Heron, 1971.

Of Mice and Men [and] *Cannery Row*. Harmondsworth, Eng.; New York: Penguin, 1978.

The Grapes of Wrath, *The Moon Is Down*, *Cannery Row, East of Eden,* [and] *Of Mice and Men*. London: Heinemann, 1976.

John Steinbeck, 1902–1968. [*Tortilla Flat, Of Mice and Men*, and *Cannery Row*]. Lim. ed. Franklin Center, PA: Franklin Library, 1977.

The Short Novels of John Steinbeck [*Tortilla Flat, The Red Pony, Of Mice and Men, The Moon Is Down, Cannery Row,& The Pearl*]. Introd. Joseph Henry Jackson. New York: Viking, 1981.

Novels and Stories, 1932–1937. New York: Library of America, 1994.

The Grapes of Wrath & Other Writings, 1938–1941. [*The Long Valley, The Grapes of Wrath, The Log from the Sea of Cortex,& The Harvest Gypsies*]. New York: Library of America, 1996.

Miscellanea

- *Their Blood Is Strong.* San Francisco: Simon J. Lubin Society of California, 1938. Pub. as *The Harvest Gypsies: On the Road to the Grapes of Wrath*. Berkeley: Heyday, 1988.
- *A Letter to the Friends of Democracy*. N. p.: Overbrook , 1940.
- *Sea of Cortez.* With Edward F. Ricketts. New York: Viking, 1941. Pub. as *Sea of Cortez: A Leisurely Journal of Travel.* New York: Appel, 1971. Rev. ed. *The Log from the "Sea of Cortez": The Narrative Portion of the Book, "Sea of Cortez."* New York: Viking, 1951. Rpt. New York: Penguin, 1977.
- *Bombs Away: The Story of a Bomber Team.* New York: Viking, 1942.
- *A Russian Journal.* Photog. Robert Capa. New York: Viking, 1948.
- *Travels with Charley: In Search of America.* New York: Viking, 1962. Rpt. New York: Penguin, 1980.
- *America and Americans.* New York: Viking, 1966.
- *Journal of a Novel: The "East of Eden" Letters.* New York: Viking, 1969.
- *Steinbeck: A Life in Letters.* (See Works Cited.)
- *The Acts of King Arthur and His Noble Knights: From the Winchester Manuscripts of Thomas Malory and Other Sources.* Ed. Chase Horton. New York: Farrar, 1976.
- *Letters to Elizabeth.* (See Works Cited.)
- *Working Days: The Journals of the Grapes of Wrath.* Ed. Robert DeMott. New York: Penguin, 1989.

Appendix B: Selective Bibliography

Annual Steinbeck Bibliography. John Steinbeck Society of America. English Dept. Ball State Univ. Muncie, IN.

Astro, Richard. *John Steinbeck and Edward F. Ricketts: The Shaping of a Novelist*. Minneapolis: U of Minnesota P, 1973.

———and Hayashi Tetsumaro, eds. *Proceedings of a Conference Sponsored by Ball State and Oregon State on Steinbeck: The Man and His Work*. Corvallis: Oregon State UP, 1971.

Beegel, Susan F., ed. et al. *Steinbeck and the Environment*. Tuscaloosa: U of Alabama P, 1997.

Benson, Jackson J., ed. *The Short Novels of John Steinbeck: Critical Essays with a Checklist to Steinbeck Criticism*. Durham, NC: Duke UP, 1990.

Bryer, Jackson R., ed. *Fifteen Modern American Authors: A Survey of Research and Criticism*. Durham, NC: Duke UP, 1969.

———*Sixteen Modern American Authors*. Vol. 2 of *Survey of Research and Criticism*. Durham, NC: Duke UP, 1990.

Buerger, Daniel. "'History' and Fiction in *East of Eden*." *Steinbeck Quarterly* 14 (1981): 6–14.

Coers, Donald V., ed. *After The Grapes of Wrath: Essays on John Steinbeck in Honor of Tetsumaro Hayashi*. Athens: Ohio UP, 1995.

Cox, Martha Heasley. "Steinbeck's Family Portraits: The Hamiltons." *Steinbeck Quarterly* 14 (1981): 23–32.

Davis, Robert Murray., ed. *Steinbeck: A Collection of Critical Essays*. Englewood Cliffs, NJ: Prentice, 1972.

———Rev. of *The Working Days: The Journals of The Grapes of Wrath, 1938–1941,* by John Steinbeck and edited by Robert DeMott. *World Literature Today* 64 (1990): 120–21.

DeMott, Robert J. *John Steinbeck: A Checklist of Books by and about John Steinbeck.* Bradenton, FL: Opuscula, 1987.

———"Cathy Ames and Lady Godiva: A Contribution to *East of Eden*'s Background." *Steinbeck Quarterly* 14 (1981): 72–83.

———"'Culling All Books': Steinbeck's Reading and *East of Eden*." *Steinbeck Quarterly* 14 (1981): 40–51.

Ferrell, Keith. *John Steinbeck: The Voice of the Land.* New York: Evans, 1986.

———*John Steinbeck's Fiction Revisited.* New York: Twayne, 1994.

Gannett, Lewis. *John Steinbeck: Personal and Bibliographic Notes.* New York: Viking, 1939.

Garcia, Reloy. *Steinbeck and D. H. Lawrence: Fictive Voices and the Ethical Imperative.* Steinbeck Monograph Ser. 2. Muncie, IN: Steinbeck Society, 1972.

———"The Rocky Road to El Dorado: The Journey Motif in John Steinbeck's *The Grapes of Wrath*." *Steinbeck Quarterly* 14 (1981): 83–93.

Gladstein, Mimi R. "Ma Joad and Pilar: Significantly Similar." *Steinbeck Quarterly* 14 (1981): 93–104.

Goldhurst, William. "*Of Mice and Men*: John Steinbeck's Parable of the Curse of Cain." *Western American Literature* 6 (1971): 123–35.

Govoni, Mark W. "'Symbols for the Wordlessness': The Original Manuscript of *East of Eden*." *Steinbeck Quarterly* 14 (1981): 14–23.

Gray, James. *John Steinbeck.* Ser. 94. Minneapolis: U of Minnesota P, 1971.

Gurko, Leo. "*Of Mice and Men*: Steinbeck as Manichean." *University of Windsor Review* 8.3 (1973): 11–23.

Harmon, Robert B. *Steinbeck Bibliographies: An Annotated Guide.* Metuchen, NJ: Scarecrow, 1987.

Hayashi, Tetsumaro, ed. *A Handbook for Steinbeck Collectors, Librarians, and Scholars.* Steinbeck Monograph Ser. 11. Muncie, IN: Steinbeck Society, 1981.

———ed. *Steinbeck and the Arthurian Theme*. Steinbeck Monograph Ser. 5. Muncie, IN: Steinbeck Society, 1975.

———ed. *Steinbeck's Literary Dimension: A Guide to Comparative Studies*. Metuchen, NJ: Scarecrow, 1973.

———ed. *Steinbeck's Literary Dimension: A Guide to Comparative Studies*. Ser. 2. Metuchen, NJ: Scarecrow, 1991.

Hyman, Stanley Edgar. *Some Notes on John Steinbeck*. Yellow Springs, OH: Antioch, 1942.

Jones, Lawrence W. *John Steinbeck as Fabulist*. Ed. Marston LaFrance. Muncie, IN: Ball State UP, 1973.

Loewen, Nancy. *John Steinbeck*. Mankato, MN: Creative Education, 1997.

McCarthy, Paul. *John Steinbeck*. New York: Ungar, 1980.

McDaniel, Barbara. "Alienation in *East of Eden*: The 'Chart of the Soul.'" *Steinbeck Quarterly* 14 (1981): 32–39.

McElrath, Joseph R. et al., eds. *John Steinbeck: The Contemporary Reviews*. New York: Cambridge UP, 1996.

Marks, Lester J. *Thematic Design in the Novels of John Steinbeck*. The Hague: Mouton, 1971.

Millichap, Joseph R. *Steinbeck and Film*. New York: Ungar, 1983.

Owens, Louis. *John Steinbeck's Re-Vision of America*. Athens: U of Georgia P, 1985.

Reef, Catherine. *John Steinbeck*. New York: Clarion, 1996.

Salinas Public Library. *John Steinbeck: A Guide to the Collection of the Salinas Public Library*. Eds. John Gross and Lee Richard Hyman. Salinas, CA: The Library, 1979.

Simmonds, Roy S. *Steinbeck's Literary Achievement*. Steinbeck Monograph Ser. 6. Muncie, IN: Steinbeck Society, 1976.

Smith, Thelma M. and Ward L. Miner. *Transatlantic Migration: The Contemporary American Novel in France*. Durham, NC: Duke UP, 1955.

Swisher, Clarice, ed. *Readings on John Steinbeck*. San Diego: Greenhaven, 1996.

Timmerman, John H. *John Steinbeck's Fiction: The Aesthetics of the Road Taken*. Norman: U of Oklahoma P, 1986.

Watt, Ian. John Steinbeck. New York: Grove, 1962.

Wilson, Edmund. *The Boys in the Back Room: Notes on California Novelists*. San Francisco: Colt, 1941.

Appendix C: Letters from Steinbeck

Sheffield refers to numerous correspondence throughout the text. For convenience the letters are numbered here and cross-referenced with the published letters of Steinbeck by his fourth wife Elaine and Robert Wallston. (Editor's note: RCS refers to Ruth Carpenter Sheffield, first wife of CAS; MA is Marion Adams, sister, and PC is "Pat" Covici, publisher and friend.)

LETTER	TO	DATE	GOOD COMPANION	LIFE IN LETTERS
1	CAS	2 Mar 1964	Pref xviii	796–98
2	RCS	June 1926	86–88	12–14

Gramercy Park, NYC. Sidenote: Sheffield married second wife Maryon Crane on January 26, 1929.

LETTER	TO	DATE	GOOD COMPANION	LIFE IN LETTERS
3	CAS	25 Feb. 1928	94–95	64–65

Lake Tahoe, CA.

LETTER	TO	DATE	GOOD COMPANION	LIFE IN LETTERS
4	CAS	21 June 1933	146–51	74–77

The famous "Phalanx Theory" letter in which Steinbeck discusses group behavior in detail.

LETTER	TO	DATE	GOOD COMPANION	LIFE IN LETTERS
5	CAS	30 June 1933	152	78

Salinas, CA.

The *LL* version is truncated and deletes the "phalanx" outline here.

LETTER	TO	DATE	GOOD COMPANION	LIFE IN LETTERS
6	CAS	28 Sep. 1962	158–59	744

The "bullrunning" reference makes this another discrepancy between *Good Companion* and *LL*, which notes the date of this letter as 1 Nov. 1962.

LETTER	TO	DATE	GOOD COMPANION	LIFE IN LETTERS
7	CAS	1938	160	Unpub.

Dook is mistaken; the year is most likely 1939.

LETTER	TO	DATE	GOOD COMPANION	LIFE IN LETTERS
8	CAS	9 July 1940	165-66	207–09

Los Gatos, CA

9	CAS	23 June 1939	170	186–87
10	CAS	13 Nov. 1939	171	197–94
11	CAS	27 Sep. 1944	171-72	272–73
12	CAS	12 Apr. 1944	173	268–70

NYC

13	CAS	27 Sep. 1944	174–75	272–74
14	CAS	25 Feb. 1952	175	Unpub.
15	CAS	10 Sep. 1952	176	456–57

"Fifty is a good age . . ."

16	CAS	16 Oct. 1952	177-78	458–59

[Of Cathy's character in *Cannery Row*, *Life in Letters*: "You *won't* believe her, many people don't." CAS: "You *don't* believe her . . . " [editor's emphasis].

17	CAS	3 Dec. 1952	178	462–63

"The Book—it's been capitalized in my mind . . ."

18	CAS	2 Nov. 1953	180	473–75
19	CAS	23 Sep. 1955	180	473–75

Sheffield includes a portion unpublished by *Life in Letters*: "Youv'e [sic] got to be real smart to be a good show girl . . . The era of the dumb blonde is definitely over. It's going to be a very good show." Dook claims this refers to *Pippin IV*, but Steinbeck and Wallston aver that it is an entirely experimental work that JS "never felt sufficiently satisfied with to show it to anyone else" (*LL* 513). If true, that would be only the second attempt at an experimental narrative since the "Dissonant Symphonies" JS allegedly wrote at the time of *Pastures of Heaven*.

20	CAS	Oct. 1955	181-82	Unpub.
21	CAS	Nov. 1955	182–83	Unpub.
22	MA	27 June 1961	184-85	708–11

Dook earlier refers to JS's "light tap on the shoulder" remark—a reference to the Grim Reaper and the beginning of his decline in health, from the letter to Marion that resumed the correspondence between JS and CAS.

23	CAS	8 Nov. 1962	188-89	753–54

JS compares the Nobel to winning "Lettuce Queen of Salinas" title.

24	CAS	1 Dec. 1962	189	Unpub.

Dook claims JS began the letter on 28 Sep. and completed it by this date.

25	CAS	26 Apr. 1965	191	821

Death of Mary Dekker, the sister JS affectionately called "Sir Mary."